A TIME

TO

HOPE

A TIME

—— TO ——

HOPE

365 DAILY DEVOTIONS
FROM GENESIS TO REVELATION

Naomi Reed

Authentic

First published 2020 by Authentic Media Limited,
PO Box 6326, Bletchley, Milton Keynes, MK1 9GG.
authenticmedia.co.uk

British Library Cataloguing in Publication Data
A catalogue record for this book is available from the British Library.
ISBN: 978-1-78893-144-1
978-1-78893-145-8 (e-book)

Cover design by Mykola Shelepa
Printed and bound by CPI Group (UK) Ltd, Croydon, CR0 4YY

A note from the author

When I first began this writing project, I was filled with excitement. I was drawn to the challenge of capturing the sweep of the Bible, from Genesis to Revelation, in an accessible, engaging devotional book. I didn't realise how hard it was going to be, or how long it was going to take! But I have been greatly blessed in the writing. I have spent the year deeply immersed in Scripture and I have encountered God again, in all his glorious holiness and faithfulness. I have lifted my eyes to his plans and purposes for the world, through his Son, the Lord Jesus . . . and I have fallen in love with Jesus again. That is a year well spent! My prayer for this book is that you too will be blessed through the Scriptures and that you will fall in love with Jesus again. So please take your time and enjoy the immersion in God's word and don't stress if you fall behind in the days. Take five years if you like! I pray that as you do, you will find yourself drawn back to the Lord Jesus, in a wonderful, life-changing way.

Naomi

With special thanks to my husband, my sons, my editing friends, my pastors and my prayer partners – for their immeasurable input into this book and my life.

Out of the void

'In the beginning God created the heavens and the earth.'
Genesis 1:1

Read Genesis 1:1–25

Every now and again, it's good to remind ourselves that we are small in God's ongoing, cosmic plan for the universe. This is God's world! In the beginning, there was God. He was always there – holy and good and unfathomably great. And God created the heavens and the earth. He made order and beauty out of disorder. He made everything! The narrative also has a beautiful repetition. *'God said . . .' 'And it was so.' 'And God saw that it was good.'* God formed all things out of the void – deserts and ostriches and photosynthesis, as well as Himalayas and jungles and hyenas. The universe, every part of it, was made by God and for God. He named it and enjoyed it. It was good! Then, incredibly, after God formed the oceans and the rivers, the plants and animals, the stars and the moon . . . he formed humankind in his own image (the pinnacle of his creative work!) for the purpose of intimacy with him. It's astounding! But as individuals, we are not the beginning of things, nor the centre of things. Instead, we serve a God who is eternally, graciously, incomprehensibly holy and good. He is the centre of things, and he will continue to bring about his sovereign plans for his world, in his time, for his glory.

- - - - - -

Pray

> *'Lord, we thank you for your vast, ordered world, and for the way it shows us what you're like – holy and generous and beyond time and unfathomably great. Help us to sit quietly today in the scope of your world, and your good plan.'*

In his image

'Then God said, "Let us make mankind in our image."'
Genesis 1:26

Read Genesis 1:26–31

It's breathtaking, isn't it? After forming everything, out of nothing, out of the void, God chose to make humankind in his own image – *'in the image of God he created them'*. Many scholars have debated what it might mean to be made in the image of God, or to be uniquely human – perhaps to have moral choice, or rationality, or self-awareness. I remember sitting in Nepal with a group of people who had suffered from leprosy. They were physically deformed. They had been rejected from their villages. Reading Genesis 1 was incredible to them. We are not made in a hierarchy, like the Hindu scriptures say. We are made in the image of God! And slowly they began to see the most astounding truth. Our purpose for existence as humans is defined by being in relationship with God – loved by God, and uniquely part of his story. What makes us 'human' is our rich relationship with God, and with each other. David Atkinson, in his commentary on Genesis 1, refers to the story of *The Velveteen Rabbit*. In that story, he says, when a child loves you for a very long time, you become 'real'. In the same way, we become real (we become more human) through our relationships of love with God and each other, through the Lord Jesus. It's an amazingly rich reminder today.

- - - - - -

Pray

> *'Lord, it's easy to forget that your design and plan for humankind is astounding. Help us to lift our gaze today, and remember that we are here to live in relationships of love with you and each other. Help us to nourish those relationships today.'*

Rest

'By the seventh day God had finished the work he had been doing; so on the seventh day he rested from all his work.'

Genesis 2:2

Read Genesis 2:1–3

It's good to think about the word 'rest'. It can be confusing. Perhaps we think of a quiet afternoon, or a comfy chair, or the absence of work. In the Bible, though, we read about 'God's rest' – the wonderful invitation to share his fellowship. In Genesis 2:1–3, there's a picture of a flourishing world, where God rests and humans are given responsibility and joy and delight in service. Later in the Scriptures, God encourages his people to rest on the Sabbath day, keeping it holy, actively praising him (Exodus 31:15, Psalm 92). Rest was, and still is, a glorious gift from God. *'My Presence will go with you and I will give you rest'* (Exodus 33:14). It's also interesting that God's rest is a noun as well as a verb. God *gives* us rest for our souls as we spend time with him. Of course, in the gospels the word gets even larger. Jesus said, *'Come to **me**, all you who are weary and burdened, and I will give you rest'* (Matthew 11:28). Jesus, carrying our burdens, and fears, and failures, took them to the cross to be dealt with for ever. He offers us rest today, in whatever we're doing, because of the cross and the empty tomb. It's the invitation we all need amidst our worries and concerns.

- - - - - -

Pray

> *'Lord, we thank you for your good gift of your rest. Help us to find and receive rest today in the Lord Jesus, and to look forward to a place of rest for ever.'*

Work

'The LORD God took the man and put him in the Garden of Eden to work it and take care of it.'

Genesis 2:15

Read Genesis 2:4–24

From the beginning of Genesis, there is reference to work as well as rest. In Genesis 2, in the second creation account, the Lord God formed a man, breathed life into him and then put him in the garden to work it and take care of it. Also, in the most breathtaking way, God formed a woman as a companion to the man, and as a helper in the work of tending the garden. For me as a garden-lover, I love this narrative! It reminds me that all of us, as humans, are formed and designed for the purpose of good work. The work is dignified and beautiful and deliberate and collaborative. It is not necessarily clocking on and off in a particular office space until retirement. The work is vast – it is to care for this world, and its people, in a myriad of different, creative, beautiful ways. And we are designed to do that together as partners, which is wonderful. In Genesis 2, 'work' is definitely not a burden. It reminds us of Paul's words much later in the Bible to the church in Colossae, *'Whatever you do, work at it with all your heart, as working for the Lord'* (Colossians 3:23). The word 'whatever' is challenging to me though – whatever we do in the kitchen, or at the shops, or in the car, or as we sit at the computer . . . let it be for the Lord.

- - - - - -

Pray

'Lord, help us to be thankful for the gift of work today, and to let your Word change the way we see all of work and engage in it.'

Everything was tarnished

'Cursed is the ground because of you; through painful toil you will eat food from it all the days of your life.'
Genesis 3:17b

Read Genesis 3:1–23

The beginning of Genesis is a grand saga, calling us to imagine a God who is good and holy and unfathomably great, and who wanted one, important thing: to be with his people, in a sharing together, dwelling kind of way. In the beginning, that's exactly how it was. God was with his people, in all his glorious holiness, and they felt no shame or need to hide. But it didn't last long. God gave his people a choice and, at the same time, a strange figure arrived – a snake, who called the people to imagine something else, something distorted. And the people chose it – their own way, and their own food, and their own answers, and knowledge. The choice changed everything. Soon, all that was good in the beginning became irrevocably tarnished and askew. Every time I read Genesis 3, I feel the immense and ongoing weight of it. This choice (that was not so far removed from us) produced pain, dysfunctional rule and hard toil – evil alongside good, ugliness alongside beauty, and dying alongside life. The people themselves were driven away from the glorious presence of God. It's simply awful to imagine. It's confronting. We too hide in our shame. We long for God. And the narrative sets up one all-consuming, penetrating question. Will the people be able to return? What will God do to bring them home? Will there be someone who will 'crush the serpent's head' (see 3:15)?

- - - - - -

Pray

'Lord, help us to sit with the pain of our ongoing, self-absorbed, self-protective choices, and to be moved to pray for your answers, in the Lord Jesus.'

Cain and Abel

'While they were in the field, Cain attacked his brother Abel and killed him.'

Genesis 4:8b

Read Genesis 4:1–26

Every time I read Genesis 4, I'm stunned by how quickly the account moves from beauty and generosity to disobedience and judgement, and even envy and murder. It's so immediate! The two sons of Adam and Eve (Cain and Abel), both brought an offering to the Lord. Abel's offering came from a grateful, trustworthy heart; Cain's did not. So the Lord spoke with Cain, but transformation did not occur. Instead, Cain went out into the field and murdered Abel in cold blood. How can this be? Why did unrighteous Cain prosper, and righteous Abel didn't even have a voice in the narrative? What was God doing? How is this account fair or just? We have so many questions. And yet, thousands of years later, the writer of Hebrews refers to Abel, saying that Abel was commended as righteous, and he *still speaks today*, even though he is dead (Hebrews 11:4). It's remarkable. It's the heart of the gospel message. Even in his death, Abel wasn't forsaken by God. He still lives and speaks! And somehow, his blood anticipated a 'better' blood and a more significant death to come – that of Jesus, who ultimately paid the price for human sin and brought victory over death for ever. It's amazing. In the meantime, we do well to pause at the story of Abel and to put our trust in God, whose ways are not always fathomable but they are always good.

- - - - - -

Pray

> *'Lord, there is so much we don't understand. But we do trust you, and we trust that you will bring about your sovereign, good purposes in everything, even in the face of untold suffering.'*

The Lord regretted

**'The LORD regretted that he had made human beings on the earth, and
his heart was deeply troubled.'**

Genesis 6:6

Read Genesis 6:1–22

We need to read this portion of Scripture very carefully . . . and sit with the
heaviness and disobedience of the human race, as well as the grieving heart
of God. It would be easier, of course, to skip it and get to the end of the
flood story. But our human capacity to sin is so very great, and it grieves
the Lord. In Genesis 6, we read that every kind of evil and wickedness
flourished, including greed and desolation and envy. It was so awful that the
Lord was *deeply troubled*, and he regretted that he had made human beings
on the earth. That's the point where I pause. This is the loving heart of God,
who grieves over our human choices, and who 'regrets'. Perhaps, if we don't
sit with the extent of God's regret, we will find it hard to fathom his grace,
or his promise, or his patience. The flood story reveals it all in the most
astounding way. God was deeply troubled, yet he remained committed to
the human race. He brought about judgement, but he also brought about
an answer – a righteous person, a rescue plan, a saving boat, and the promise
that would come out of the chaos of the water. God saved his people. He
remained gracious. And in that grace, he pointed ahead to his final saving
act, through Christ.

- - - - - -

Pray

> *'Lord, thank you for Jesus, and for your grieving, loving heart. We ask that
> you remind us today of the cost you bore to save us.'*

In the middle of it

**'The animals going in were male and female of every living thing, as God
had commanded Noah. Then the LORD shut him in.'**

Genesis 7:16

Read Genesis 7:1–24

One of the hardest things about being human is that we never know how
any particular struggle is going to turn out. If we did, we might relax and
breathe a bit! But we don't know. I often try to imagine Noah and his wife
and family in the middle of the flood – in the middle of the rain and the
surging water that went on for a year. Noah was an obedient, faithful man.
He had been given a promise that God would save his family and establish
a covenant with him. But Noah was not told how long the rain or the flood
would go on for, or what would happen next. Did the family ever despair
in the middle of it? Did they wonder if they would spend the rest of their
lives on a floating ark? Or, did they notice the small acts of God in the
middle of it? Did they hold onto the character of God when all they could
see was rain? One verse in particular strikes me. *'The LORD shut him in'*
(7:16). Noah and his wife must have noticed that miraculous, caring detail!
And I hope that we also notice the small acts of God in the middle of our
struggles . . . because it's often the little things that help us to hold on to
God's larger, ongoing plan to save us, and the world, through Jesus.

- - - - - -

Pray

*'Lord, we thank you for your presence and for your promise to save. Help
us to notice your small acts of kindness that remind us of your ongoing
plan and good character.'*

God remembered

'But God remembered Noah and all the wild animals and the livestock that were with him in the ark, and he sent a wind over the earth, and the waters receded.'

Genesis 8:1

Read Genesis 8:1 – 9:17

After a year of rain and surging water, we read these two words – *'God remembered'*. This is what God is like. He remembers. He never forgets. He acts. He is faithful to his promises, always. In this case, he restrained the waters and made dry land appear. Then, when Noah and his family left the ark, he gave them a promise. *'Never again will all life be destroyed by the waters of a flood; never again will there be a flood to destroy the earth'* (9:11). It must have been so reassuring. Having come through the judgement of the flood, Noah and his family could rest in God's faithfulness. There was a calling to a new life of intimacy with God, and a promise that God would never destroy humanity again. The narrative also gives an endnote that reminds us of human sinfulness, but even within that we see the pattern of salvation and rescue that is repeated throughout the Bible. God remembers. He rescued his people from watery chaos, and then later from slavery in Egypt, and despair in the desert, and from foreign nations and idols, and from exile in Babylon, and then, of course, from the desolation of the human heart itself through the one completely righteous person, the Lord Jesus. This part of Genesis makes us raise our heads and remember. One day, God will make everything completely right.

- - - - - -

Pray

'Lord, we thank you for your patient, rescuing heart. Please help us to find refuge in you, today.'

The tower of Babel

'Come, let us build ourselves a city, with a tower that reaches to the heavens, so that we may make a name for ourselves.'

Genesis 11:4

Read Genesis 11:1–9

In the beginning, God invited human beings to work in his good world, to take care of it and fashion and shape it in good, collaborative, creative ways. The invitation reflects both the essence of God and our humanity. God designed us with a boundless imagination, and capacity for new ideas and inventiveness within a flourishing world. Yet that design was so quickly distorted and misused – tarnished in the same way that our relationships with God and each other have been tarnished. In Genesis 11, the people planned to build a tower that would reach the heavens, so they could *'make a name for [them]selves'.* The phrase immediately alerts us to something – the hidden desire lurking within all of us – to matter, to be known, to be seen, or to control, or even to be divine. The gift of innovation in Genesis turned into something else, contrary to God's good purposes. Back then, of course, God came down and he caused lasting consequences, which included the scattering of people. It makes us wonder, though, about our current innovative striving. Is our human pride and inventiveness leading us to distraction, to loss of community, to a longing to be the source of our own security, or to be divine? Does it ever deaden us to prayer, or to the ways of God? I wonder what God would say to us today.

- - - - - -

Pray

'Lord, speak to us today, and help us to listen; to dwell deeply in your word, and to find our security in you, rather than our own grasping need for control or status.'

The nations

'And all peoples on earth will be blessed through you.'
Genesis 12:3b

Read Genesis 12:1–9

In the sweep of the Bible, this passage in Genesis 12 is a key moment. After feeling weighed down by the hopelessness of sinful humanity in the previous chapters, God's heart and plan for the world are beautifully revealed. He will bring hope and blessing to counteract the curse. It's interesting that the word 'blessing' is used five times in this passage, and that God especially wants to bless the *nations* – all peoples on earth who believe in him. It's so important. From the beginning, God's plan has been for the nations. He will bring about a lavish banquet in the garden, for the nations, and he will do that, he says, through one man, Abraham, and through the nation that he and his descendants will become. What an amazing promise! Of course, as we read the narrative today, we know what happened to the descendants of Abraham. We know about Isaac and Jacob and Joseph and all of the others up to David, and then to the Lord Jesus himself. But Abraham didn't know that back then, and neither did Sarah. They didn't know how long it would take. Back then, though, we hope they heard the stress on the word *'I'*. God said to them, *'I* will make you into a great nation.' *'I* will bless you.' *'I* will make your name great . . .' They didn't need to know how he would do it. They needed to know in whom to put their trust. It's the same for us today.

- - - - - -

Pray

'Lord, help us to put our trust in you, to hold onto the truth that you will bring about your purposes through the Lord Jesus, even when the way appears very dim.'

Is anything too hard for the Lord?

'Now the LORD was gracious to Sarah as he had said, and the LORD did for Sarah what he had promised.'

Genesis 21:1

Read Genesis 12:10 – 21:7

I find this section of Genesis strange every time I read it. God announced his great plan of salvation history, for the world, through Abraham . . . and then the events that followed were not easy or smooth or clear at all. Firstly, the Canaanites were already in the land. Then, Abraham failed, twisting the truth of Sarah's identity in order to be treated well in Egypt. Then, Lot took the better part of the land. And most importantly, Abraham and Sarah were so old and barren that they were unable to bear a child. After years of distress, they chose Hagar to be the child-bearer. What sort of narrative is this? Couldn't God have made it a whole lot simpler, or chosen healthier, more obedient people? But two things are striking. Firstly, God kept speaking and revealing his covenant. He was, and is, patient and faithful. Nothing is impossible for him. And secondly, by the time Isaac was finally born (25 years after the initial promise), Abraham and Sarah must have been so profoundly aware of their own failures and weaknesses that they knew, without a doubt, that Isaac was a gift from a sovereign, generous, promise-keeping God whom they could trust. It was not their doing or cleverness! It was God's plan to save. And in Abraham and Sarah, we see ourselves – helpless and dependent, longing to put our trust in God who is faithful to his promises for the world.

- - - - - -

Pray

'Lord, help us to come humbly to you today, painfully aware of our own weaknesses, and trusting in your good purposes in everything.'

The Lord provides

> **'Do not do anything to him. Now I know that you fear God, because you have not withheld from me your son, your only son.'**
>
> **Genesis 22:12b**

Read Genesis 22:1–19

If the family history of Abraham and Sarah strikes us as strange early on, then there was worse to come. When Sarah finally bore their child Isaac, we all smiled with her and rejoiced. We could almost feel the warm baby flesh in our own ageing arms, and sense her joy and wonder at the good plans of God, and the fulfilment of the promise. So why, then, did the wonder turn so quickly to fear? Why did God test Abraham with the hardest of all questions? Why did God ask Abraham to give up his only son – the one through whom multitudes would be given life? It makes no sense to us. And how did Abraham actually do what he was told when we would have run screaming off into the bushes? The text tells us that Abraham got up and obeyed. He took with him two servants, and his son Isaac, and the wood. Then, after walking for three days, he placed Isaac on the altar at Mount Moriah. The entire story horrifies us. But Abraham obeyed, and the Lord intervened and provided a ram as a substitute. Somehow, Abraham passed the test. He trusted God. And in doing so, he pointed ahead to the incredible day when the Lord would offer his own beloved Son as a substitute for us.

- - - - - -

Pray

'Lord, we don't understand this story, but we sit with it, and we thank you. We know that you are faithful. Please develop perseverance and faith in us, even in the midst of trials.'

Isaac and Rebekah

'So she became his wife, and he loved her.'
Genesis 24:67b

Read Genesis 24:1–67

There is much to enjoy about this chapter. Isaac, the son of Abraham and
Sarah, needed a wife, and his servant was sent to Paddan Aram in search
of one. Rebekah was found as a gracious and almost miraculous answer to
prayer. It's lovely! But the story seems to be about more than a timely union,
or a handy meeting of souls. God's plan for the world mattered enormously.
He would provide a way of salvation for all people and he would do it
through this one family, so their family and descendants mattered. Yet it's
also striking that within God's large plan for the world, these individual,
ordinary people mattered. Each of them had a distinct and important role
to play. The servant prayed and trusted. Rebekah appeared at the well at
just the right moment, and spoke the words the servant was waiting to hear.
Even the family requirements were met, seemingly effortlessly. So much so,
that everyone remarked on the Lord's provision. *'This is from the LORD'* they
said (24:50). I often wonder, though, about the later years, when life became
hard. Did Isaac and Rebekah look back on that day and continue to draw
encouragement from God's provision and guidance? I hope they did . . . and
I hope that we do too in hard times. It's a challenge to actually lean on the
character of God and to recall his gracious intervention when it doesn't
easily come to mind.

- - - - - -

Pray

> *'Lord, thank you for the way you answer prayer, now and in the time of Isaac.*
> *Help us to notice and lean on your character on all the days when it isn't clear.'*

Patience

'Isaac prayed to the LORD on behalf of his wife, because she was childless.'
Genesis 25:21

Read Genesis 25:19–26

It's a noticeably short description in Genesis 25, telling us that Isaac was 40 years old when he married Rebekah, and he prayed to the Lord on behalf of her because she was childless. Then *'the LORD answered his prayer'* and Rebekah became pregnant and gave birth to twins. It sounds simple, except that it took 20 years! Isaac was 60 years old when Rebekah gave birth to twins (v. 26). God waited to act for 20 years. It's stunning. Even though the Lord had graciously promised to provide descendants and salvation through Abraham and then Isaac, the path (in this case to childbearing) was not easy or simple. Did Isaac and Rebekah have questions or doubts during those 20 years? Did they pray for patience? I remember when we were living in Nepal and I was home-schooling our three sons on a monsoonal Himalayan ridge, through a civil war, I often prayed for patience. In my mind, I imagined that God would pour a golden bowl of patience onto my head, making everything easier. It didn't work out that way! The rain and the war continued, and God gave me a path where patience was required. Reading this chapter, I imagine Isaac and Rebekah praying and growing in patience and trusting in God as they waited. And I imagine millions of people on the path behind them, also growing in patience – waiting firstly for the Messiah to come and now, today, waiting for him to return in glory.

- - - - - -

Pray

'Lord, please grow patience in us today, in the small things as well as the large, on the path where patience is required.'

In need of transformation

'The first to come out was red, and his whole body was like a hairy garment; so they named him Esau. After this, his brother came out, with his hand grasping Esau's heel; so he was named Jacob.'

Genesis 25:25–26

Read Genesis 25:22–34

It's a little bit disappointing. After waiting so long for the descendants of Abraham to be born (and for God to do something wonderful through them), the twins that were born to Isaac and Rebekah both seem, at first glance, to be a bit defective. Esau, the first, was red and hairy and careless, and Jacob, the second, was self-seeking and grasping. In fact, one day, Esau was so focused on his appetite that he sold his birthright to Jacob and, in doing so, gave away the Lord's blessing to his younger, deceitful brother. This was a serious event with enormous consequences! What was God doing? The narrative causes us to stop and wonder. We know that in the rest of Genesis, God used Jacob and his family. A nation came from Jacob, and it ultimately led to the saving work of Jesus. Jacob was self-seeking, but God was able to transform him over time for his good purposes. It reminds us that if he can do that with self-seeking, grasping Jacob, then he can also do that with us, in all our faults, to bring about his purposes and make his name known in the world. It's a comfort and an encouragement today in the face of our flaws.

- - - - - -

Pray

'Lord, it's easy to feel disappointment. Help us to notice the way you slowly transform your people through your Spirit, and you bring about good things even through our flaws.'

Deception and duplicity

'Jacob said to his father, "I am Esau your firstborn. I have done as you told me. Please sit up and eat some of my game, so that you may give me your blessing."'

Genesis 27:19

Read Genesis 27:1–41

Normally, we think that justice will be served. The person who lies shouldn't benefit from those lies. Trickery won't be condoned. Deceitfulness is wrong! So why did Jacob receive the blessing from Isaac (the most important death-bed blessing) after blatantly lying? It doesn't make sense, again. What has happened to the Lord's good plan, or even worse, to the Lord's good values? Is everything going to derail here in chapter 27? Has the Lord lost control? No. In this narrative, every character was tainted with duplicity, even Isaac and Rebekah who were pitted against each other with their scheming. But if nothing else, it reminds us of ourselves and the entire human race. We too are tainted with duplicity, and are inherently self-serving. Incredibly, we can come to the Lord in repentance and faith. We can say sorry. Amazingly, because of the Lord's own sacrifice through Jesus, we can receive grace. Perhaps, more than anything, this narrative forces us to sit with the extent of our own sinfulness and the mercy of grace. Even within this most flawed situation, God still remained sovereign, and he was not surprised. Jacob received the blessing and he was sent off to Paddan Aram to find a wife.

- - - - - -

Pray

Lord, please speak to us today. Remind us that as humans we are not good, or deserving of grace. Instead, you have showered us in love and mercy. Let it sink in again today.'

I am with you

'I am with you and will watch over you wherever you go.'
Genesis 28:15

Read Genesis 28:10–22

Jacob did as he was told. He left Canaan for Paddan Aram, and on the way there he had a dream. The Lord said, *'I am the LORD, the God of your father Abraham and the God of Isaac. I will give you and your descendants the land on which you are lying. Your descendants will be like the dust of the earth, and you will spread out to the west and to the east, to the north and to the south. All peoples on earth will be blessed through you and your offspring. I am with you and will watch over you wherever you go, and I will bring you back to this land. I will not leave you until I have done what I have promised you'* (28:13–15). It was the same promise given to Abraham and now repeated to undeserving Jacob. He must have woken up in awe. He certainly responded in faith. But within that all-encompassing plan, Jacob must have noticed the small, intimate phrase, 'I am with you.' The God of his father and grandfather was with him! It was the most precious promise ever given to anyone. It was the promise that would be repeated to numerous individuals in the generations to come, and then ultimately to us, through the Lord Jesus. In Matthew 28:20, Jesus said to the believers, *'And surely I am with you always, to the very end of the age.'*

- - - - - -

Pray

'Lord, we thank you that you promised your followers something far greater than ease of life or prosperity. You promised that you would be with us in everything, today and for ever. Thank you.'

From Leah's perspective

'When morning came, there was Leah!'
Genesis 29:25

Read Genesis 29:14b – 30:24

With interesting echoes to Isaac's story, Jacob continued on his journey and he met beautiful Rachel by the well in Paddan Aram. He fell in love with her, and Rachel responded in kind. Nice! But Rachel also had a sister with 'weak eyes' and she had a scheming father, Laban. Laban bargained with Jacob over the bride price (which became seven years of labour) and then, after seven years, Laban deceived Jacob and gave him Leah instead of Rachel. Awful! Jacob, the deceiver, had been deceived himself, and he needed to work for another seven years in order to marry Rachel as well. As I read this story, though, I often think about Leah. How did she feel that morning when she heard Jacob's rant? Did she bury her head in the pillows and cry, wishing she was her sister? Possibly. But there is a line in the text that is surprising and lovely. *'When the LORD saw that Leah was not loved, he enabled her to conceive'* (29:31). It is strangely unexpected. This God of Abraham is compassionate and kind and merciful. He knew Leah's heart and he gave her a child. Stunningly, even after Jacob had fathered twelve sons, via four different women, it was through one of Leah's sons (Judah) that the Saviour of the world, Jesus, would eventually come. We sit in quietness at this narrative. There is much that we don't understand, but we trust in a God who is compassionate and kind, as well as faithful.

- - - - - -

Pray

> *'Lord, thank you for your unexpected kindness. Thank you that you know our hearts. Help us to respond to your mercy today.'*

Jacob wrestled with God

'I am unworthy of all the kindness and faithfulness you have shown your servant.'

Genesis 32:10

Read Genesis 30:25 – 32:32

After Jacob had married both Rachel and Leah (and their maidservants), and fathered 11 sons, the family headed home. Reading the account, though, it's clear that those 20 years had not been easy. Even the dialogue between the sisters and Jacob is brutal in its honesty, brimming over with jealousy and anger, as well as attempts at vindication. Then, Jacob tricked Laban out of all his best livestock and left. Was that okay? Jacob, who knew the truth, *fled with all he had . . . and headed for the hill country of Gilead'* (31:21). Of course, it wasn't the end of the story. Laban, Esau and God all caught up with Jacob. God (the man) wrestled Jacob. It's difficult to picture, but the thing that is most striking is that immediately before the wrestle, Jacob prayed in repentance. For the first time, Jacob knelt down and admitted to God that he was unworthy and unable. Most of us spend an inordinate amount of time and energy trying to prove ourselves to each other. But before God, we can, and must, be completely honest. God knows us. Jacob admitted his dire need before God and then later, God wrestled him, leaving him with a painful limp. Jacob saw God face to face, and yet he stayed alive, humbled and dependent. We too can learn from this, because God, who is powerful and gracious, has the right to confront us, and we need to kneel.

- - - - - -

Pray

'Lord, we acknowledge your power and rule and authority. We submit in humility. And we thank you that because of Jesus we will never feel the full force of your judgement.'

The gift called need

**'So Rachel died and was buried on the way to Ephrath
(that is, Bethlehem).'**
Genesis 35:19

Read Genesis 34 – 36

There is a gift called 'need'. It causes us to pray more urgently. It causes us
to stop and plead with God, and to accept the truth that the best of our
cleverness won't fix things. At those times, we pray more desperately, 'Lord,
please act!' Reading chapters 34 – 36 of Genesis feels a bit like that. The
immorality within Jacob's extended family continued. Jacob's daughter,
Dinah, was raped by a Canaanite. Two of her brothers (Simeon and Levi)
acted violently in response. Many men died. Then, Jacob's beloved wife
Rachel died in childbirth, and his eldest son Reuben slept with his own
concubine Bilhah. This is not an admirable family history! It was shameful
and tragic. It is noteworthy that the stories were even recorded. Surely,
anyone who wanted to write an inspiring story about the family of God
would not include these. But no, the stories reveal the extent of our own
need and God's redeeming hand. We are not so far from these chapters. We
too need God's grace within our need. In the sweep of the Genesis narrative,
the story isn't over. The focus will soon turn to Joseph, the son of Jacob,
through whom God's grace will transform this family, and then the world.
In the sweep of our own lives too, the story isn't over. God's grace is able to
transform us today and we can trust him in our need.

- - - - - -

Pray

*'Lord, some days we come to you desperate. We can't see a way forward. We
are wearied by our own efforts and our own scheming. Please work your
grace in us and in those we love.'*

Hints of grace

"'Here comes that dreamer!" they said to each other. "Come now, let's kill him.'"

Genesis 37:19–20

Read Genesis 37:1–36

The early description of Joseph's life seems unremarkable. He was a young man of 17, busy tending the flocks with his brothers. But it didn't stay that way. Jacob, who loved Joseph more than the others, made him an ornate robe – a brightly colourful statement of his love. And the brothers were angry. As a mother of sons, and as a sibling myself, I can imagine this. I know how family rivalry works. And, of course, the brothers' anger only intensified when Joseph told them about his dreams in which his brothers bowed low before him. They were more than annoyed. They plotted to kill him, and they would have succeeded if Reuben hadn't convinced them to throw him in the well, and if Judah hadn't convinced them to sell him to the Midianite merchants for 20 silver shekels. The brothers, of course, then returned to Jacob, who wailed at the news of Joseph's death by wild animals, as well he should. But the thing that is striking through this whole story is the character of Joseph. At no point do we hear Joseph scheming or using deceit. He didn't voice anger or a need for retaliation. He was obedient. After a deluge of disappointing characters, it's welcome relief. In Joseph's story we sense grace, and we want more. The narrative beckons us to read on because there is more of grace to come.

- - - - - -

Pray

> *'Lord, thank you for your glimpses of grace and transformation. Help us to see that all of grace comes from you.'*

In favour, or in prison

> 'But while Joseph was there in the prison, the LORD was with him; he showed
> him kindness and granted him favour in the eyes of the prison warder.'
>
> **Genesis 39:20–21**

Read Genesis 39:1–23

The description of Joseph's life in this chapter appears to be one of extremes.
At the beginning of the chapter, Joseph was in favour in Egypt, in charge
of everything in Potiphar's house. But by the end of the chapter, he was
in prison. The contrast is striking and yet the narrative is also one of
similarities. When Joseph was in Potiphar's house, he lived faithfully and he
was given responsibility. He acted without malice, even when tempted by
Potiphar's wife and then falsely accused. But equally so, when Joseph was
in prison, he lived faithfully and he was given responsibility while confined
behind bars. It's really challenging – the reminder that we will all experience
extremes of life – measures of success, as well as suffering. For Darren and
I, moving from the comfort of Australia to civil war and curfews in Nepal,
and then back to opportunities (and their associated anxieties) in Australia,
has felt similar. In all cases, how will we respond? Will we be faithful? Will
we seek the Lord in the same manner, in all situations? It's also striking that
in Genesis 39, in both situations, *'the LORD was with him'* (v. 2,21). In a
spiritual sense, to God there was no difference at all. God was at work, in
Joseph and through him. The temptations and the settings differed, but in
God's eyes it was faithfulness that mattered. It's the same for us today.

- - - - - -

Pray

> *'Lord, challenge us to serve and love you faithfully, whether in plenty or in
> need. Thank you that you are with us equally in both.'*

An unexpected plot

> **'The chief cupbearer, however, did not remember Joseph;**
> **he forgot him.'**
> **Genesis 40:23**

Read Genesis 40:1–23

For a story to grip the reader, it has to have twists and turns and surprises. Joseph's story certainly has those. In prison, Joseph attended the cupbearer and the baker of the king of Egypt. The two men were in prison for offending their master, and after some time they both had dreams, and Joseph interpreted the dreams for them. The narrative seems like it's finally becoming clearer. Joseph's dreams and word pictures are a gift from God. Surely God will soon act to favour Joseph and release him, through the dreams. But Joseph wasn't released. The cupbearer (who was released) forgot all about Joseph, and Joseph stayed in prison for two more years. It teaches us again that God's ways and timing aren't anything like ours. We leap to conclusions and use human logic to guess what God will do next (in our personal lives, or in the world), and every time he surprises us. Incredibly, though, God is never surprised. He is able to use every seeming twist in the plot, and unexpected outcome, both then and now, for his purposes – to make Christ known, and to grow each of us in our walk with him.

- - - - - -

Pray

> *'Lord, we see unexpected twists in our lives and families every day. Mostly, we wish it were simpler, or even a little bit predictable. Help us to see twists in the path through your lens, not ours.'*

Pharaoh's dream

"'I cannot do it," Joseph replied to Pharaoh, "but God will give Pharaoh the answer he desires.'"

Genesis 41:16

Read Genesis 41:1–57

For some of us, strangely, it can be harder to trust God when things are going well than when they're hard. Perhaps we become spiritually complacent, or feel less of a need to pray, or to remember the Lordship of Christ in everything. Not so with Joseph! After two more years in prison, the king of Egypt had an inexplicable dream, and the cupbearer, who had previously forgotten all about Joseph, suddenly remembered him. Hooray! Joseph was released from prison, cleaned up, and brought before Pharaoh. It was a wonderful answer to prayer but, incredibly, Joseph didn't focus on the opportunity, or his own ability to meet it. He kept his eyes on God. Pharaoh asked Joseph if he could interpret his dream and straight away Joseph said, *'I cannot do it, but God will'* (41:16). In one sentence, Joseph admitted his own frailty and he pointed to God as the giver of gifts and the Lord of all. He remembered God, even when things were going well. And then Joseph was enabled by God to give Pharaoh the dream interpretation as well as the wisdom to plan his future. Pharaoh, of course, was overwhelmingly thankful and he placed Joseph in charge of the entire palace and the land, because he saw that God's spirit of wisdom was in him. It challenges us to stop and pray and humbly depend on God when there is outward ease, or affirmation, as well as in its absence.

- - - - - -

Pray

'Lord, help us to remember that you rule always – even in the times that seem less desperate to us.'

Joseph wept

'Deeply moved at the sight of his brother, Joseph hurried out and looked for a place to weep.'
Genesis 43:30

Read Genesis 42:1 – 43:34

As foretold by Joseph, the famine in Egypt was severe and it affected the other lands as well, bringing Joseph's family back into the picture. The brothers suddenly found themselves dependent on Joseph, bowing down before him without even recognising him. The interaction is fascinating. Joseph, with all the power to do anything he wanted, didn't use it for revenge or mockery. He focused on finding out whether Benjamin was okay. It's also fascinating that even though more than 20 years had passed, the brothers still felt guilt over Joseph when questioned. As humans, we do carry the weight of past deeds or misdemeanours, or our failures to live well. It hangs on us. And yet within all of that, Joseph was gracious. He displayed a grace that could only come from God. Firstly, he wept over his brothers, and he gave them bags of grain and provisions for the journey. Then, when they returned with Benjamin, he was so overwhelmed by his own emotion that he left the room to weep. The weeping, perhaps, makes us wonder. Would we have done that? Would we have kept the injustice from our voice? Would we have put pride aside? Did Joseph learn that degree of generosity and grace while in prison? Did he work hard to keep the bitterness out of his soul? Was he somehow so mindful of God's grace that he could respond in kind, and with weeping?

- - - - - -

Pray

'Lord, we thank you for your grace. We can't drum it up in ourselves, but we can receive it from you, in Christ, and then pour it out.'

Joseph revealed himself

'And they threw themselves to the ground before him.'
Genesis 44:14b

Read Genesis 44:1 – 45:7

In another twist to the narrative, Joseph deliberately planted a silver cup in Benjamin's sack. Why did he do that? If it wasn't for vindication, then why? Did he need to detain Benjamin? Did he need to discover what was beneath the polite exterior of his brother's words? He certainly found out. They returned to him and tore their clothes. They threw themselves before him and pleaded with him. And that was when Joseph revealed to them who he was. It's breathtaking. Joseph was overcome by emotion, and they were terrified, unable to speak. No wonder! They were probably thinking he would kill them. But in some of the most remarkable words ever spoken, Joseph said to them, *'Do not be distressed and do not be angry with yourselves for selling me here, because it was to save lives that God sent me ahead of you'* (45:5). Here is a person who was so focused on God's saving plan that he was able to put his own ego and needs out of the way. He spoke grace to them. In doing so, he pointed ahead to Jesus, who would speak words of grace on the cross to the angry crowd before him, *'Father, forgive them, for they do not know what they are doing'* (Luke 23:34). It's the grace of God that overwhelms us today. We are forgiven by the blood of Jesus, and the weight of sin need no longer drag heavily on our shoulders. We freely receive mercy from God.

- - - - - -

Pray

> *'Lord, help us to pause today and say thank you for the blood of Jesus.'*

Attributing everything to God

'God has made me lord of all Egypt. Come down to me; don't delay.'
Genesis 45:9b

Read Genesis 45:7 – 47:31

It's the extravagant generosity that is striking in these chapters. Joseph didn't merely forgive his brothers. He poured out gifts on them – clothing and grain and silver shekels. He invited them to return with their father, and he gave them the best land in Egypt. But in everything, Joseph attributed the events to God. He kept saying that *God* placed him there, and *God* allowed him to rule. In response, of course, Jacob was unable to contain himself. *'My son Joseph is still alive'* (45:28). It must have felt like a miraculous resurrection to Jacob. And then, the reunion was beautiful. Restoration is possible, under God! But as well as that, there is a lovely promise in chapter 46. Jacob was 130 years old by then, but God spoke to him on the journey, repeating the promise and affirming their relocation to Egypt. He said to Jacob, *'I will make you into a great nation there . . . and I will surely bring you back again'* (46:3–4). As the reader, it's remarkable to notice that God was setting up the exodus even here. But for Jacob in that moment, he needed affirmation and God gave it to him. He needed the reminder, as we do, of God's character and promises.

- - - - - -

Pray

> *'Lord, thank you that you speak to us through your Word and your Spirit.*
> *Help us to hear your voice today and to hold on to your promises, in every*
> *stage of life.'*

God meant it for good

'You intended to harm me, but God intended it for good to accomplish
what is now being done, the saving of many lives.'

Genesis 50:20

Read Genesis 48:1 – 50:26

The final chapters of Genesis are very hopeful. The promises given to Abraham
in Genesis 12 were passed on to Jacob's offspring. Through one of Judah's line,
a ruler would come to whom the nations would submit; and through Joseph's
line, there would be abundant blessings because God had been his helper.
As well as that, the family were reassured that God would come to their aid
in Egypt, and take them back to the land of promise. Wonderful! And then,
almost to sum up the book, Joseph spoke to his brothers after their father
died. They were probably still feeling guilty and worried about what Joseph
might do to them, so Joseph told them not to be afraid. *'You intended to harm
me, but God intended it for good to accomplish what is now being done, the saving
of many lives'* (50:20). It's the kind of statement that couldn't have been spoken
lightly, and we mustn't read it lightly. Joseph had developed a profound sense
of knowing God and trusting in his purposes, through years of struggle and
betrayal and false accusations. He knew, more than anything, that God was a
God who saves. In Egypt, it was from starvation, but for us today, he saves us
from everything that keeps us apart from him. So we ask him to make us into
the people he wants us to be.

- - - - - -

Pray

> *'Lord, help us to see your good, saving purposes, through Christ . . . in
> everything, even the parts of our life, and ourselves, that we would never
> choose.'*

Moses is born

'But when she could hide him no longer, she got a papyrus basket for him and coated it with tar and pitch.'

Exodus 2:3

Read Exodus 1:1 – 2:10

It's a curious thing. God's promise to Abraham regarding the size of his family, actually happened. The Israelites increased in number! But then, their sheer numbers threatened the Egyptians and the new Egyptian king put slave masters over them, and years of terrible toil resulted. The Israelites suffered and groaned, baking bricks and labouring in the hot sun. It was bitter and ruthless for everyone. What was God doing? How was this part of his good plan? But then the plan seemed to worsen. The king of Egypt ordered that every Hebrew boy born must be thrown into the Nile. We can almost hear the mothers wailing. We would have wailed. But God, who had not forgotten his people, caused a baby to be born. And the baby was going to be the rescuer. There is a wonderful clue in the text. The baby's mother placed him in a *'papyrus basket'* (2:3). It's the same word used in Genesis 6 for the ark that Noah built. The baby, who would be the rescuer, was placed in a tiny ark, in the water, the place of chaos . . . and then rescued by the Pharaoh's own daughter, and nursed by his own mother. It's an amazing story! The God of the Israelites is able to rescue. Nothing is beyond him, but he often works in quiet, upside-down ways. We need to remember that, for the times when we also walk an unclear path.

- - - - - -

Pray

'Lord, we often fail to trust you in the chaos. Please grant us again a vision of your plan in Christ.'

Eighty long years

'The Israelites groaned in their slavery and cried out.'
Exodus 2:23b

Read Exodus 2:11–25

It's a good story, but it's long. The child Moses lived and grew up, and it took 80 long years for anything to seemingly happen. As a child, Moses was nursed by his mother and then raised in the palace as the son of Pharaoh's daughter. It's hard to imagine how that was for Moses. Did he see himself as a Hebrew or an Egyptian? Did he grow up worshipping Egyptian gods or the God of his ancestors? Did he understand the difference? At age 40, Moses went to the place where his people were slaving away, and he saw an Egyptian beating a Hebrew, so he killed the Egyptian. That's one way to deal with oppression, but it's not God's way. The murder became known and, as a result, Moses fled to the desert for another 40 years. He was a hot-headed failure. What did his family think of him now? Did they hear the news and assume that their only glimmer of hope had disappeared for ever in the sand dunes? We don't know, but we do know that God was still at work in the life of Moses, in ways that went largely unnoticed. This is typical of God. He also works in our (unexceptional) lives, through times of trial and waiting and preparation. Our path is very different to that of Moses, but the Lord longs to grow us and teach us and to mould us for his purposes. Our lives of faith will also require much perseverance, and it's often the times of waiting that develop it.

- - - - - -

Pray

'Lord, we often wait, unseeing. Help us to develop perseverance, and to see time and events through your eyes.'

Yahweh

'God said to Moses, "I AM WHO I AM."'
Exodus 3:14

Read Exodus 3:1–22

After another 40 long years, the Lord met Moses in the desert. He suddenly appeared from within a burning bush, and he spoke to Moses, calling him by name. Imagine being Moses that day. Imagine the hot ground beneath his feet and the fear inside him. Imagine the terrible surprise, after years of tending sheep and assuming that life had passed him by. There was the Lord, calling him by name, and telling him that he'd heard the cry of the Israelites, and he had a rescue plan. I think I would have been on the ground, unable to speak or breathe. After all those years! But then God told Moses to go to Pharaoh, and bring his people out of Egypt. Moses was worried. He questioned why it should be him. I love the Lord's reply. He said, *'I will be with you.'* It makes all the difference. It's enough! It's the same promise given to Jacob in Genesis 28, and then throughout Joseph's life. God will be with him. But there was even more than that. God told Moses his own name, *'I AM WHO I AM,* Yahweh' (3:14). It's a stunning revelation. It's so intimate. It's the first revelation of his name. The human relationship with the almighty God had suddenly become even more personal and intimate. The Lord had a name, and he revealed it to Moses and then, in consequence, to all of us who would come after him.

- - - - - -

Pray

> *'Lord, sometimes we think that you are distant or theoretical. Remind us today that your purpose is intimacy and rich relationship. Thank you that we can speak to you today by name.'*

Who gave you the capacity to speak?

'The LORD said to him, "Who gave human beings their mouths?"'
Exodus 4:11

Read Exodus 4:1–17

Even after God promised to be with Moses and revealed his name to him, Moses was still worried, especially that the Egyptians wouldn't believe him or listen to him. So then the Lord revealed his power to Moses through three miraculous signs. This is how they will believe! But Moses still didn't want to go. He wasn't good enough. He'd never been eloquent, and he was slow of speech and tongue. So God replied, asking Moses the most probing of questions, *'Who gave human beings their mouths? Who makes them deaf or mute? Who gives them sight or makes them blind? Is it not I, the LORD?'* (4:11). It's the reminder we all need. Every capacity Moses has (and every capacity we have), is from God. He gave us our mouths to speak. On top of that, every good or wise thought is from God. We speak it, or write it, but God gives it. And while this is a specific reminder for Moses, it helps us too. God works his ongoing, saving plan through unexceptional, weak people, like babies and slaves and us. In fact, it's often in our weakness that God works even more powerfully. In Exodus 4, God told Moses to go again, but Moses still didn't want to go. So then, with unbearable patience, God gave Moses a helper, his brother Aaron. It's wonderful, because it means that we too are recipients of God's mercy and patience. Though we are weak, he has given us all that we need to serve.

- - - - - -

Pray

> *'Lord, thank you for your unbearable patience, and the reminder that all that we have is from you, and it's enough.'*

Then you will know

'But I will harden his heart so that he will not let the people go.'
Exodus 4:21b

Read Exodus 4:18 – 6:12

It's so difficult to understand. Moses returned to Egypt, in obedience to the Lord, and he took his family with him. Along the way, they met with Aaron and the elders of the Israelites. After explaining to them what the Lord had said and done, the Israelite leaders bowed down in worship. It was good! But then, when Moses and Aaron actually went to Pharaoh and asked him to let their people go, Pharaoh simply refused. He ordered the Israelites to work even harder! He treated them more harshly! Surely, this wasn't meant to happen. Surely, this God who is more powerful than our human minds can ever imagine, could enact his plan better than this? But there is a truth hidden away in chapter 4. God told Moses that he would deliberately harden Pharaoh's heart. Why did he say that, or do that? No wonder Moses went back to enquire of the Lord. And God repeated the same promise that he would rescue and redeem his people. But he added something new. *'Then you will know that I am the LORD your God, who brought you out from under the yoke of the Egyptians'* (6:7). Then you will know. Perhaps when the way is smooth or easy, our 'knowing' of God is not embedded in our souls. It's superficial. And more than anything, God wants us to utterly depend on him, in everything.

- - - - - -

Pray

>*'Lord, we don't know why you hardened Pharaoh's heart, but we do know that you want each of us to know you more, so teach us again, we pray.'*

The awful plagues

'But I have raised you up for this very purpose, that I might show you my power and that my name might be proclaimed in all the earth.'
Exodus 9:16

Read Exodus 7:1 – 10:29

Moses and Aaron returned to Pharaoh, as the Lord commanded them. They were old men by then, possibly white-haired and unsteady on their legs, but amazingly, they performed miracles in front of Pharaoh, by the power of God. Moses' staff became a snake, hissing on the ground. Then he reached it across the Nile, turning the river to blood and causing the fish to die. But that didn't convince Pharaoh. He wouldn't let the Israelites go. So the Lord sent plagues – frogs and gnats and flies everywhere, buzzing in the Egyptian's hair and in their eyes, and even in the palace. It must have been awful. But the cycle continued. Pharaoh showed signs of relenting and then his heart hardened again. So the Lord sent more plagues – festering boils, and hail storms, and devouring locusts, and then complete darkness for three days. It was a wholesale display of God's absolute power over everything. But it makes us question. Couldn't God have revealed his power and glory in other ways, or perhaps quicker? Yet again, there is a quiet clue in the text. Through this, *'the Egyptians will know that I am the Lord'* (7:5). Pharaoh himself was raised up, so that *'my name might be proclaimed in all the earth'* (9:16). God was not content to reveal himself only to the Israelites. He wanted to make himself known in all the earth! And even today, we trust that God is doing exactly that.

- - - - - -

Pray

'Lord, help us to widen our view of your work in the world today. Please help us to see, and be part of your proclamation.'

The final plague

> **'The blood will be a sign for you on the houses where you are, and when I see the blood, I will pass over you.'**
>
> **Exodus 12:13**

Read Exodus 11:1 – 12:36

I remember reading this section of Exodus while we were living through civil war in Nepal. Many of our Nepali friends were groaning. They had lost children and livelihood and education. I often cried out to God, 'Lord, when will you hear them? When will you do something?' In that context, though, reading parts of Exodus confused me. I knew, as I read Exodus, that God planned to deliver the Israelites. He would give *them* a message to the nations and a Saviour . . . but what about the people of Nepal? What could we hope for? Then I came to the final plague. On the entire land, apart from the houses marked by the lamb's blood, a plague came that wiped out every firstborn child. Then, Pharaoh commanded the Israelites to go and to worship the Lord. They left Egypt, with their unleavened bread in their bags. Ultimately, though, the people were not following Pharaoh's command; they were following Yahweh's. Yahweh had told them to smear blood on their doorframes. Yahweh had saved them and passed over them. For any of us suffering in other lands, the comfort is real. We don't know that God will rescue us from current suffering, but we trust him. Why? Because we know that 1,500 years later, his perfect Son shed his blood for us that we might be saved, not from the Egyptians, but from our own feeble attempts to live life without God. We also have been rescued with his mighty hand.

- - - - - -

Pray

> *'Lord, you are good, you are holy, you are trustworthy. Help us to accept your saving grace.'*

The people were delivered

'The LORD is my strength and my defence; he has become
my salvation.'

Exodus 15:2

Read Exodus 12:37 – 15:21

When Jacob and his family arrived in Egypt, they numbered 66 descendants; and when they left Egypt, they numbered 600,000. They had multiplied! It was exciting. God led the Israelites out of Egypt by the desert road towards the Red Sea. It was his wonderful plan. But then, the Egyptians pursued them and overtook them! And God, who had somehow caused this to happen, was still God. He would gain glory for himself. Of course, the Israelites were terrified. Some of them even wished they'd stayed behind in Egypt! But Moses told them not to be afraid. The Lord would fight for them. And he did! The Lord caused the Red Sea to part in two. All night long, the Lord drove back the sea with a strong east wind, and the Israelites walked through on dry ground. I love the description of the Lord's presence. All through their journey, he led the way in a pillar of cloud by day, and a pillar of fire by night. Then, during that entire night, the Lord moved between them and the armies of Egypt. He even caused darkness and light to co-exist. This is what God is like! And when the people reached the other side, they celebrated. They danced and they sang! They praised the Lord with tambourines because he had brought them out of Egypt. They were amazed at his power and glory! Thousands of years later, we rest on this story, and we still sing. This is what God is like, and this is still his saving heart.

- - - - - -

Pray

'Lord, let us not miss your power and your glory and your saving heart today.'

Then they grumbled

'So the people grumbled against Moses, saying, "What are we to drink?"'

Exodus 15:24

Read Exodus 15:22 – 17:7

Prior to the Lord's great saving act of the exodus, he had told them to remember – to commemorate the day, and celebrate the Passover, and eat the unleavened bread, and consecrate their firstborn. Why? So they would remember him. The commemorating would be like a sign on their hands and a symbol on their foreheads. The Lord knew they were in danger of forgetting! And then, three days after God's greatest saving act ever, the people forgot. They walked for three days in the desert and they grumbled about the lack of water. But even then, the Lord provided for them and reminded them to listen to him and do what was right in his eyes. It worked for a time, but by the next month they were grumbling again, this time about food. So the Lord rained down manna and quail from heaven, enough for each person, and enough for each day. He wanted them to trust him. He wanted them to know who he was! At the same time, he told them to rest on the seventh day. They could gather food on six days, but they were to rest on the seventh day, a holy day to the Lord. He would provide for them. The rhythm was good and generous, but so quickly the human response became tarnished. They wanted more. And we see ourselves in this narrative. We too want more, and we become anxious. We forget the Lord and his good rhythm for our days. We fail to honour him as the giver of all things.

- - - - - -

Pray

'Lord, forgive us for gripping onto your gifts, and forgetting who you are as the giver.'

'As long as Moses held up his hands, the Israelites were winning.'
Exodus 17:11

Read Exodus 17:8–16

When any of us take a journey, we're sure to meet threats along the way.
The threats might be physical or relational. We want more food, or we
argue with each other and complain. But at other times, the threats might
be external. In this case, the Israelites journeyed to Sinai, and they met
both. The external threats took the form of the Amalekites. We may have
questions at this point. Why did the Lord plan to blot out the name of
Amalek from under heaven? What kinds of evil did they do? But within our
questions, the emphasis is on God. He wanted the Israelites to be utterly
dependent on him, and to look to him. He wanted them to remember who
he was. So, Moses stood on the hill and he held up the staff of God – that
great reminder of God's power and saving might in the exodus. As long as
Moses held up the staff, the Israelites were winning. When Moses got tired,
Aaron and Hur helped him to hold his hands up and point to God. And the
Lord said, *'Write this on a scroll as something to be remembered . . .'* (17:14).
It was important then, and it's important today. God wants our focus to be
on him as the source of all things and the reason for all things. When we get
tired or weary, we need to help each other to look to his strength and rule,
trusting that he will bring the change that he wants.

- - - - - -

Pray

> *'Lord, we pray again today, and we ask that you would teach us about
> persistent trust in an era of instantaneity.'*

'Now if you obey me fully and keep my covenant, then out of all nations you will be my treasured possession.'

Exodus 19:5

Read Exodus 19:1 – 20:26

There is something wonderful happening in this section of the biblical narrative. The promises that were given initially to Abraham and his descendants, were now extended to the whole nation of Israel. All of Israel would now be God's treasured possession. And as his treasured possession, they had been given everything they needed. So, in that context, God appeared to Moses on the mountaintop, and he gave him the ten words – the exciting vision for how the Israelites were to belong to him, and live in harmony with him and each other. God had already given them everything they needed, so they didn't need to covet, or murder, or worship idols, or take anything that belonged to anyone else. It was a distinct way to live out their love for God. It still speaks to us today, because even today, our walk with God can degenerate into rule-keeping, or smug self-righteousness. We either think that we're good enough, or that we're *not* good enough and need to try harder. But in Exodus, the law and the Ten Commandments were not given to save! They were given to guide God's people who had already been saved by his grace. And today, we too have been saved by God's grace and initiative, in Christ. We too need the Holy Spirit to convict us of sin, but we will certainly never qualify by our own merits or law-keeping.

- - - - - -

Pray

'Lord, we thank you and we confess the times when we have slipped into smug self-righteousness, or judgement. Convict our hearts and remind us of our need for your freely given grace.'

A sapphire pavement

'But God did not raise his hand against these leaders of the Israelites; they saw God, and they ate and drank.'

Exodus 24:11

Read Exodus 24:1–18

In reading this part of Exodus, we don't want to miss something very important. When Moses went up the mountain to speak to God, there was a moment, in chapter 19, when God came down. The text says that the Lord descended in a thick cloud and billowing smoke . . . and the whole mountain trembled as he did (19:18). It's an incredibly strong image of the consuming holiness of God. And the people needed it! We need it today! God is not some kind of wish-granting, grandfatherly, benign sort of being. He is holy! He is so holy that the text says that if the people were to actually see him they would perish (19:21). That's why the following event in chapter 24 is stunning. Moses and Aaron, Nadab and Abihu and the 70 elders went up, and actually saw the God of Israel. They ate and drank with him. And as they did, they saw a dazzling sapphire pavement under his feet. What an incredible image. This holy, glorious, covenant-keeping God (with his feet on a sapphire pavement) was fellowshipping with the elders. And in fact, the amazing fellowship was the point of it all. It's why they (and we) were created. It feels like a preview of the relationship with God that is possible through Jesus, but also the relationship that we will have with God for eternity. Imagine that extended, glorious fellowship!

- - - - - -

Pray

> 'Lord, we shudder at your consuming holiness, and at the same time we
> respond to your invitation to fellowship. It stuns us that the two images
> occur concurrently.'

God's longing to dwell with us

> **'Then let them make a sanctuary for me, and I will dwell among them.'**
>
> **Exodus 25:8**

Read Exodus 25:1 – 30:38

After all of that – the words to Moses, the covenant, the trembling mountain, and the appearance of the Lord himself – you'd think it would be enough . . . yet the people drifted again into disobedience. So, to help them remember and to give them something very tangible, the Lord told them to build a tabernacle. The description was so exact. It was a tent with an altar in it, and an ark of acacia wood with the covenant law inside. It was a place where they could meet with God himself. It was a sanctuary and a reminder, day after day, that God wanted to *dwell* with them. I love all the details – the exact measurements of the curtains and the shape of the table and the lampstand and the altar and the washbasin and the courtyard. It was so colourful and exact. But in all the detail, the Lord was pointing to the purpose of it. God is a God who dwells with us! He is not far away and ethereal. He was present and holy! And because of his holiness there were exact requirements for meeting with him – offerings and priestly garments and anointing oil – and then he said, *'I will dwell among the Israelites and be their God'* (29:45). It's an incredible extension of the promises to Abraham and, of course, it culminated in the Lord Jesus Christ – God himself, *dwelling* with us. I wonder how our moments might change if we truly grasped God's deep longing to dwell with us.

- - - - - -

Pray

> *'Lord, sometimes we shy away from you. We are not worthy of your presence. And yet you want to dwell with us. Help us to respond today.'*

The golden calf

'When the people saw that Moses was so long in coming down from the mountain, they gathered around Aaron and said, "Come, make us gods who will go before us."'

Exodus 32:1

Read Exodus 32:1–35

It feels shocking to me. How could the Israelites turn away so quickly, mere days after the Lord himself had appeared to them on a dazzling sapphire pavement?! How could Aaron agree to their demands and make a golden calf out of their earrings? And how could they bow down to that calf after what they'd seen of Yahweh's glory and rescue? It's the human heart on vivid, confronting display. We are all full of good intentions, yet we are incapable of carrying them out. We are weak. We are drawn to ease and comfort and protection, in any possible form. No wonder Yahweh burned with anger and wanted to destroy them. He is holy and righteous. He can't abide it. And yet Moses stayed there and pleaded with him. And the Lord relented. This is also what God is like! Even within his righteous anger, the Lord's nature is to redeem. So Moses went down the mountain and he saw what the people had done and he too burned with anger. He broke the stone tablets into pieces and burned the golden calf into dust. There was a plague. There was forgiveness, but there was also consequence. The human heart needs more than this to redeem it. At this point, and all through the Old Testament, we long for Jesus.

- - - - - -

Pray

'Lord, thank you that we live on this side of Jesus' sacrifice for us. Thank you that we will never suffer the extent of your burning, righteous anger.'

The dance of friendship

'The LORD would speak to Moses face to face, as one speaks to a friend.'
Exodus 33:11

Read Exodus 33:1–23

One aspect that draws us to God is his steadfastness. We know that he is unchangeable and holy, bringing about his plan since the beginning of time. And yet, we also see something lovely and relational in his interactions with Moses. After the golden calf incident, the Lord repeated the promises to Moses, telling him to leave that place and go to the land he promised his forefathers. But he would not go with them because they were a stiff-necked people and he might destroy them along the way! The people, when told, were naturally distressed and they mourned, as well they should have. But Moses kept on meeting with the Lord. He spoke to him as a friend, face to face. And during those interactions, there was a remarkable honesty. Moses longed to know the Lord more. The Lord was pleased with Moses. Moses pushed the conversation, arguing for the Lord's reputation, and that if he didn't go with them, how would the people be distinguished from anyone else? And then, incredibly, the Lord relented. He showed Moses his glory, passing by him, while Moses lay sheltered in the cleft of a rock. It reminds us today that the relational nature of God is not something we can ignore. He is not static or immovable. Even now, we can bring our concerns to God honestly, trusting that we have a two-way interaction. We too can dance in friendship, because the Lord Jesus removed the need for a veil, or even a cleft in the rock.

- - - - - -

Pray

'Lord, thank you for showing us that you listen and respond. You are not static. Help us to let that truth change the way we pray today.'

The Lord is a jealous God

'Then the LORD said to Moses, "Write down these words, for in accordance with these words I have made a covenant with you and with Israel."'

Exodus 34:27

Read Exodus 34:1–28

As a result of the Lord's interaction with Moses, new stone tablets were carved out and given to the people. A covenant was again established between the Lord and Israel. The Lord said he would go with them. But, in turn, the people should obey the commandments and not make treaties with anyone else living in the land, or worship other gods, *'for the LORD, whose name is Jealous, is a jealous God'* (34:14). This is a strong sentence. The Lord's name is Jealous. Sometimes, I'm inclined to think that the Lord's commandments to not worship other gods are mostly because it's good for *us*. The Lord knows that those gods of stone are empty. They cannot speak or help us. When we were living in Nepal, I would watch the craftsmen make small Hindu gods in the bazaar, and think, 'How can they help us?' But then I would consider the emptiness of all the other things I idolise. They are all impotent, so it doesn't make sense to worship any of them. But here in this interaction with Moses, the Lord told the people not to worship other gods, because of *him*. He is a jealous God. His name is Jealous! It's a profound insight into the passion of God. And it causes us to consider a God who is deeply impacted by our choices and worship.

- - - - - -

Pray

> *'Lord, let this truth sink in deeply to our souls. Forgive us for bowing down in other places. Teach us to worship you alone.'*

Willingly

'Everyone who was willing and whose heart moved them came and brought an offering to the LORD for the work on the tent of meeting.'
Exodus 35:21

Read Exodus 35:1 – 40:38

The final chapters of Exodus give a wonderful glimpse of the community coming together in service of the Lord. They each used their different skills to build the tabernacle and the ark, and they did it willingly. Some worked with precious stones or linen, others with silver and bronze, some spun yarn from goat hair, or provided spices and olive oil, and still others were teachers and designers. But together, they were enough. In fact, there was a time when Moses gave an order to prevent any more giving, *'because what they already had was more than enough to do all the work'* (36:7). I love the sense of willingness and generosity. It doesn't sound like resentment, or a sense of fatigue from being on too many church rosters. The people *wanted* to serve together. It teaches us about the body of Christ today, in our communities and around the world. We have been given a beautiful diversity of gifts and resources, and when we work together willingly, there will be enough. In the text, though, after the tabernacle was perfectly complete and everything was in its place, the glory of the Lord filled the tabernacle! It must have been breathtaking! At the beginning of Exodus, the Israelites were slaves in Egypt, building a palace for Pharaoh; but by the end of Exodus, they were free, worshipping the Lord in all his glorious holiness, in the way he'd commanded them, together.

- - - - - -

Pray

> *'Lord, thank you for this glimpse of your people working together in service of you. Help us to be those willing, generous people today.'*

Atonement

'You are to lay your hand on the head of the burnt offering, and it will be accepted on your behalf to make atonement for you.'

Leviticus 1:4

Read Leviticus 1:1 – 16:34

During the time that the Israelites were camped at Mount Sinai, God gave Moses extensive instructions about how they should live and worship him. Reading the detail of Leviticus nowadays can feel quite overwhelming. Why did the Israelites need so many laws? Can we skip this? Actually, I think if we were to skip it, we would miss the enormity of God's holiness, our human need for atonement and, ultimately, the exorbitant price of grace, paid through the Lord Jesus. Leviticus sets the stage for grace. Back then, the purpose of every offering was atonement. The people were acutely aware that they were sinful and could not be made right before a holy, powerful God. But what's amazing here is that the atonement that God provided for them became personal and individual, as well as corporate. At Sinai, the new pattern meant that at the right time each year, the high priest would take a perfect goat and sprinkle its blood in the Most Holy Place, and then each person could lay their own hand on its head and receive forgiveness and life. I picture them each standing there and feeling that deep sense of owning up to their sins, and then receiving complete payment. I wonder if we also sense that deep forgiveness today. Jesus has become our perfect sacrificial lamb and our debt is gone. We can come to God as individuals, forgiven.

- - - - - -

Pray

> 'Lord, we thank you that the debt has been paid. Help us to understand the enormity of our sin, and the freeing nature of your grace in Christ.'

Be holy

'Be holy because I, the LORD your God, am holy.'
Leviticus 19:2b

Read Leviticus 17:1 – 27:34

The other thing that becomes obvious in reading Leviticus, is that the people had an incredibly clear sense of the holiness of God. He was so holy that even Moses couldn't enter the tent of meeting and approach him safely (Exodus 40:35). That was a problem! So, the first half of Leviticus describes the sacrifices required for atonement, and then the second half describes the path to purity in all of life. Every tiny detail mattered, including food and hygiene and sex and bodily fluids. But in everything, the purpose of purity was for deep fellowship with God. Indeed, it was the purpose since the beginning of time. And yet, as humans, it's so easy to lose sight of that goal and to become obsessed with the rules. I remember one time, a few years ago, we stayed in Jerusalem in a flat belonging to a strictly Jewish lady. She had lists of rules everywhere, especially regarding food and the Sabbath. I understood the need for the rules, and I could sense the appeal of the law. It would be simpler, in many ways, to have a list of laws and then find our own merit by keeping them. But we can't. And even back then for the Israelites, the law was like an X-ray machine. It revealed what was wrong and pointed them to the answer. In the same way now, we are convicted of sin by the Holy Spirit, and pointed to the answer in Christ, who has become our perfect sacrifice, for ever.

- - - - - -

Pray

'Lord, we come to you again and confess our sinfulness and even our drive to fix it ourselves. Remind us of your answers in Christ.'

Guidance

'Whenever the cloud lifted from above the tent, the Israelites set out; wherever the cloud settled, the Israelites set up camp.'

Numbers 9:17

Read Numbers 1:1 – 9:23

After the Israelites had been camped in the desert of Sinai for more than a year, receiving the commandments, the narrative suddenly shifted. One day, the Lord told Moses to take a census and arrange the tribal camps in a specific pattern – three tribes were to camp on each of the four sides of the tabernacle. I love the sense of deliberate order here. Nothing, and nobody, was random or unimportant. Everybody was part of the community and accounted for. Then, as a group, they began to march. Imagine how exciting that must have been after so long in the desert. They were on their way! But it was even more exciting than that. The Israelites were led by the Lord, on his command. The cloud that indicated his presence, lifted when they were to set out, and then settled where they were to stop and camp. How reassuring must that have been? Surely they couldn't go wrong with the Lord's presence to guide them? It reminds me of all the times when I've longed for specific guidance from the Lord. What exactly should we do now? Where should we live? What role should I take on? On occasions I have felt the Lord's answers to be very clear, but at other times not at all. And yet, I wonder. Today, we have the very words of Jesus, in print, in our language, and yet we disregard them. We have the gift of the indwelling Holy Spirit, and yet we don't listen.

- - - - - -

Pray

'Lord, we are quick to want more. Help us to dwell in your word, and listen to your Holy Spirit today.'

The consequence of grumbling and comparison

'Is the LORD's arm too short? Now you will see whether or not what I say will come true for you.'

Numbers 11:23

Read Numbers 11:1 – 12:16

It didn't take very long. Even with the cloud of the Lord directing their every step, the Israelites grumbled. They became fed up with manna, and began to crave the food that they'd had when they were in slavery. Surely not! No wonder the Lord was angry with them. Fire consumed the outskirts of the camp, and then the Lord sent quail so thick that the stench came out of their nostrils, and many people died of plague. As the reader, we are forced to sit with the serious consequences of grumbling. Be satisfied with the Lord's good gifts, is the message! But the graves were hardly covered before something more insidious occurred. Miriam and Aaron began to talk against Moses. They were jealous of him. *"'Has the LORD spoken only through Moses?" they asked. "Hasn't he also spoken through us?"'* (12:2). It's such a recognisable human wiring – the jostling for power, the envy of another person's status, or the secret jealousies. Perhaps, because it's so common, we treat it lightly or we brush it off as normal. But in this case, the Lord came down in a pillar of cloud. His anger burned against them, and Miriam's skin became leprous. It sounds so harsh. And yet anything that takes our eyes off the Lord is a danger. Jealousy can distract our best efforts, as can grumbling. Instead, we need to remember that the Lord will bring about his purposes, through whom he pleases. We are not all Moses!

- - - - - -

Pray

'Lord, thank you for this harsh reminder. Please forgive us our secret jealousies and help us to keep our eyes on you as the provider of all things.'

Unbelief

'No one who has treated me with contempt will ever see it.'
Numbers 14:23b

Read Numbers 13:1 – 14:45

After the grumbling and jealousy, something even worse happened. The Lord told Moses to send a team of leaders to explore the land. They did, and after 40 days they returned bearing fruit. But when they spoke to Moses, fear overtook them. Yes, there was fruit, they said, but the people living in the land were strong and powerful. They were as big as Nephilim, and their cities were fortified. We can't go in, they said! From the narrative, it's a little unclear. Did the leaders actually see anyone? Did they make it up? But what we do know is that they failed to trust in Yahweh. All of them failed except Joshua and Caleb, who tore their clothes and told the people that Yahweh would go with them. But it was too late. The Lord appeared and said he would strike them all down. Yet once again Moses pleaded on their behalf and the Lord's response is striking. It was mercy *and* justice. No, he wouldn't strike them down. He would forgive them, but he would bring justice. None of the generation who had failed to trust him would enter the land. As a result, they wandered. That whole generation suffered and died in the desert for 40 years. The story sits heavily with us. It's not easy. Humanity is rebellious. We struggle to believe and trust. But if anything, it reminds us of our desperate need for Jesus. Without him, we cannot fix ourselves or enter the new kingdom. With him, we have a sure hope of eternity and the gift of his presence, for ever.

- - - - - -

Pray

'Lord, we have also treated you with contempt and failed to trust you.
Thank you for Jesus.'

The need for a priest

'You are to be responsible for the care of the sanctuary and the altar, so that my wrath will not fall on the Israelites again.'

Numbers 18:5

Read Numbers 18:1–32

Throughout the early books of the Bible, there is a strong focus on the need for a priest – someone who would go into the tabernacle and offer sacrifices on behalf of sinful humanity. The Lord was too holy to tolerate the presence of sin, so a priest was needed. In fact, it was such an important position that the priest needed to dress in a certain way, and be consecrated, and be holy in his behaviour. For me, as I read these sections, I'm again tempted to skip them. We don't need a priest anymore! If I were to skip these sections, though, how would I ever fathom the gift of Jesus as our perfect High Priest? How would I ever appreciate the sacrifice that he made for the world? In Hebrews, it compares the Old Testament sacrifices with what Jesus has done, *'But he has appeared once for all at the culmination of the ages to do away with sin by the sacrifice of himself'* (Hebrews 9:26b). Today, we can sit here thankful. We can read about the endless requirements of the priests, and we can trust that the Lord has given us an answer, for all time. We can come to God, ourselves, because of Jesus.

- - - - - -

Pray

'Lord, thank you that Jesus has taken our burden of sin once and for all. Thank you that he entered heaven itself, not just the tabernacle in the desert. Fill us with a grateful response today.'

Moses failed

'Because you did not trust in me enough to honour me as holy in the sight of the Israelites, you will not bring this community into the land I give them.'

Numbers 20:12

Read Numbers 20:1–13

Reading Exodus and Numbers does, in some ways, highlight the faithfulness of Moses. He struggled early on, but mostly he showed patience. He trusted Yahweh, and pleaded with him on behalf of his people. And yet, in this chapter, in one small moment, Moses failed. Of course, we know that he was under pressure. His sister Miriam had recently died, and the people were grumbling about the lack of water. So the Lord told Moses to gather the people, speak to the rock, and it would pour out water. Moses did as he was commanded, but then he struck the rock twice, and spoke in a manner that wasn't humble. He dishonoured the Lord, and there was judgement. As a result, Moses wouldn't bring his people into the land. It's awful. But reading this chapter also forces us to think about times of pressure for all of us. We all live through harsh times of testing and, within them, it's easy to lash out in anger or haste. We fail, like Moses. And yet we know that thousands of years later, Jesus came and he didn't fail, even within 40 days of severe testing in the desert (Matthew 4). He stayed true. And because Jesus didn't fail, we have hope. We know that we will have times of testing, but we will be given strength to endure. In everything, God longs to produce character and humility in us.

- - - - - -

Pray

> *'Lord, do your good work in us during harsh times. Help us to choose holiness over grumbling, and humility over bitterness, in our hardest moments.'*

A donkey

'He answered, "Must I not speak what the LORD puts in my mouth?"'
Numbers 23:12

Read Numbers 22:1 – 24:25

There are many puzzling narratives in the Bible, and this is one of them. As the Israelites journeyed through the desert, they met other people groups. Over time, it became clear to the other groups that the Lord was with the Israelites, protecting them. In fact, the other groups became so convinced of this that they were fearful of the Israelites. In one instance, the king of Moab enlisted the help of Balaam, a non-Israelite prophet, to put a curse on them. But what's striking about this is that the Lord actually spoke *to* Balaam, the non-Israelite prophet. The Lord told him what to do, and then later, he spoke *through him* and his donkey. It's so strange and unexpected, and yet in every sentence the focus is on the Lord. '*The LORD opened the donkey's mouth*' (22:28). '*The LORD opened Balaam's eyes*' (22:31). '*The LORD put a word in Balaam's mouth*' (23:5). The Lord can do whatever he likes! And the words that Balaam spoke were words of blessing to the Israelites, as well as a prophecy regarding a future ruler from the house of Jacob (24:19). It's amazing! The Lord can do as he pleases and speak through whom he pleases, for his purposes and glory. For us, we need to remember that, especially on the days when we're tempted to limit God, or to reduce what is possible for him. He is our holy, powerful, glorious, puzzling, everlasting God, and we need to remember that.

- - - - - -

Pray

> '*Lord, forgive us for thinking that we can put you in a box – or explain to others what you can do, or can't do. Challenge our imaginations today, as we serve and love your people.*'

Hopeful, again

'Take Joshua son of Nun, a man in whom is the spirit of leadership, and lay your hand on him.'

Numbers 27:18

Read Numbers 26:1 – 36:13

By the end of the book of Numbers, the narrative is feeling hopeful again. The entire generation that failed to trust in Yahweh has died out after 40 years wandering in the desert, and there is a brand-new people, all accounted for, and waiting on the edge of the land. Once again, the Lord spoke to Moses about obedience and sacrifices and celebrating the Passover. It was important. The people must remember him, distribute the land well, and destroy any carved images (33:52). They must not forget who he is. As well as that, the Lord appointed a new leader – Joshua would succeed Moses and lead the people. It was all good! But we still wonder. Will the new generation really be able to remember the Lord when they arrive in the land? Will they really leave behind their old habits and keep their promises? It sounds hopeful, but it's an untried hope, as it is for us every day that we get out of bed. We may want to wholeheartedly serve the Lord Jesus, but we face daily threats to our faith. How will we respond in our time? There's one abiding message from the book of Numbers. Despite extreme provocation, God didn't abandon his people. He continued to lead and guide them because of his covenant love for them. And we trust that he won't abandon us either. He has made a covenant with us through the blood of his own Son, Jesus, and he will never forget us, no matter what.

- - - - - -

Pray

*'Lord, thank you for a new day in which to wholeheartedly serve you.
Help us to respond to your covenant love today.'*

Tell God's story

'The LORD your God has blessed you in all the work of your hands. He
has watched over your journey through this vast wilderness.'

Deuteronomy 2:7

Read Deuteronomy 1:1 – 3:29

The book of Deuteronomy is pastoral. It captures the final words of Moses
to the Israelite people as they waited on the edge of the land. Every time I
read it I appreciate the way Moses begins. There he was, perhaps sitting on
the Moab plains, using his hands, telling the people their story. Their story
was important – they were so flawed, and God was so faithful! And there
was the crowd that day, a whole new generation, perhaps leaning forward,
listening to Moses. Did they appreciate again the ways that the Lord had
led them? Did they squirm when they heard about the times when they'd
failed to trust and obey him? Moses didn't leave out the hard bits, or gloss
over them. And we all need this reminder. Trust and obey the Lord. He is
powerful and good and holy and faithful. He is bringing about his purposes
to redeem his world, through Jesus – back then in the desert, and now, in
the world, even through our personal trials and failure. We can trust him,
even when we can't see any evidence of his work. And we must tell each
other his stories. As we do, we will remember that we're part of the Israelite
story, grafted in thousands of years later to the Lord's redeeming plan, by the
blood of his Son, Jesus. It's amazing!

- - - - - -

Pray

*'Lord, thank you for your long story of redemption. Help us to share it
with each other.'*

Don't let it fade

'Watch yourselves closely so that you do not forget the things your eyes have seen or let them fade from your heart as long as you live.'

Deuteronomy 4:9

Read Deuteronomy 4:1–14

As Moses reminded the Israelites of their story in the desert, he also urged them to keep the commandments. At first, his focus seems similar to the corresponding sections of Exodus, Leviticus and Numbers, but there was a new dimension as well. Moses told the Israelites to observe the law carefully because this would *'show [their] wisdom and understanding **to the nations**'* (4:6). Previously, the focus had been on the Israelites being set apart as holy to the Lord, so they could be in relationship with him. But now, as the Israelites obeyed the Lord, the other nations would notice and say, *'Surely this great nation is a wise and understanding people'* (4:6b). It's a wonderful reminder for us as well, because as we obey and love the Lord, there will be people who will notice our God. It will flow naturally from a life of faithfulness. But, in case it ever becomes a duty, Moses told the people it was about their hearts. He said, 'Don't let the things you've seen fade from your hearts.' 'Teach them to your children and your children after that.' It's a long-term, daily, faithful, heart-felt response to God. Moses was probably looking ahead and imagining generations of people knowing and honouring God. And we're part of that! What a privilege! As we revere God, others will see him too.

- - - - - -

Pray

> *'Lord, this is a humbling thought as well as an exciting reminder. Please help us to be people who point to you today and to your great love for the world.'*

If you fail

'When you are in distress and all these things have happened to you, then in later days you will return to the LORD your God and obey him.'
Deuteronomy 4:30

Read Deuteronomy 4:15–31

The message that Moses gave to the Israelites on the edge of the land was also a warning. He knew that it was going to be hard for the people in the land, so he reminded them not to make an idol, in any shape or form, and to not bow down to the moon or the stars, or worship anything the Lord had made. They could perish as a result. It was serious! But at the same time, Moses said something deeply encouraging to them, *'But if from there you seek the LORD your God, you will find him if you seek him with all your heart and with all your soul'* (4:29). He knew they would fail . . . and when they did, they were to seek the Lord, because they would find him, no matter what they'd done. It's such a deeply needed message for us today. We will also fail, daily. We cannot be holy, or good enough for a holy God. Even this morning, we failed. But every time, we're able to seek the Lord. We can come to him because of Jesus. Even when we think we're beyond help, or full of shame, or that if someone really knew us they'd walk away . . . even then, we can seek the Lord with all our heart and soul, because he is a merciful, compassionate God.

- - - - - -

Pray

'Lord, help us to seek you today, with all our heart and soul, and to ponder what that might mean in the midst of failure.'

The Lord is God

> **'You were shown these things so that you might know that the LORD is God; besides him there is no other.'**
>
> **Deuteronomy 4:35**

Read Deuteronomy 4:32–40

I love the reminders of God's glory and wonder that are dotted throughout Deuteronomy. One minute, Moses was giving the people a serious warning about their behaviour in the years to come, and then the next minute, he was overcome by the wonder of God himself, and needed to talk about him! God's character and glory is central in everything! Remember him! In this section, Moses suddenly asks the people to imagine the former days, long before their time, when God created human beings on earth. Has anything so great as this ever happened? Have any other people heard the voice of God speaking out of the fire? Have any other people been the recipients of his miraculous hand, in order that they might know him? No! It strikes me as I read this section that I also need to pause and ask myself similar questions. Can I sit with the glorious wonder of God today, who formed human beings in his image for the purpose of a wonderful intimacy? Has anything so great ever happened? Has anything like this ever been heard of? No! As we also pause to consider God, it brings to light the truth at the heart of everything. The Lord is God. And even if the worst thing happens tomorrow, or the most mundane thing, he will still be God. We will still trust him. At the end of everything, we will hold onto these four words, *'The Lord is God.'*

- - - - - -

Pray

> *'Lord, thank you that at the centre of everything, you are. Help us to pause in wonder today.'*

Love the Lord your God

'Love the LORD your God with all your heart and with all your soul and with all your strength.'

Deuteronomy 6:5

Read Deuteronomy 6:1–25

In the gospels, when Jesus was asked about the greatest commandment, he replied, *'Love the Lord your God with all your heart and with all your soul and with all your mind'* (Matthew 22:37). It's a well-known and loved reply. It's the answer to every question we've ever had. And Jesus was quoting Moses. When Moses summed up the whole law for the people, he said, *'The LORD our God, the LORD is one. Love the LORD your God with all your heart and with all your soul and with all your strength'* (6:4–5). It's an all-of-life response, and it has always been crucial – back in the time of Moses, and then in the time of Jesus, and now in our time. Indeed, how could we not love the Lord when we consider who he is and what he has done for humanity and the world? Yet in this section of Deuteronomy, there is a seriousness that captures us. Moses also said, tie these commandments as symbols on your hands, and bind them on your foreheads. Write them on your doorframes, and talk about them as you walk along the road. They're strong, deliberate actions, in all of life – equally when it's hard and when it's comfortable – because even then you may forget the Lord your God (6:12). We also need to hear this, in our time. Within comfort and satisfaction, we may be in danger of forgetting the Lord and losing our love for him. Let that not be the case today.

- - - - - -

Pray

> *'Lord, thank you for who you are. Help us to love you, even on the days when comfort or satisfaction surrounds us and numbs us.'*

It wasn't anything you did

'But it was because the LORD loved you.'
Deuteronomy 7:8

Read Deuteronomy 7:1–26

It can be easy to think that we're loved because we're lovable, or that we're liked because we did something good. It makes some sense, and it's how human relationships often work. But in our journey with God it is altogether different. In this passage, Moses reminded the Israelites that the Lord didn't set his affection on them because of anything they did or were (certainly not because of their numbers), but simply because he loved them. He loved them because of who *he* was. He kept his oath to them and he redeemed them, because he is a faithful, covenant-keeping God who will continue to love them for a thousand generations (7:9). It's actually a foreign thought to us and something difficult to accept. Perhaps we prefer to be loved because we did something good, or deserve it! Some years ago, one of our close friends became very unwell with a brain tumour. Towards the end of his life he said to us, 'I've spent my whole life being busy, serving the Lord and my family. And now for the first time I can't do anything at all. I can't even get out of bed. But I have to realise that God loves me just as much today as he did before, when I was busy.' It was a profound thought for him, and it's a profound challenge for us today. Whether we're busy, or bedbound, or limited by chronic pain, we are loved by God because of who he is.

- - - - - -

Pray

'Lord, it's strange how hard this is to accept. Please help us to fathom your love for us, and your character today.'

Whose work is this?

'But remember the LORD your God, for it is he who gives you the ability to produce wealth, and so confirms his covenant, which he swore to your ancestors.'

Deuteronomy 8:18

Read Deuteronomy 8:1–20

Sometimes we struggle with our work or vocation, particularly on days when it's not going well. On those days, I think that I'm kidding myself. I can't even correct my punctuation, let alone write this book. Why am I doing this? But on other days, of course, work can seem to go well. Maybe we receive good feedback or feel affirmed in our gifts and choices. Perhaps we receive an email telling us to keep going. I received one of those emails recently, which was lovely, and then I started to think that I could do it in my own strength – even punctuation. I'm good at this! We all need the reminder in Deuteronomy 8. It's the Lord who has done this. The Israelites were reminded that it was the Lord who had led them in the desert for 40 years, to humble them and test them. It was the Lord who had brought them to the edge of the land and provided for them. It was the Lord who had given them their abilities, even when they were tempted to think it was the work of their own hands, or their own power or strength or righteousness. And that's a message for all of us in our work today. It's the Lord who has given us our abilities and it is the Lord who sustains our work, on every kind of day.

- - - - - -

Pray

'Lord, we thank you for the reminder that even on the good days when we seem clever, it is your faithful work in us that keeps us going.'

The final reminder

'Be strong and courageous.'
Deuteronomy 31:6

Read Deuteronomy 31:1 – 32:47

Towards the end of Moses' life and message to the people, after he'd reminded them of the laws and the need to be generous, and to never worship any other gods of stone, he then repeated the most important thing. He told them that Yahweh had made a covenant with them, and that they needed to respond to him. If they obeyed the Lord out of love, then things would go well. If they didn't, there would be judgement and struggle and curse. Then Moses said one last thing, *'Be strong and courageous. Do not be afraid or terrified because of them, for the* LORD *your God goes with you; he will never leave you nor forsake you'* (31:6). It's an interesting use of the words 'strength' and 'courage'. I wonder if the Israelites first thought of physical strength – the courage they would need for battle against the Anakites, or to take possession of the land. Possibly. But what about the strength and courage they would need to keep Yahweh's law, and to love him, and trust him? What if that was the greater strength and courage after all? What if it is for us? In either case, the second part of the verse remains incredibly assuring. The Lord your God goes with you; he will never leave you nor forsake you. It's in that promise alone that we find our strength and courage, for the life he has given us to lead.

- - - - - -

Pray

> *'Lord, help us to come to you as the source of strength and courage, and to realise that it's only in your strength and courage that we continue to follow you.'*

Moses died

'And Moses the servant of the LORD died there in Moab.'
Deuteronomy 34:5

Read Deuteronomy 32:48 – 34:11

As we consider the life of Moses, it feels unique in every way. Early on, Moses struggled with violence and temper, and then questions and doubts. But the Lord did an incredible work in him, over years, to the point that he became renowned for his humility (Numbers 12:3). Moses regularly fell on his face before the Lord and pleaded for his people. In fact, his very stance and humility makes the reader worried in his absence. Who will plead for the Israelites now that Moses is gone? Will they cope without him? Mostly, it puts a longing in us for someone just like him (a new and better Moses) who will plead our case for ever. Of course, we know that to be Jesus, but there is something else at the end of Deuteronomy. After all those years, Moses didn't get to go in to the land. He died. It feels disappointing, but it was actually not the end. Reading ahead, in Luke's gospel, we notice that Jesus went up a mountain to pray, and *'two men, Moses and Elijah, appeared in glorious splendour, talking with Jesus'* (Luke 9:30). Moses did eventually go into the land! It seems a strange and fitting end to this unique story. The man who was a hot-headed failure was transformed by God, for his purposes. And God can also work in our lives in the same way, for his purposes, as we quietly humble ourselves before Jesus.

- - - - - -

Pray

'Lord, we are not Moses, but we learn from the way you work in human hearts and we ask you to do the same work of humility in us.'

Anticipation

'Three days from now you will cross the Jordan here to go in and take possession of the land the LORD your God is giving you for your own.'
Joshua 1:11b

Read Joshua 1:1 – 2:1

There's a wonderful sense of anticipation in the first chapter of Joshua. Finally, after hundreds of years of preparation and wanderings, the Israelites were about to enter the land that the Lord their God had promised them back in Genesis 12. Finally, it was going to happen and, as the reader, we are about to see it! The words from the Lord to Joshua, and then from Joshua to the people, were deeply encouraging, as were the responses of the people themselves who told Joshua that they would do whatever he said, knowing that the Lord was with him. Great! Then, Joshua sent in two spies and they went to visit the Canaanite prostitute Rahab. What? It seems like an unexpected action and sentence. Do we know what their intention was? What kind of story is this? It's the Lord's story. From the beginning, the Lord's plan is, and has always been, for Israel and *for the nations* – for the outsiders, and the ones we would never expect. Indeed, centuries later in Luke 14, when Jesus was teaching the people about hospitality, he told them to invite the poor, the crippled, the lame and the blind to their banquets. As we read the book of Joshua, we need to pause. What would surprise us most today about the way God might work in the people in our community? Why is that surprising?

- - - - - -

Pray

'Lord, forgive us for our hardened assumptions and ongoing prejudices, despite what we know of you. Please bring about your work in your world, in the hearts of people you love.'

Extravagant risk

'I know that the LORD has given this land to you.'
Joshua 2:9

Read Joshua 2:1–11

There are so many surprising things about Rahab's story. When the king of Jericho heard about the Israelite spies, he sent Rahab a message, telling her to bring them out. But she had already hidden them. She gave the king a reply, deliberately sending him off in the wrong direction. What lay behind her actions? Why did she risk her life for two men whom she had only just met, who were the enemies of her people? We find out in the next amazing dialogue. Rahab told the spies that she had heard about their God – the one who had dried up the waters of the Red Sea, and destroyed the Amorite kings, and given the Israelites the land. In fact, her people were melting in fear because of Yahweh! It is striking that Rahab had heard the reports, along with, presumably, everyone else, but she *believed* them. She simply knew it to be true in her heart; so much so, that she risked her life for the spies. It reminds us that there is also deep knowing in our own hearts – a moment when we hear the message of Jesus and we sense its utter truthfulness. It's the moment of faith. And it's the faith that then causes us to risk everything – at home, at work, at school, wherever we are.

- - - - - -

Pray

> *'Lord, we thank you for your gospel – that we know it to be true in our hearts. Please let it bring a new sense of extravagant risk today.'*

Rahab believed and asked

'So she sent them away, and they departed. And she tied the scarlet cord in the window.'

Joshua 2:21b

Read Joshua 2:12–24

Rahab's surprising faith in the God of the Israelites – the God in heaven above and on earth below – led her to immediate action. She knew that the Lord God was powerful, so she asked the spies to remember her and her family in the ensuing battle. The spies said yes. They organised a scarlet cord in the window so they could spare her when the time came. It's an amazing story, and it seems even more amazing in the chapters to come, but at this point it's worth considering the wonderful link between Rahab's belief and actions. She believed, so she acted, immediately. She knew that the God of the Israelites was powerful, and that he could work to spare her, so she asked to be spared. Centuries later, of course, James wrote about faith and actions. He said that faith without actions was dead, and he even mentioned Rahab in his letter, saying, *'Was not even Rahab the prostitute considered righteous for what she did when she gave lodging to the spies and sent them off in a different direction?'* (James 2:25). James knew that faith and actions go together, as in the case of Rahab. And it's the same for us today. We also put our faith in Jesus, the one who sits on the throne with all power over heaven and earth and, because of that, we act in a myriad of different, daily, surprising ways, out of our trust in him.

- - - - - -

Pray

'Lord, please remind us that our faith in you, as Lord of all, leads to daily, surprising action.'

Crossing the Jordan

'The water from upstream stopped flowing.'
Joshua 3:16

Read Joshua 3:1 – 5:12

After the encounter with Rahab, Joshua told the people to consecrate themselves, for the Lord was about to do amazing things among them. And he did! In a striking echo of the exodus event, the new generation of Israelites reached the Jordan River, as commanded by the Lord, and as soon as their feet touched the shores, the Lord caused the entire river to pile up in a heap a great distance away. It simply stopped flowing – the river that was normally in flood at harvest time. And the entire nation of Israelites walked through on dry ground. Amazing! Then they commemorated the event, and celebrated the Passover, and ate the fruit of the land. It was the first time in years that they didn't need to eat manna! The whole event was a cause for thanksgiving, and I love the way Joshua described it to the people. *'The LORD your God did to the Jordan what he had done to the Red Sea . . . He did this so that all the peoples of the earth might know that the hand of the LORD is powerful and so that you might always fear the LORD your God'* (4:23–24). There is an interesting double-barrelled reason here – the Lord did it so that all the peoples of the earth might know that the hand of the Lord is powerful, and also so that *you might know.* Both have been, and always will be, important – the enormous, worldwide witness to the Lord, and our personal response of faith today.

- - - - - -

Pray

> *'Lord, help us to grasp this – that you are always making your power and glory known to the world, and also to us, one by one, through Christ. Help us to respond in wonder.'*

Jericho fell and Rahab was remembered

'When the men gave a loud shout, the wall collapsed; so everyone charged straight in, and they took the city.'

Joshua 6:20b

Read Joshua 5:13 – 6:27

There are so many striking things about this text. The Lord met with Joshua and gave him specific instructions about what to do: seven days of marching around the city of Jericho, and then on the seventh day they would shout, and the walls of the city would simply collapse. And they did! Can you imagine being inside the wall during the lead up to this? Can you imagine being Rahab? There she was, probably watching from her window and catching sight of the army as they marched past, six days in a row. Did she worry, or wonder if they would remember her? They did. Every wall of that fortified city crumbled in a terrible heap, except for the wall surrounding Rahab and her family. Every living thing in that city was destroyed, except for Rahab and her relatives. They were taken to a safe place outside the Israelite camp. Yahweh remembered Rahab, the Canaanite prostitute – the one who had been the outsider, but who had put her trust in Yahweh. Rahab was taken away from the burning city and included in the Lord's family (6:25). Later, we know that Rahab married Salmon, and gave birth to Boaz, and became part of the line to the Lord Jesus himself (Matthew 1:5). Rahab became an insider! It tells us that in Yahweh's world, everything is upside down. He loves us because he loves us.

- - - - - -

Pray

'Lord, thank you that Jesus became the outsider and that, because of him, we are freely invited in to your place of safety.'

The consequence of coveting

'Achan replied, "It is true! I have sinned against the LORD, the God of Israel."'

Joshua 7:20

Read Joshua 6:20 – 7:26

Apart from saving Rahab and her family, the rest of this section describes the terrible destruction on the city of Jericho. It's so hard to comprehend. How does it sit with the saving, compassionate nature of Yahweh? We can only think that he was beginning again, and he needed to set his people and their land apart so they could know him and worship him, and so that he could be known. When Joshua spoke with the commander of the army of the Lord, prior to this event, the emphasis was on the holiness of God, who was neither for the Israelites nor their enemies. He would be worshipped, and anything that would tempt or distract the Israelites needed to be destroyed, including the 'devoted things'. The destruction then occurred. But in the next chapter, there is another shock. After that grand, all-consuming victory, *the Israelites were unfaithful in regard to the devoted things'* (7:1). A man named Achan took some of them, and coveted them . . . so the Lord's anger burned against Israel. It only took one man's sin! But then, in Yahweh's anger, Achan himself was consumed, and the people were defeated in battle. The episode sits heavily. It surely convinced the people then (and the reader today) that it is serious. Yahweh is holy and his presence and faithfulness are never to be taken for granted. It makes me wonder what I take for granted today, in my own walk with Jesus.

- - - - - -

Pray

> *'Lord, we know that your judgement for sin is utterly serious. We're amazed that, in the right time, you took it on yourself, for all time. Thank you.'*

But what does it look like?

'Do not be afraid of them; I have given them into your hand.'
Joshua 10:8

Read Joshua 8:1 – 10:15

I remember the first time I read the book of Joshua, I kept expecting to read a scenic description of the Promised Land. After so much anticipation, I wanted to know what the land looked like! But a scenic description never came and, instead, there were lots of stories of victory in battle, and the renewal of the covenant, and the actions of nearby kings and their treaties. But then I realised that I was actually seeing something far more important than the land itself. I was seeing what was happening *on* the land. The Lord's fame was spreading, and so was the understanding of his character. At one point, the Lord spoke to Joshua and said, *'Do not be afraid of them; I have given them into your hand'* (10:8). Yahweh didn't say that he *would* give them, he said he *had* given them. It was present perfect tense. The Israelites were somehow to believe before they saw it, and to trust Yahweh before they experienced it, because *he had already given it to them*. Perhaps it's not dissimilar to what the Lord requires of us today. We also trust that God is with us, without seeing him, and we trust in his future plans and purposes through Christ because we know that he has already achieved them, eternally.

- - - - - -

Pray

'Lord, please open our eyes to your purposes today, and to trust in your hand and character in all things, seen and unseen.'

The trajectory of peace

'Then the land had rest from war.'
Joshua 11:23b

Read Joshua 10:16 – 11:23

After a great deal more gruesome battles, the Lord finally gave the Israelites peace in the land. As the reader, we breathe a huge sigh of relief. It's been a jarring, unsettling read. How can we make sense of this degree of violence? The exceptions, of course, are helpful. Rahab was included in the land, as a non-Israelite, and Achan was excluded, even as an Israelite, because of his sin. Ethnicity itself was not the reason for battle. Yet, even so, isn't Yahweh a God of peace? Yes, he is. We know that Yahweh was setting apart a nation for himself, and the nation needed to be distinct from the other nations. But there was more to it as well. The book of Joshua is read within the whole sweep of Scripture, and within that whole sweep there is an ongoing, wonderful trajectory towards peace. By the time we read Isaiah, for example, the glimpses will be more tangible. There will be a startling promise that the prince of peace is coming and that, one day, the lion will lay down with the lamb, and that warfare will cease entirely. This is God's plan and purpose! The redeemed world, when Jesus returns, will be one of peace, made possible through the Lord Jesus, the prince of peace. The book of Joshua stirs in us a deep longing for that day, and to pray for that day, but also to be vocal, committed agents of peace in our communities and our world today, until he comes.

- - - - - -

Pray

'Lord, please do your good work in us, so that our longing for peace turns into our service for peace, in every part of life, because of Jesus.'

God's story was growing

'Every promise has been fulfilled.'
Joshua 23:14b

Read Joshua 15:1 – 24:33

After the victory in the land was won, and after the land was divided amongst all the clans of Israel, the tabernacle was erected in the middle, at Shiloh. Then, after many more years, Joshua called the people together and gave them a final message. He told them to be strong, and to be careful to obey everything in the law, and to love the Lord their God. His words were similar to those of Moses back in Deuteronomy. There would be covenant blessing if they obeyed, but also curse if they disobeyed. And then he told them their story again, beginning with Abraham and Isaac, and their descendants in slavery in Egypt, and then the rescue through the Red Sea, and the protection in the desert, and the miraculous crossing of the Jordan, and all the victories that had occurred in the land. The story was growing! And his hearers must have had a strong sense that they were part of it. They surely wanted to respond, in daily faithfulness, to their amazingly faithful God. Yet even Joshua knew it would be hard. His words at the end of the book give us reason for doubt and concern. Will the people remember? Will they be able to serve the Lord, who is holy? Will we? On this side of the cross of Christ we have a different viewpoint, but it's still amazing that our small stories are part of God's big, grand story. And the question is ongoing. How will we respond today, in service of our God who is holy?

- - - - - -

Pray

> 'Lord, we often treat your calling to faithfulness lightly. Please grant us strength and wisdom through your Holy Spirit, to honour you today.'

Failure

'They aroused the LORD's anger because they forsook him.'
Judges 2:12b–13

Read Judges 1:1 – 2:23

The first line in the book of Judges is immediately worrying. The Israelites had no leader. Joshua died without passing the mantle on to anyone, and it was clearly a problem. How would the Israelites function? Unfortunately, this is the sad story of Judges. But the lack of leadership wasn't their only problem. On entering the land, the Israelites failed to drive out all the original inhabitants, and that was a breach of the covenant and disobedience to Yahweh. Of course, Yahweh told them it would become a trap and a snare (2:3) and in response the people wept, but it didn't really help. Time passed, and all the original generation died out, and the new generation knew neither the Lord nor what he had done in Israel. *'Then the Israelites did evil in the eyes of the LORD'* (2:11). It's an awful line, and it's sadly repeated in the chapters and decades to come. And for us, as the reader, it can be easy to sit in the comfort of our own homes, or churches, and feel a little bit proud that we're not like them. But the story is not only an account of the Israelites back then, it's reflective of our human wiring. It's you and me. It's our numerous good intentions and failures to carry them out. It's our failure to love the Lord our God with all our heart and soul. It's desperately awful. It's our naked state, deserving of judgement, needing grace.

- - - - - -

Pray

'Lord, we gloss over the hard bits, and judge others, and avoid the depths of our own failure. Please move us to confess today and receive your forgiveness. Thank you that we can, in Christ.'

He hears us

'But when they cried out to the LORD**, he raised up for them a deliverer.'**
Judges 3:9

Read Judges 3:1 – 5:31

Throughout all of Scripture, there's an ongoing tension. God is infinitely holy and righteous, and he demands obedience to his covenant law. Yet at the same time, he is infinitely gracious and loving, a Father who will not give up on his people. How will this tension work out in the end? Will Yahweh override his promises, or will he overlook the sin of his people? In the book of Judges, the tension worsens. The Lord allowed the other nations to stay in the land and, in fact, he used them to test disobedient Israel. But every time, when the Israelites cried out to the Lord, he heard them and answered them. Every time, God raised up a deliverer to lead them and save them . . . and there was peace for a while, until the cycle of disobedience continued. As the reader, we're meant to sit with the weight of it. As humans, we cannot fix our wiring, back then or now. But within our frail humanity, we can cry out to the Lord and he hears us. He has done something, for all time, and he has stayed true to both his holiness and his grace. He didn't override his promises, and he didn't overlook the sin of the people. He sent his own Son, the Lord Jesus Christ, to bear it for us. And it's because of Jesus that we can cry out to him today, with groans of honesty and repentance . . . and we can know with assurance that he hears us.

- - - - - -

Pray

'Lord, we do cry out to you. We have failed. We need your grace and mercy. Thank you that you hear us today.'

Gideon's fleece

'Then I will know that you will save Israel by my hand, as you said.'
Judges 6:37b

Read Judges 6:1 – 8:35

Occasionally, in conversations regarding choices or decisions, a person might say, 'Well, I actually put out a fleece,' and they're referring to Gideon, who asked for a sign from God in the form of dew on a fleece. And we wonder. Is it okay to ask God for specific assurance? Are we testing God, who is always true to his promises? Did Gideon do the right thing, or the wrong thing? The text reveals that Gideon, who was called by God, was initially reluctant in service. He had questions, and he asked for signs, and God graciously provided them, even though he'd already spoken to him. Afterwards, God also provided victory, even though Gideon was not trusting or obedient. It's an interesting account, once again revealing Gideon as a flawed leader (as the entire nation of Israel was flawed), yet the main point is made even clearer. It was the Lord who gave them victory and strength in the face of their weakness. It was the Lord who grew faith in them, as he saw fit. And still today, the Lord wants to grow our faith in Jesus. He has given us the greatest sign of all in the resurrection, and he longs for us to trust him. Yet God is also gracious with us and our extra questions. He can choose to lead us and guide us in all the ways he pleases. But in everything, he longs to grow faith in us.

- - - - - -

Pray

'Lord, please build our faith and confidence in you, in all the ways that you choose to do that.'

Samson disappoints

'He grew and the LORD blessed him.'
Judges 13:24b

Read Judges 13:1 – 16:31

After more disappointments and confronting accounts in Judges, the
Lord promised Israel a saviour of sorts – a Nazirite named Samson who
would deliver them from the hands of the Philistines. Wonderful! Even the
introduction to Samson sounds promising. It has Messianic overtones. Yet
as soon as Samson took centre stage, the disappointment became real. Even
though the Lord 'blessed him' and the Spirit of the Lord was upon him in the
form of strength, Samson wasn't focused on the concerns of the Lord. Firstly,
he married a Philistine woman, and then he was coerced by her against his will,
and then he wreaked havoc in a corn field, and then later, he was manipulated
by Delilah. What was God doing through Samson? It's hard to know . . . except
that in the end, after the Philistines seized Samson and gouged out his eyes, he
was brought before them, blind and helpless, as a prisoner. In that moment of
helplessness, Samson prayed to the Lord, and the Lord answered him. Samson's
strength returned, and the temple was destroyed. Interestingly, hundreds of
years later, the writer of Hebrews mentions both Samson and Gideon in the
list of people who are part of the great cloud of witnesses, calling us to faith
in Jesus (Hebrews 11:32). It's unexpected and encouraging. Within the most
disappointing of leaders, God still performs acts of transforming grace. And we
too are disappointing. We disappoint ourselves, our friends, our community,
and our Lord. Incredibly, God still works small acts of grace in us, and he
points us to the true Saviour, who will never disappoint.

- - - - - -

Pray

*'Lord, we are people who disappoint you. We thank you that we are also
people in receipt of your transforming grace.'*

Beautiful love and loyalty

'So the two women went on until they came to Bethlehem.'
Ruth 1:19

Read Ruth 1:1–19

The period of the judges was dire, an awful state of affairs for Israel at a time when they were without a king, and where *'everyone did as they saw fit'* (Judges 21:25). And yet, within that same time period, there was a glimpse of something beautiful. An Israelite woman named Naomi went to Moab because of the famine in Israel. While she was there, her husband and two sons died, leaving only herself and her two daughters-in-law, who were Moabite women. Over time, the grieving Naomi decided to return to Israel, and she told the two women to return to their own people. One of them did that, but the other decided to stay with Naomi, saying, *'Where you go I will go, and where you stay I will stay. Your people will be my people and your God my God'* (1:16b). It's a beautiful, unexpected profession of love and loyalty from Ruth, especially after the gruesome acts of revenge in Judges! It feels like God is doing a wonderful work in the heart of one outsider, in a similar way to the story of Rahab. For some reason, Ruth longed to follow Naomi and her God, even though all the logic in the world would tell her the opposite. This is what God is like! He can perform small acts of hope and redemption, one family at a time, one person at a time, through his son Jesus, even within our heavy times of grief and sadness.

- - - - - -

Pray

'Lord, we've all had times of sadness. Thank you that even now, within grief or hardship, you can work beautiful stories of redemption, one heart at a time.'

A change of heart

'He is one of our guardian-redeemers.'
Ruth 2:20b

Read Ruth 1:19 – 2:23

Ruth showed love and loyalty towards Naomi in accompanying her to
Bethlehem. But for Naomi, it was still a time of anguish of soul. She even
blamed Yahweh, vocally. It was all his doing! But then, something lovely
happened. The barley harvest began and a good man by the name of Boaz
showed kindness to Ruth. His generosity was striking, given that Ruth
was a foreigner and a member of a despised people. Ruth, the outsider,
was blessed! It seems like the wonderful promise to Abraham in Genesis
12, of God's heart for the nations, was quietly being fulfilled in this one
family. And there was more! Not only did Ruth have rest and water and
food to take home but, in the process, Naomi's heart softened. After years
of bitterness and blame, Naomi's heart moved to thankfulness, and it was
all at the hand of Yahweh. It reminds us that there are times in our own
lives when our hearts can turn very hard. Or perhaps the hearts of those
we know have become bitter and resentful. And while there can be good
reason for that, we must remember that there is no heart too hard for the
Lord. Yahweh is not only a God who parts the waters and causes city walls
to tremble, he is also the Lord who reaches the nations, one person at a time,
and who tenderly softens hearts, even when they've been broken by the
awful winds of grief. He is close to the broken-hearted (Psalm 34:18).

- - - - - -

Pray

*'Lord, this is a beautiful story of your love. Let it seep into our own hearts
today and remind us of what you're like, as a tender redeemer.'*

The wedding and the genealogy

'So Boaz took Ruth and she became his wife.'
Ruth 4:13

Read Ruth 3:1 – 4:22

I love this part of the story. Boaz continued to do the right thing. One evening, he found Ruth at his feet and, whilst surprised, he acted honourably. Then, after the proper process, he married her. Of course, a wedding is always a joyful thing, but we can imagine how this particular wedding brought such happiness to these two widows. And there was more! The Lord enabled Ruth to conceive and she gave birth to a son. It actually moves me to tears every time I read the next lines: *'The women living there said, "Naomi has a son!" And they named him Obed. He was the father of Jesse, the father of David'* (Ruth 4:17). That small boy, born of Ruth and Boaz, grew up to become the grandfather of King David, in line to the Lord Jesus himself (Matthew 1:5). The child of the outsider, the grieving foreigner, became the one through whom every single person in the world would be blessed and invited as an insider. And there was more! Later, we find out that Boaz himself was actually the child of Rahab and the spy Salmon. What an amazing story. God was weaving his grand plan together through unlikely outsiders who responded to his name. He was bringing about the threads of restoration and hope that he had imagined since the beginning of time. And all these years later, we can only marvel at his good purposes in the lives of ordinary people, and outsiders, for the world.

- - - - - -

Pray

> *'Lord, lift our eyes today to see your beautiful story of provision through the generations to your Son, the Lord Jesus, and then from him to us today.'*

Hannah's prayer

'There is no one holy like the LORD.'
1 Samuel 2:2

Read 1 Samuel 1:1 – 2:11

In about 1040BC, the history of Israel was about to shift again and, in this case, God was at work through the tears of one faithful woman, Hannah. She was childless. Strangely, the text tells us that *'the LORD had closed [her] womb'* (1:6) and we perhaps wonder why he did that. Are obstacles required to point more gloriously to the Lord's provision and plan? But then, after many years of weeping and of pouring out her soul, the Lord remembered Hannah, and she gave birth to a son and named him Samuel. Wonderful! Of course, there's a sense in the text that Samuel is going to be used by God to bring about his saving purposes, but the part that strikes me most is Hannah's prayer. After she had waited and wept for Samuel, and after she had birthed him and then given him up, she prayed, *'My heart rejoices in the LORD; in the LORD my horn is lifted high . . . I delight in your deliverance. There is no one holy like the LORD; there is no one besides you; there is no Rock like our God'* (2:1–2). I find it incredibly encouraging that Hannah prayed like this. Within despair and provocation, as well as within thanksgiving and sacrifice, she found herself in the same position – before her holy God, whom she trusted and honoured and praised. It challenges us to also find our deepest focus on God, who knows all things, who brings death and makes life, who sends poverty and wealth . . . because the foundations of the earth are his.

- - - - - -

Pray

'Lord, we call to you in need, but we can forget you when it's easy. May your glory cause us to worship and praise you today.'

The Lord called Samuel

'In those days the word of the LORD was rare; there were not many visions.'
1 Samuel 3:1b

Read 1 Samuel 2:12 – 3:21

At the time of Samuel, there was a priest by the name of Eli who had wicked sons. Amongst other things, they treated the Lord's offering with contempt. So, in response, the Lord replaced them. He said he would raise up a new, faithful priest, who would do *'according to what is in my heart and mind'* (2:35). It's a lovely description of service. And then the Lord called Samuel by name, in a beautifully, persistent manner – four times, because at first Samuel didn't respond, not having heard the Lord's voice before. Then, in the years to come, Samuel obeyed. We read that *'The LORD was with Samuel as he grew up, and he let none of Samuel's words fall to the ground. And all Israel from Dan to Beersheba recognised that Samuel was attested as a prophet of the LORD'* (3:19–20). It's an amazing reminder of the way God works. When he wants to make his word known, in a new and widespread manner, he will do it. All of Israel recognised Samuel! And incredibly, in the life of Samuel, the Lord once again pointed ahead to Jesus who would come and live a life of complete, faithful obedience, even unto death. Verse 35 is worth re-reading though. What would it mean if *we* also lived and served according to what was in the Lord's heart and mind?

- - - - - -

Pray

> *'Lord, we stray easily. We do all the things on our own mind. Please reveal your heart and mind again to us and help us to follow you.'*

Putting God in a box

'Let us bring the ark . . . so that he may go with us.'
1 Samuel 4:3b

Read 1 Samuel 4:1 – 7:2

We all long for certainty. We see it in the Israelites at the time of Samuel. They went out to fight against the Philistines and were defeated. So, in an attempt to win favour back with Yahweh, or perhaps to control him, or the outcome, they brought the ark of the Lord (the great symbol of the Lord's living presence) back into their camp, imagining they could move him in a box. But then, they were still defeated and, worse than that, the ark was captured and taken by the Philistines. How could that be? It's such a strange story, particularly when the ark was placed by the Philistines in their temple and their stone god Dagon fell on his face before the ark, twice! And then the Philistines broke out in awful tumours so, after a time, they sent the ark back to the Israelites. More than anything, the narrative reminds us that the Lord God is extraordinary and holy. He cannot be placed in a box, or confined or controlled. He will be worshipped. And the Israelites also realised that, saying, *'Who can stand in the presence of the LORD, this holy God?'* (6:20). It was a needed question for them, and it's a needed question for us today, as we're also tempted to control God, or the outcome. We too need to remember his power and holiness, and then shudder at the thought that because of Jesus, we can stand before him, forgiven.

- - - - - -

Pray

> *'Lord, forgive us for the ways we have been tempted to confine you this week. May your holiness strike us again today, along with the grace required to approach you.'*

The addiction to certainty

'Now appoint a king to lead us, such as all the other nations have.'
1 Samuel 8:5b

Read 1 Samuel 8:1–22

We understand the longing for certainty. It's inbuilt in all of us. And we know that the Israelites were living in a violent, shaky world, surrounded by their enemies. So, after they attempted to move the Lord in a box, they asked Samuel to give them a king, like all the other nations had. They thought that a king would fight for them, and assure them success. They knew that by then, Samuel was old and his sons weren't trustworthy, so they needed a king. But we can almost hear the terrible sadness in Yahweh's voice as he replied to Samuel, *'It is not you they have rejected,* **but they have rejected me** *... as they have done since I brought them up out of Egypt'* (8:7b–8). The Israelites hadn't realised the Lord was their true King, and he was the one who would fight for them. But even so, even within all the warnings, the Lord gave them a king. He gave them what they asked for. Within a failure of faith, and a rejection of the Lord himself, and every mixed motive, Yahweh still gave them what they asked for, knowing what the outcome would be. We too live in a chaotic, scary world where terrible things happen all around us, and we long for certainty and assurance in a myriad of different ways. Indeed, our addiction to certainty is always present. Yet we need to pause and consider, because certainty, more than anything, is the opposite of faith.

- - - - - -

Pray

'Lord, humble us today. Remind us of who you are, as our true King. Show us that faith in you replaces our addiction to certainty, and is freeing.'

Outwardly impressive Saul

'Kish had a son named Saul, as handsome a young man as could be found anywhere in Israel, and he was a head taller than anyone else.'
1 Samuel 9:2

Read 1 Samuel 9:1 – 11:15

It shouldn't really surprise us, given the back story, that the first king the Lord provided for Israel was outwardly impressive. The Israelites had asked for someone who could lead them in battle and assure them of victory against the nations. And so, the man chosen to be the first king was a tall, handsome man named Saul, from the tribe of Benjamin . . . and after he was anointed by Samuel, there was an immediate victory against the Ammonites. That's what they wanted! And then the battle was followed by celebration, as handsome Saul was crowned king. But be wary. Outward success is not always a barometer of faith. Even the words of the Lord prior to the battle cause us to pause. It wasn't really what God wanted. It was still a rejection of himself (10:19). And any time, as humans, that we place our complete trust in a human, even a tall or impressively handsome one, it can diminish our trust in Yahweh. Our allegiance is flimsy at best, and our affections fleeting. We need the Lord to change our hearts, and we need him to help us to trust him.

- - - - - -

Pray

'Lord, you moved the stars into position and set up dominion over the earth. We potter about here, wishing that humans could meet our need of certainty. Please remind us that the most certain things are in you.'

Looking to self

'And the Lord regretted that he had made Saul king over Israel.'
1 Samuel 15:35b

Read 1 Samuel 12:1 – 15:35

Sometimes it's not the big things that undo us, or the big moments, but the smaller choices along the way. In this passage, Saul kept making choices that didn't put Yahweh first. He looked to his own strength and his own ability. Early on, he failed to enquire of Yahweh over whether they should go into battle with the Philistines, and then he made a strange ruling over the eating of food, and then he didn't carry out Yahweh's instructions in battle with the Amalekites. All the way through, Saul's heart wasn't quite right. He even set up a monument in his own honour (15:12), rejecting the word of the Lord. So the Lord rejected Saul as king. It's a tough passage because it reminds us so clearly of ourselves. We also look to our own abilities. Maybe the more strength or outward abilities we have, the more we're tempted to rely on them. And the more our society regards and rewards outward strength, the more we will seek it. But the Lord looks at the heart. He humbles us, and shows us the right way. He seeks to grow faithfulness. And he modelled it. When the Lord Jesus took on flesh, he didn't choose a palace or an outward display of power or beauty. He humbled himself to death on a cross for us. The Scriptures remind us that God longs to grow faithful servants, because of his faithful servant.

- - - - - -

Pray

'Lord, help us to be more concerned with your honour than in building a monument to our own. Please work in our lives to make us more like you.'

David trusted

'People look at the outward appearance, but the LORD looks at the heart.'
1 Samuel 16:7b

Read 1 Samuel 16:1 – 17:58

The contrast is striking. After the outwardly impressive Saul was rejected as king, the Lord chose David, the smallest and most unlikely of them all, because his heart was right – he was a man after the Lord's own heart (13:14). That's a lovely description! And not long after David was anointed by Samuel, he had an encounter with the Philistine giant Goliath, where his faithful heart was certainly on show. David looked to the Lord for strength, and he trusted that victory was in the name of the Lord. Even more than that, he longed for the whole world to know that *there is a God in Israel* (17:46). And they did! When the Philistines saw what had happened to their warrior Goliath, they turned and ran, no doubt telling each other about the young man who trusted in the Lord God, and who triumphed with a sling and a stone. But we also know that throughout his lifetime David failed. He didn't always honour God. He made terrible mistakes. And more than anything, it makes us long for the shepherd king to come who would be perfectly faithful, the Lord Jesus. He did not fail! But we also draw strength from David's story. When he did show strength in battle, it was not his strength, it was the Lord's strength. We have also been given treasure in 'jars of clay' to show that this all surpassing power is from God, and not from us (2 Corinthians 4:7).

- - - - - -

Pray

'Lord, remind us today that the strength we have is from you, and not us. Please help us to use it in ways that make you known, even to the ends of the earth.'

In the middle of it all

'I know that you will surely be king.'
1 Samuel 24:20

Read 1 Samuel 24:1 – 31:13

It seemed to take a really long time for David to become the rightful king – years and years of twists and turns, and ongoing rivalry on the part of Saul, who tried to keep the kingship away from David. But it didn't work. The Lord continued to protect David. Interestingly, when David had a number of opportunities to take revenge on Saul, he didn't use them. Instead, he waited . . . and even Saul acknowledged that David was more righteous than he (24:17). But the wait feels frustratingly long. If Yahweh decides something, why doesn't he just bring it about? We so often ask the same questions. Why does the Lord wait so long to bring about his good purposes? And the answer remains the same – we simply don't know. What we *do* know is that he is growing faith and obedience in us. And it takes a lifetime to learn that! Imagine if someone were to write a book about each of our lives, documenting all the hidden twists and turns, and the years it took for us to learn patience or obedience to the Lord. We might not want to read those books! But finally, after many years, David became king, and it was a new beginning for Judah and then for Israel. But we must not discount the in-between years. I love the verse in the middle of chapter 30. *'But David found strength in the LORD his God'* (30:6b). May we also find strength in the Lord Jesus, in our in-between years.

- - - - - -

Pray

'Lord, there are so many inexplicable years in between. Please help us to find our strength in you as we wait.'

Worship with abandon

'David and all Israel were celebrating with all their might before the Lord.'

2 Samuel 6:5

Read 2 Samuel 5:1 – 6:23

When David was finally made king over all Israel, he took up residence in a fortress in Jerusalem. And then, once settled, he went to Judah to bring the ark of the Lord to Jerusalem. It sounds like he was careful in the arrangements, no doubt having heard what happened the last time the ark was moved. But even so, a man named Uzzah died after touching the ark accidentally. God's presence and name were still utterly holy, even in the symbolic form used back then. And that's a reason for celebration! I love the description of the way David rejoiced and celebrated before Yahweh. Amidst the huge crowds, he danced before the Lord with *'all his might'* (6:14). I wonder when was the last time we exerted all of our energy – perhaps in a sporting competition, or during hard physical labour, or in front of an audience cheering us on. But David used all his energy and might before the Lord, to worship him and to give him thanks, because that's what the Lord was due. Even later, when David's wife complained, he told her that he would celebrate and become *'even more undignified'* (6:22) in response to the Lord himself.

- - - - - -

Pray

> *'Lord, we so often expend our energy on less-worthy things. Please create a heart in us that dances before you in worship, with everything we have, with all our might.'*

The One who will rule for ever

'But my love will never be taken away from him.'
2 Samuel 7:15

Read 2 Samuel 7:1–29

In my Bible, I have highlighted passages. This is one of them! There was David, sitting in his palace, enjoying peace on all sides . . . and turning his thoughts to the ark of the Lord. Surely, he thought, they should build a temple for the Lord? But then, immediately after that thought, Nathan the prophet spoke to David, telling him there would be something even more important than a dwelling place for the ark (although that would also happen) but the 'something better' would be a permanent home for his people, for ever, through one of David's line. *'The LORD himself will establish a house for you: when your days are over . . . I will raise up your offspring to succeed you, your own flesh and blood, and I will establish his kingdom. He is the one who will build a house for my Name, and I will establish the throne of his kingdom for ever. I will be his father and he shall be my son'* (7:11b–14). Imagine what David thought in that moment! He praised the Lord, and how could he not? Yahweh had promised them an everlasting ruler in David's line! And yet for us, as we sit and read this promise, we can praise the Lord even more. We read it and understand the reference to Solomon, the son of David who built the temple for the Lord, but we also understand the reference to the Lord Jesus Christ, who was born in David's line and established his kingdom amongst us for ever.

- - - - - -

Pray

'Lord, thank you for your stunning promise to David 3,000 years ago. Thank you that it's still true today, in Christ, and for ever.'

The terrible temptation within glory

'But the thing David had done displeased the Lord.'
2 Samuel 11:27b

Read 2 Samuel 8:1 – 11:27

For a while, there was a wonderful high point in the history of Israel. The Lord not only gave David the Davidic covenant (described in chapter 7), but also victory over his enemies everywhere he went. Imagine that! In the process, of course, David became famous: *'David reigned over all Israel, doing what was just and right for all his people'* (8:15). It's a wonderful description of faithful service. And yet, in the middle of all of that glory, David abused his power. He subdued his enemies, but he didn't subdue his own heart and passion. It was springtime and he sent his army out to fight, yet he stayed home and desired a beautiful woman, Bathsheba. He took her, but she wasn't his. And then, when she became pregnant, David added to his sins. He ordered that Bathsheba's husband, Uriah, be sent back to battle in order to be killed. And Uriah was killed. This is a sobering, awful account. Even David, the anointed receiver of God's good promises, was not above the law. He sinned. He lost his sense of perspective, and he abused the power he'd been given. And it displeased the Lord. We must take this seriously. No matter who we are, and what accolades we have received, we must not rest on past success or stories. God requires faithfulness today.

- - - - - -

Pray

'Lord, you know everything, even the things we have not admitted to anyone. Forgive us.'

A story about sheep

'Then David said to Nathan, "I have sinned against the LORD."'
2 Samuel 12:13

Read 2 Samuel 12:1–31

Stories are powerful. Jesus himself used stories all the time – to convict people and to compel them towards faithfulness. In a similar way, the prophet Nathan told David a story about sheep. He said that once there were two men: a rich man with many sheep, and a poor man with one ewe lamb. And the rich man took the poor man's ewe lamb and he killed it for a meal. David, on hearing the story, was outraged. How could the rich man do that? And then, of course, Nathan told David that the story was about him. We can only imagine David's cry of repentance as he realised the nature of his sin and its consequences, but also the depth of sin against the Lord himself. And the consequences were dire. Bathsheba's child died. Later, she conceived again and gave birth to Solomon, whom the Lord loved (12:24), but in many ways it was too late. The history of Israel would carry ongoing repercussions from David's actions. Indeed, the Lord said that the sword would never depart from David's house because he had despised the Lord. In the years to come, there would be ample evidence of that, but in this section it's worth noting that David also repented. He got up, and he began again. He must have suffered unimaginable anguish and regret, but he still began again, with the Lord. It's possible for us also, because of Jesus.

- - - - - -

Pray

> *'Lord, there is much we have also done that we regret. Help us to repent, receive your forgiveness and to move on again in ways that honour you.'*

The fear of the Lord

'So David sought the face of the LORD.'
2 Samuel 21:1

Read 2 Samuel 13:1 – 24:25

There are vast sections of the recorded history of Israel that we'd perhaps rather not read, or skip over quickly. This is one of them. Amnon, son of David, sinned dreadfully by raping his sister Tamar. Absalom, another son of David, then sought revenge and murdered Amnon. Later, Absalom himself was murdered. There were repercussions for decades, and it makes us wonder about David's own failure to deal well with his sons. And yet within the whole narrative, we see small, wavering glimpses of faith and repentance. Even within the worst of it, David sought the face of the Lord (21:1). He wept and he mourned (18:33). He admitted that he'd done foolish things (24:10). He submitted to God, telling him to deal with him in whatever way seemed good to him (15:26). The account is, if nothing else, honest. It doesn't gloss over human sin or its consequences. And there is something encouraging about David's honesty. We are also wired to do wrong and to fail. Yet within our failure, we have the opportunity to humbly confess, before God, because of Jesus. And there is something worse than failure – it's the tendency to do wrong and then justify it, or defend our actions bullishly in the face of wrong. No. Instead, come humbly before God, and admit our foolishness. David, the king of Israel, who fought and failed in equal measure, seemed to keep one thing constant in his life – he lived with a fear of the Lord. May we also come to the Lord in honesty, admitting our foolishness, and seeking his face in everything.

- - - - - -

Pray

'Lord, forgive us our pride and defensiveness. Soften our hearts today, to seek you.'

Except

'Observe what the LORD your God requires: walk in obedience to him.'
1 Kings 2:3

Read 1 Kings 1:1 – 4:34

At the beginning of Kings, it feels like all the promises to Abraham had finally been fulfilled. The people were *'as numerous as the sand on the seashore'* (4:20), they were living in their own land, and they had peace on all sides. David, in his old age, had passed on the kingship to his son Solomon, and reminded him to walk in obedience to the Lord. David even told Solomon about the new promise, saying that if he obeyed the Lord, he would always have a successor on the throne of Israel (2:4). It was hopeful! Solomon also received great wisdom from God, as a gift to govern wisely. Surely, this could be the end of the story! And yet there is one word that alerts us – 'except'. *'Solomon showed his love for the LORD by walking according to the instructions given to him by his father David, **except** that he offered sacrifices and burned incense on the high places'* (3:3). It wasn't all fine. And it wasn't going to be fine in the future. In every human life there is the presence of the word – 'except'. We cannot be good enough. We may put on an impressive outward show, or have marvellous gifts of wealth and wisdom but, in the quiet of the night, there is a phrase that describes us, beginning with the word 'except'. We too need the grace of Christ. We need more to the story.

- - - - - -

Pray

> *'Lord, we read about Solomon and notice our own choices and half-hearted attempts to love and obey you. We live with the word 'except'. Thank you for the grace of God, in Christ, today.'*

Power and glory, and the temple

'He began to build the temple of the LORD.'
1 Kings 6:1b

Read 1 Kings 5:1 – 9:28

It took Solomon seven years to build the temple of the Lord, and the result was magnificent. The interiors were panelled with cedar and overlaid with gold. There were carvings in the form of cherubim, palm trees and open flowers. There was an altar, and a table made from burnished bronze. Then, when the ark of the Lord was placed inside it, there was a wonderful ceremony of dedication – countless sheep and cattle were sacrificed. Imagine the smoke that day! And then, more amazingly, the glory of the Lord filled the temple (8:11). It must have been a dazzling occasion! Afterwards Solomon prayed powerfully to the Lord. He clearly worshipped him. He knew who the Lord was and where he dwelt. He knew that forgiveness was only found in him, and he prayed earnestly that others might hear of the Lord's great name. It's an incredible account and yet, also, slightly unsettling. Is it unsettling because of the contrasts? Back in Exodus, when the people were building the tabernacle, there was a body at work together – each one bringing their own gift and following the Lord's instructions, willingly (Exodus 35:21). Yet in this case, Solomon seemed to work by himself, according to his own mind. It was a different situation, yet it unsettles us . . . as it should when any leader takes power and glory for themselves. But even more than that, we can be unsettled by our own tendencies to enjoy power and glory, or to bask in our own reputation and achievements, when the better way to live would be to point to the Lord.

- - - - - -

Pray

'Lord, you know our hearts. Turn them back to you today.'

The source of wisdom

'Solomon answered all her questions.'
1 Kings 10:3

Read 1 Kings 10:1–13

Solomon was wise. And because of his wisdom, many people came searching for him, including the Queen of Sheba. But what seems amazing about this account is the way it occurred straight after Solomon's prayer at the dedication of the temple. Solomon prayed that people living far away might come and hear about Yahweh (8:41–43), and then the Queen of Sheba actually came. She'd heard of Solomon's fame and his relationship to the Lord . . . so she came to test him. Imagine the two of them sitting in the grandeur of Solomon's palace, with the finest of food, and having the most robust of conversations – perhaps about the rhythm of the stars, or the heart of man, or the origin of time itself. The queen was so overwhelmed by Solomon's wisdom that she said, *'Praise be to the LORD your God, who has delighted in you and placed you on the throne of Israel'* (10:9). The queen recognised Yahweh as the giver of all things, and she even mentioned Yahweh's eternal love for Israel. Then, she returned to her own country. Of course, we don't know what happened to her after that, and perhaps we don't need to know. On so many occasions, it's enough to notice the seeds and the incredible answers to prayer, and then to leave the outworking of faith in the hands of the Lord, who flung the stars into space himself and who is the source of all wisdom, from the beginning of time.

- - - - - -

Pray

> *'Lord, we pray today for people far away as well as for the people in our street – that they may come to know you and love you.'*

It went wrong

'So Solomon did evil in the eyes of the LORD.'
1 Kings 11:6

Read 1 Kings 10:14 – 11:43

Back in the time of Moses, the people of Israel received a warning about
kingship. Their king must be a fellow Israelite, and he must not acquire a
great number of horses, or take many wives, or accumulate large amounts of
silver or gold (Deuteronomy 17:16–17). Five hundred years later, Solomon
received 666 talents of gold every year (10:14), and had 12,000 horses
(10:26), and loved many foreign women (11:1–3). The text tells us that as he
grew old, his heart was not fully devoted to the Lord and he *did evil in the
eyes of the LORD'* (11:6). It's an awful downward spiral in the life of Solomon.
But it's also strangely predictable. The kind of person who builds a grand
palace for themselves, and who sits every day on an ornate throne carved with
12 lions, may struggle to live humbly. The person who is sought by rulers
around the world for his wisdom and influence, may easily forget where
it came from. The person who holds lightly to the Lord's commands, and
acquires many loves, may find himself bowing down to anything, or anyone.
No wonder Paul warned his readers against the love of money (1 Timothy
6:6–10) and Jesus himself said we cannot serve both God and money (Luke
16:13). It's difficult to have great wealth or power and not succumb to its
temptations. In the end, Solomon's grand palace and ornate throne didn't
save him. He died, and the kingdom was torn away from him by Yahweh.

- - - - - -

Pray

*'Lord, help us to pause at the life of Solomon and to hear your words to us
about wealth and power, and the way we should use it in obedience to you.'*

The boy lived

'The LORD heard Elijah's cry, and the boy's life returned to him, and he lived.'
1 Kings 17:22

Read 1 Kings 17:1–24

After the death of Solomon, the descent of the Israelites into murder and mayhem was astonishingly quick. The kingdom disintegrated into north and south (Israel and Judah), and the kings prostrated themselves before other gods. In response, the Lord was angry, and he told them they would be uprooted and scattered. Judgement would come. But within that awful disobedience, there were quiet glimpses of hope. Elijah, the prophet, suddenly appeared in the northern kingdom and announced a drought. His voice was clear and welcome at that difficult time; however, his impact was initially small and mostly unnoticed. The Lord sent Elijah to stay in a ravine and the Lord fed him. Then, when the water dried up, he sent Elijah to stay with a widow. The widow was poor and had no food, so the Lord quietly and miraculously provided food for the family and Elijah. Then, the widow's small son died, so the Lord quietly raised him to life! There was life amidst the evil and mayhem. In that incredible moment, Elijah took the small boy to his mother and he said, *'Look, your son is alive!'* (17:23). And the mother believed. It's a beautiful story of resurrection life amidst sin and rebellion. This is the power of God, anytime and anyplace! And of course it points us ahead to the moment when God would raise his own Son, Jesus, back to life and bring life for us all.

- - - - - -

Pray

'Lord, thank you for new life, and the resurrection that you offer all of us because of Jesus.'

The showdown

'When all the people saw this, they fell prostrate.'
1 Kings 18:39

Read 1 Kings 18:1–46

The descriptions of Ahab, the evil king of Israel, are extreme. He served and worshipped Baal, and caused Israel to do the same. So, into that arena, Elijah announced a showdown on Mount Carmel – Baal versus Yahweh. The prophets of Baal would place a diced bull on one pile of wood, and Elijah would place a diced bull on the other pile of wood. And they would call on Baal and Yahweh to bring down fire, and the God who answered by fire – he would be God. It's a fairly confident way to reveal God's identity! They began their task. But from Baal, there was no response. No one answered, even when the people pleaded and shouted frantically. Baal was silent. In contrast, even with extra gallons of water on the offering, Yahweh sent a consuming fire that licked up everything in response to Elijah's prayer. And everyone cried out, *'The LORD – he is God!'* (18:39). It's amazing that in the worst time of Israelite history, when it seemed like evil had won, Yahweh was not silent at all. He was as powerful and glorious as he had ever been! And it's an encouragement to us today. God is still powerful and present. We may not hear him, but that doesn't mean he is silent. He has shown us in Christ that he reigns. And so our response is to trust him and honour him and bring faithful witness to him, even when surrounded by other gods.

- - - - - -

Pray

'Lord, thank you that you still answer Elijah's prayer – that they may know you and that their hearts may be drawn back to you. Help us to whisper it today.'

The gentle whisper

'I have been very zealous for the LORD God Almighty.'
1 Kings 19:14

Read 1 Kings 19:1–18

There is a place of rest and retreat in Thailand specifically designed for missionaries who have been engaged in full-time gospel ministry and who are exhausted. Darren and I stayed there once during our years in Nepal, and we loved it! We were gently cared for at a time when we sorely needed it. In this section, Elijah was also exhausted. He had witnessed a miraculous work of God in answer to his prayer, and yet afterwards he felt empty and scared. He even ran for his life on receiving a death threat from Jezebel (19:3). We understand! There was Elijah, curled up beneath a broom tree. And then a beautiful thing happened. God spoke to Elijah gently and tenderly. He didn't ask him what was wrong, or harangue him for his loss of faith, he just said, *'Get up and eat'* (19:5). Then Elijah was given food, and he ate and slept. When he felt strengthened, he travelled 40 days to Horeb. He felt better, but he was still hiding. So the Lord appeared to him again – not with force or might but with a gentle whisper. The Lord listened to Elijah, and told him what to do next, and gave him what he needed. And Elijah, refreshed, went from there, to serve. The Lord also knows what we need today. There are times when our giving and service has been exhausting, even in the face of miracles. We also need to pause and be renewed by the Lord's gentle care and direction.

- - - - - -

Pray

'Lord, thank you that you are the God of all power and might, and yet you came to us gently, in Christ, that we might be restored.'

Abundance

'This is an easy thing in the eyes of the LORD.'
2 Kings 3:18

Read 2 Kings 2:1 – 4:44

After Elijah was taken up into heaven (in a whirlwind!), Elisha inherited his gift and calling. It seems that the Lord often works through pairs of people. Moses died and passed on the role of leadership to Joshua. Elijah died and passed on the role of prophet to Elisha. Even in those dark days, the Lord was still providing a clear voice of hope. Elisha began by prophesying that the Lord would fill the entire valley with water (3:17) . . . and he did! Then, Elisha spoke to a widow who had no food left. The widow did as Elisha suggested and the oil kept flowing (4:6)! Then, Elisha prophesied to a Shunammite woman, telling her that she would bear a son in a year's time (4:16). And she did! The child was born . . . but afterwards the child fell sick and died, and Elisha prayed for the boy, and the boy returned to life! It's a remarkable set of strange and wonderful life-giving stories at a time when the Israelites were turning away from the Lord. They needed to know that the Lord would never turn away from them. He was still at work in powerful, life-giving ways, and he was greater than Baal. Not long after that, Elisha met a hungry crowd and spoke to a man with 20 loaves of bread and some ears of corn. Afterwards, everyone ate and had enough! It reminds us of the Lord's generosity, and the time ahead when Jesus would come and provide abundantly – death to life, scarcity to abundance, and despair to hope.

- - - - - -

Pray

> *'Lord, thank you for your life-giving hope even in the face of evil and despair. Help us to trust you today.'*

'Now I know that there is no God in all the world except in Israel.'
2 Kings 5:15b

Read 2 Kings 5:1–27

It's almost deliberately surprising. In the worst of times, God brought hope and healing to an unexpected outsider, and he used a weak, unexceptional servant girl in the process. Naaman was a foreigner, a valiant and important soldier (on the enemy's side!) and he suffered from leprosy. But then, a young captive Israelite girl said, *'If only my master [Naaman] would see the prophet who is in Samaria [Elisha]! He would cure him of his leprosy'* (5:3). It's such a lovely, simple expression of faith. The girl was a captive at a time when all of Israel was deserting the Lord, but she believed in him. She pointed Naaman to Yahweh and believed he could heal. So Naaman went to see Elisha and he was made clean, after the Lord dealt with his pride. Naaman's flesh was restored and he believed in Yahweh! It's amazing. Naaman was an outsider! He was not one of the chosen people, but Yahweh chose to heal him. The Lord cares for the outsider, and his plan from the beginning of time has been *for the nations* (Genesis 12:3). At first it was fulfilled in ones and twos – Rahab, Ruth, Naaman. It feels slow at this point, but soon it will be thousands upon thousands (Acts 2), and then in every part of the globe.

- - - - - -

Pray

> *'Lord, thank you for your plan for the nations . . . and that we're a part of the nations, welcomed in by you because of Jesus. Help us to have faith in you, like the captive girl.'*

'All this took place because the Israelites had sinned against the LORD their God.'

2 Kings 17:7

Read 2 Kings 17:1–23

Generally speaking, the book of Kings is a terrible, downward spiral. The people of Israel and their kings became more and more disobedient. They did evil in the sight of the Lord. Some of the kings were better than others, particularly in Judah, but most of them failed, badly. And then in about 720BC, Yahweh allowed the Assyrians to come and lay siege to Samaria, capturing the northern kingdom entirely, and deporting the people to Assyria (17:6). It's shocking. It must have been desperate times. Did the people of Israel understand why they were exiled? Did they think it was because their enemy was more powerful than Yahweh? Or did they realise it was judgement on their sinfulness? It's interesting to note that the book of Kings was primarily written for the Israelites in exile so that they would know why they were there. They had sinned and forsaken Yahweh, and so they had received judgement. But sometimes, nowadays, we describe God solely in terms of his grace and mercy and compassion. This is truly his character, but we forget that his grace is required because of the enormous judgement that we all deserve. Jesus is the answer because God chose to take that judgement on himself. And we can never fully fathom that sacrifice if we do not sit with the weight of the problem. Here it is, in all its darkness, in Kings.

- - - - - -

Pray

'Lord, thank you. We know you have the power and right to judge because you are holy. Thank you that you took the judgement upon yourself, in Christ. Help us to remember today.'

Laying it out before the Lord

'Then he went up to the temple of the LORD and spread it out before the LORD.'

2 Kings 19:14b

Read 2 Kings 18:1 – 19:37

There are many inspiring examples of prayer in the Bible, and this is one of my favourites. Hezekiah was a faithful king in the south. He trusted in the Lord and he held fast to his commands. He also happened to be king at the time when the Assyrians attacked the northern kingdom and carried them off into exile. Hezekiah was naturally worried! He knew the Assyrians were planning to come and do the same thing in Judah. But Hezekiah prayed. He tore his clothes, he put on sackcloth, and he *spread it out before the LORD'* saying, *'You alone are God over all the kingdoms of the earth. You have made heaven and earth. Give ear, LORD, and hear; open your eyes, LORD, and see'* (19:15–16). Hezekiah told Yahweh everything, and he acknowledged his power and might. He asked for deliverance, and he asked that people everywhere might know the Lord. The next morning, there was an incredible deliverance! All 185,000 Assyrians were struck dead. Nothing like it had ever been seen before. We may struggle to understand the ways of the Lord, yet we learn deep encouragement from this prayer. Even today, we too can spread out our concerns before the Lord – every one of them. We can tell him everything. We can remember his power and might. We can trust him for his purposes, in Christ. We can plead with him that others might know him.

- - - - - -

Pray

'Lord, we thank you that we come to you with nothing and yet you hear us. Help us to spread it all out before you today.'

Extra years

'I will add fifteen years to your life.'
2 Kings 20:6

Read 2 Kings 20:1 – 23:30

After the incredible deliverance of Jerusalem from the Assyrians, King Hezekiah became very ill. He was at the point of death, and even the prophet Isaiah told him to put his house in order. But Hezekiah prayed again, and wept bitterly. And the Lord answered him, saying, *'I have heard your prayer and seen your tears; I will heal you . . . I will add fifteen years to your life'* (20:5b–6). It's a beautiful, generous sign from God at a time when the people were mostly forsaking him. Judgement would surely come, but there was still grace in the middle of it. And then, Hezekiah's grandson Josiah became king, and he was faithful and good. He found the book of the law and he celebrated the Passover for the first time in hundreds of years. He also tore his robes over Judah and he wept in the Lord's presence. And again, Yahweh relented. He chose to grant Judah more time before the inevitable destruction. It's an interesting concept for us. Yahweh has plans and purposes, but he still responds to the tears of his faithful people. He still sees our weeping and gives extra years. Perhaps he is also, even now, giving extra years as we wait for the Lord Jesus to return in judgement. Is the Lord granting us more time now, so that more people around the world will turn to him in repentance? Is he seeing our tears, and answering?

- - - - - -

Pray

'Lord, we thank you that you are a God of mercy, and that you respond to the faithful tears of your people. Lord, please hear us today as we weep.'

The opposite of success

'He set fire to the temple of the LORD, the royal palace and all the houses of Jerusalem.'
2 Kings 25:9

Read 2 Kings 24:1 – 25:30

The book of Kings ends with devastation for Judah. It's absolutely awful. It's the opposite of a success story. In 586BC, the Babylonians came and took over Judah, and the city of Jerusalem was destroyed. The temple and palace were burnt down, and the people themselves were taken into captivity in Babylon. They must have howled. Where was Yahweh now? Why did he let the Babylonians burn down the temple – the place where he said his name would be for ever? And what about the descendant of David who would rule for ever? Where was he? And yet, as the reader, we know that the end of Kings is not the end of the long story. God was still at work, even in captivity, addressing the true, underlying problem which was that the Israelites were not able to be faithful to him. They kept worshipping other gods. And so the Lord brought terrible judgement on them, wiping out Jerusalem *'as one wipes out a dish . . . turning it upside-down'* (21:13b). It was the result of their disobedience, mentioned back in Deuteronomy. But was it really the opposite of a success story? Would the Lord be able to bring repentance and renewal? Would he bring a true king in David's line, who would turn their hearts back to Yahweh? If nothing else, the book of Kings makes us long for Yahweh to do something wonderful and everlasting – because we know that we are just like the Israelites. We are caught in our sin, and we long for Jesus.

- - - - - -

Pray

> *'Lord, we struggle, like the Israelites. We deserve judgement. We long for Jesus.'*

The prayer that took hundreds of years

'And forgive your people, who have sinned against you.'
2 Chronicles 6:39b

Read 2 Chronicles 6:1–42

In many ways, the books of Chronicles cover the same history and time period as Kings, although it focuses more on Judah in the south, rather than Israel in the north. It was also written for a later readership, and addressed a different question, 'Does God still care for us?' In reading it, I find Solomon's prayer striking. He prayed (before the exile) that the Lord would always hear his people – in times of famine and drought and plague . . . and also when they sinned. Solomon prayed, *'When they sin against you . . . and you become angry with them and give them over to the enemy, who takes them captive to a land far away or near, and if they have a change of heart . . . and pray . . . then from heaven . . . hear their prayer and their pleas . . . And forgive your people, who have sinned against you'* (6:36–39). It's striking that Solomon prayed this prayer and, 400 years later, the people of Judah were taken captive to Babylon. They stayed there for 70 years. We will read more about that later in Scripture but, incredibly, God was still answering Solomon's prayer, even then. He was listening to his people and forgiving them. It's encouraging for us today because, even now, God is still answering our prayers and those of past generations. Even the prayers we have prayed and forgotten are still being heard by God, who works his purposes over thousands of years, bringing his people back to himself.

– – – – – –

Pray

'Lord, thank you that when we turn to you, you hear us. You forgive our sins and uphold our cause. Please let that truth change the way we live today.'

The Lord moved his heart

'Any of his people among you may go up to Jerusalem.'
Ezra 1:3

Read Ezra 1:1–11

At the end of Chronicles, there was a tiny, hopeful postscript. King Cyrus of Persia would come to power and fulfil the word spoken to Jeremiah. He would send the exiles home. And then, in 539BC, King Cyrus did exactly that – he sent the first of the remnant home. It seems utterly surprising. A foreign king came to power at a certain time and place, and sent the Israelites home in remarkable accordance with the words of both Isaiah and Jeremiah – who had prophesied hundreds of years earlier that Cyrus would accomplish what the Lord pleased (Isaiah 44:28) and that the return to the land would occur (Jeremiah 29:10). It did occur. But before we read on, it's worth considering the first sentence of Ezra. *'In the first year of Cyrus king of Persia, in order to fulfil the word of the LORD spoken to Jeremiah, the LORD moved the heart of Cyrus'* (Ezra 1:1). The Lord moved the heart of Cyrus. In God's good world, and throughout history, the Lord moves hearts. He accomplishes all that he pleases for his purposes and, to do so, he moves hearts – whether it be foreign kings, judges, politicians, the Israelites themselves (Ezra 1:5), or even us today. He moves hearts through his Holy Spirit, and he accomplishes his purposes – to bring us back to him, and to help us to love him, and to serve his world.

- - - - - -

Pray

> *'Lord, thank you for your power around the world, and throughout history, to move hearts and to accomplish your purposes. Please move our hearts today in all the ways you desire.'*

There was singing

'And the sound was heard far away.'
Ezra 3:13b

Read Ezra 2:1 – 3:13

Not only did King Cyrus of Persia send the Israelites home to their land, away from captivity, but he also sent them home with 5,400 articles of silver and gold that had originally belonged to the temple! Imagine being part of the remnant at that time – 42,000 people on the road home, brimming with anticipation and excitement – finally going home to rebuild the temple! And when they got there, that's what they tried to do. Firstly, they rebuilt the altar of God and made sacrifices on it, in accordance with the Lord's commands in the time of Moses. Then, they began to work on the temple. I love the description of what happened after they laid the foundation of the temple. The trumpets came out, and the cymbals, and they sang to the Lord with praise and thanksgiving! They sang, *'He is good; his love towards Israel endures for ever'* (3:11). They all gave a great shout of praise to the Lord! It's a beautiful reminder of the most important, natural things. We sing to God and praise his name. We give thanks from our hearts. Sometimes, it's in an organised, communal way, at church or at a convention, and yet at other times it's quietly, by ourselves. We don't always need trumpets! We sing from a natural, heartfelt response to God, who is good, and whose love endures for ever – in captivity and also on the road home.

- - - - - -

Pray

'Lord, may your name be praised today, in our hearts – in songs that are both loud and communal, as well as private and personal, because you are good and your love endures for ever.'

There was opposition

'The temple was completed on the third day of the month Adar.'
Ezra 6:15

Read Ezra 4:1 – 6:22

It's a strange and yet inherent part of life that there will always be more than one emotion at play, or always more than one view on events. In the time of Cyrus, the people returned to the land and they were mostly rejoicing and singing over the rebuilding of the temple. They were glad! But there were others who wept because the temple didn't measure up to Solomon's temple 500 years earlier. And there were still others who were opposed to the building. They set out to discourage, to complain, to blame, and to frustrate the building attempts. It worked! The building of the temple came to a standstill for years. But within that, *'The eye of their God was watching over the elders of the Jews'* (5:5). No matter how discouraging or frustrating a situation may be, the Lord will still bring about his plans. In this case, nearly 20 years later, the new temple was completed and the people dedicated it to the Lord, joyfully. It encourages us today. We too will struggle with opposition or unfair criticism in gospel ministry. Some of it may be needed! But even then, we trust that God will work far beyond what we can see, or imagine. It may be that he wants to change our hearts. Or it may be that he has his own timeline. Perhaps, in another few decades, we will see the things that discourage or frustrate us today from a different viewpoint.

- - - - - -

Pray

> *'Lord, please have your way in us today, as we seek to serve you and to further your kingdom. And when we're unduly frustrated, please remind us that your eye is on your people.'*

A naked prayer

'The people of Israel . . . have not kept themselves separate from the neighbouring peoples.'
Ezra 9:1b

Read Ezra 7:1 – 10:44

The temple was rebuilt and, many years later, a man by the name of Ezra arrived with another group of returning exiles. Ezra himself was a descendant of Aaron, a Levite, and he was given wisdom to lead the people. Indeed, the hand of the Lord was on him (7:6). But it must have been hard for Ezra because, once again, the Israelites began to intermarry with their foreign neighbours, and they worshipped foreign gods. It's a terrible thought – the same choices that got them into trouble in every previous era were happening again! No wonder Ezra tore his clothes and his hair, appalled. No wonder he fell on the ground and wept. But then, he prayed. He admitted that he was ashamed and disgraced before God. He wept and confessed on behalf of his people. As he did, a large crowd of people gathered around him and they actually joined in his weeping. They agreed with him and committed themselves to change. *'You are right!'* they said, *'We must do as you say'* (10:12). It's amazing that in watching Ezra, the people longed to change and worship Yahweh again. I wonder if it was solely in response to seeing Ezra's honest, transparent prayer before God. Did they come to the same point of penitence by seeing it modelled? Do we also come to a point of change by seeing the courageous, vulnerable prayers of others? Do we dare to model the same honest prayers ourselves before God?

- - - - - -

Pray

'Lord, we are naturally private. We feel challenged by this display of naked prayerfulness and we long to learn from it today.'

Next to them

'The men of Jericho built the adjoining section, and Zakkur son of Imri built next to them.'

Nehemiah 3:2

Read Nehemiah 1:1 – 3:32

After Ezra arrived in the land, bringing much-needed spiritual reform, Nehemiah followed, bringing much-needed leadership in rebuilding the wall. There are lovely similarities, particularly in the way that both men began their work in prayer. Nehemiah also acknowledged God's holiness, and he humbly longed to help (1:11). He felt burdened by the city wall in ruins, and he enabled the rebuild to begin. But the rebuild was the work of the community. I love the detailed description of the individuals and the groups in chapter 3. They are each mentioned by name, and they worked together on their separate sections. The phrase *'next to them'* is repeated more than 40 times, as an incredible picture emerges of individuals and groups repairing their separate sections, next to each other. We need this imagery. We *need* each other . . . particularly in the crucial task of sharing God's redemptive plan for the world. We need to value each other's gifts and contribution, even when it's not as obvious as in the case of a wall rebuild. I wonder if we could make a list today of all the people who we currently rely on to share the love of Jesus. Then, perhaps we could thank them. We are indebted to each person we serve alongside, because our work will always be inferior, or unfinished, when there are parts missing.

- - - - - -

Pray

'Lord, sometimes it's easier to work alone, but we thank you that your good design for work is much better than that. Please open our eyes today to the body of people you have placed next to us.'

A response to opposition

'But I prayed, "Now strengthen my hands."'
Nehemiah 6:9b

Read Nehemiah 4:1 – 6:15

No matter who we are, or where we serve, there will always be opposition and struggle . . . even when our motives are good and we long to use our gifts to serve the Lord. (Of course, there are also times when we contribute to the struggles and misunderstanding!) But, in Nehemiah's time, the ridicule and the antagonism continued, including violent death threats. So the Israelites did three things in response. They prayed, and *'the people worked with all their heart'* (4:6), and they supported each other by placing guards at the exposed places. It's interesting that their responses didn't immediately reduce the opposition. In fact, the threats and ridicule continued. But it suggests to me that that's normal. Perhaps hoping for an opposition-free life, or ministry, would be unrealistic. But within the opposition, the Israelites continued to build, albeit at half the pace, and the whole wall was completed in 52 days (6:15). It's encouraging for us. In times of struggle, we can also respond by choosing prayerful dependence and service. We don't need to give up, rant and rave and blame, or even be surprised by opposition. Instead, we can continue to work for the Lord with all our heart in the tasks that God has given us to do. As we do, we pray that the Lord will strengthen our hands.

- - - - - -

Pray

'Lord, we are easily discouraged by opposition. Sometimes we contribute to it. Teach us to pray, and to serve you well.'

The wonderful shift

'But you are a forgiving God, gracious and compassionate.'
Nehemiah 9:17b

Read Nehemiah 7:1 – 13:30

Amidst the lists of names in Ezra and Nehemiah, there is also an important shift occurring. I wonder if the people at the time could articulate it. Did they notice there was a communal sense of repentance? Did they enjoy being able to add their own voices to the prayer of praise and confession described in chapter 9? Did they love being part of the community that rededicated itself to Yahweh in chapter 10? In previous eras, it had always been the leaders (and prophets and kings) who had heard from the Lord and passed it on to the people. And yet now, the people themselves were included. They could pray to the Lord and take part in the vows. They could rebuild the wall and praise the Lord together. As well as that, the temple area was somehow extended. The wall of their city was now dedicated to the Lord, which meant that their whole lives were somehow included in the holy place, set apart for worship. It was wonderful and yet it still wasn't enough. Even then they had problems, and they longed for more. They were still waiting for a time when the Lord would write his law on their hearts (Jeremiah 31:33) and would come himself to the temple (Malachi 3:1). There was something much greater to come in the Lord Jesus. But we, like them, also long for a time to come, the greatest shift of all time, when the Lord Jesus will return and heaven and earth will be reunited for ever.

- - - - - -

Pray

'Lord, blessed be your glorious name. Thank you for your grace towards us.
Thank you that the story is not over.'

The silent, unexpected ways of God

'So he set a royal crown on her head and made her queen instead of Vashti.'
Esther 2:17b

Read Esther 1:1 – 8:17

In around 480BC, while some of the Jews were returning to Jerusalem, others chose to stay where they were in exile. One of the Jews in exile was a man named Mordecai, who lived with his young cousin Esther. The story seems strange to us at first. It's all about a powerful foreign king who gave a banquet, and the banquet was so debauched that even his own queen refused to come. The queen's refusal meant that another queen was needed, and Esther was chosen – the young, orphan, Jewish girl, the outsider. It's another powerful reminder that God's ways are unexpected and often subversive. Indeed, the name of Yahweh isn't even mentioned in this book, but he is present in every line, bringing about his saving purposes. Mordecai happened to overhear a conspiracy early on, and it happened to be recorded. Then, when Esther risked her life to save the Jews, the king happened to have a sleepless night, and he happened to read the earlier account, at exactly the right time. God brought salvation to thousands of his people. It was a great reversal! But he did it through an unlikely outsider in exile. And God is also at work today, in unseen ways, through unexpected days and nights. He is not always mentioned or visible, but he is writing the story, causing his name to be known and his people saved, everywhere.

- - - - - -

Pray

> *'Lord, we easily forget that you are at work when we can't see you. Please remind us of your ongoing, sovereign plans and help us to be people who trust you, and who are willing to be your agents.'*

For such a time as this

**'And who knows but that you have come to your royal position for such
a time as this?'**

Esther 4:14b

Read Esther 3:1 – 10:3

Imagine being Esther. She may not have even wanted to be the queen.
She may have had other plans. Then, after hearing of Haman's evil plan
to annihilate her people, she was urged by Mordecai to go to the king and
plead with him for her people, even though it was against the law and she
could lose her own life. Mordecai responded to her concerns by saying, *'Do
not think that because you are in the king's house you alone of all the Jews will
escape . . . And who knows but that you have come to your royal position **for
such a time as this**?'* (4:13–14). It was so important. Perhaps Esther was
there for that saving moment? In hindsight, it does seem that way. God
used Esther's obedience and brought about a great reversal for his people.
But Esther didn't know that at the time. She was merely being obedient,
not knowing what was in store. And it's the calling for each of us. We don't
know why God has put us in the places where he has. We don't know the
outcome, or how long we'll be here. But we want to be obedient, faithful
people. We want to look around us and notice the opportunities the Lord
has given us, to speak of his saving grace in Jesus, and to encourage other
believers, and to do a million other things, *in a time such as this.*

- - - - - -

Pray

> *'Lord, we're not in a palace like Esther . . . but we thank you that you
> have put us here to be part of your saving plans, through Christ. Help us
> to obey today.'*

Motive

"'Does Job fear God for nothing?" Satan replied.'
Job 1:9

Read Job 1:1–22

The story of Job is striking. We don't know much about the location of Uz, or the timeline, or how the narrator overheard the heavenly conversation between God and Satan . . . but there was Job, blameless and upright and wealthy. He feared God. So then, Satan wanted to know *why* Job feared God. Did Job really fear and worship God for who he was, or because his life was going so well? It's a really important question . . . and difficult for most of us to answer. Do we really love God for who he is, or for what we might get out of him? Do we even know our own hearts? By the end of chapter 1, Job had lost everything – oxen, donkeys, sheep, servants, camels, and even his beloved children. In response, he grieved terribly. He tore his robe and shaved his head. But after a time, he said, *'Naked I came from my mother's womb, and naked I shall depart. The LORD gave and the LORD has taken away; may the name of the LORD be praised'* (1:21). And we wonder. Could we do the same? In some ways, it feels like the story could be over at that point. Satan's question had surely been answered. Job's precious things were taken away from him, and yet he *still* praised God. However, the story wasn't over. The answer was far more complex, in Job's life and in our own lives, within God's world. We need to read on.

- - - - - -

Pray

> *'Lord, we come before you quietly because our hearts are murky places and our motives untried. Please renew true praise in us today.'*

Friendship

'Then they sat on the ground with him for seven days and seven nights.'
Job 2:13

Read Job 2:1 – 8:22

Genuine friendship is a beautiful thing. It's the support we crave and the listening ear we need in our darkest times, as well as in our busy, ordinary, serious and playful times. It's the gift of presence. But it can also be hard! When Job was afflicted with severe sores from head to toe, his three friends arrived and, at first, they wept with him. They sat on the ground with him for seven days and seven nights, and they didn't say a word, because *'they saw how great his suffering was'* (2:13b). Well done to his friends! They were present *and* quiet in the midst of deep pain, which can be hard to do. We are so tempted to speak! But then, after a week, the friends began to give Job advice, and some of it was both untrue and unhelpful, especially the link between pious behaviour and blessing. If God rewards people when they're good, they thought, then suffering was a result of sinful behaviour and Job needed to repent of his sin. The friends didn't know everything. Of course, there is so much complexity within their speeches, and within Job's reply, but it speaks to me, amongst other things, about friendship. We find it difficult to sit with our friends in pain. But we need to. We don't understand everything. There can be times to speak but, usually, it's a time to be silent and present, on the ground, together.

- - - - - -

Pray

> *'Lord, forgive us our tendency to give prideful advice. Please grow in us the gift of silence and presence.'*

Job's lament

'For sighing has become my daily food; my groans pour out like water.'
Job 3:24

Read Job 3:1 – 14:22

If Job were to visit our western contemporary churches, I wonder what he would think. Would he see us all smiling and comfortable? Would he hear any honest lament? Would he assume that we've swept it beneath a carpet of superficial praise? In this narrative, Job suffered and lamented. He despaired before his friends and before God. He wished that he'd never been born (3:3). He described months of futility and nights of misery (7:3). He despised his life, and said that his days had no meaning at all (7:16). He was painfully honest, over and over again. But somehow, as we read Job's lament, it gives us permission to also feel deep anguish. We too are beset by questions and struggles. We don't know why God allows such suffering on earth, and we often find ourselves in the same space – face down on the ground, in lament. But the thing that strikes me about Job's lament is that he moves around within it. One minute he was in despair and turmoil, but then in the next phrase he had returned to a truth about God's sovereign ways. He knew that his suffering was not due to his own sin, but he didn't try to prove that he was without sin (9:20). He was humble and honest before God, as well as occasionally frustrated by his friends. It almost leaves us with a lovely blank page on which we can write our most puzzling concerns before God and know that our laments will be heard.

- - - - - -

Pray

'Lord, it astounds us that we have permission to speak to you as honestly as we can today. Please help us to groan if we need to.'

The answer

'Where were you when I laid the earth's foundation?'
Job 38:4

Read Job 15:1 – 42:17

Over time, the dialogue between Job and his friends worsened. The friends became increasingly frustrated with him, and he became increasingly adamant that his suffering wasn't due to sin. It escalated. But then, finally, the Lord spoke to Job out of the storm. I remember the first time I read Job 38. I was a recently graduated physio, and one of our young patients had just died. I felt shocked and empty. I had a million questions of God. Then I sat and read God's words to Job, *'I will question you, and you shall answer me'* (38:3). It struck me that God, who is holy and good and merciful, is also able to question us, and his questions are good. 'Where were you when I laid the earth's foundation?' 'Have you ever given orders to the morning?' 'Do you know when the mountain goats give birth?' 'Does the hawk take flight by your wisdom?' It's no wonder Job replied, *'I am unworthy – how can I reply to you? . . . I spoke once, but I have no answer – twice, but I will say no more'* (40:4–5). Afterwards, the Lord questioned Job about justice and wrath and salvation. And Job replied, *'Surely I spoke of things I did not understand . . . My ears had heard of you but now my eyes have seen you'* (42:3b–5). It's an amazing ending to a story that lifts our eyes to all the things we don't understand. But we trust in him who does know, and we love him because we know he ultimately took on suffering for us.

- - - - - -

Pray

> *'Lord, we don't understand suffering, but we ask for eyes that see you and your worthiness, today.'*

Planted by streams of water

'Blessed is the one . . .'
Psalm 1:1

Read Psalm 1:1–6

The invitation in Psalm 1 is so very compelling. *'Blessed is the one . . . whose delight is in the law of the LORD, and who meditates on his law day and night. That person is like a tree planted by streams of water, which yields its fruit in season and whose leaf does not wither'* (1:1–3). We could picture a lovely fruit-bearing tree with wide limbs and rich, green foliage. Right beside the tree is a bubbling, life-giving stream of water. We want to be like that tree! We want to be well-planted. And we can be. We can immerse ourselves in God's life-giving words, right here in the psalms. It's time to drink, and to refresh ourselves with the truths of God's ways and wonders and promises. In reading the psalms, we are invited to look over the shoulder of the psalmists and feel their amazed, songful response to God – their awe and wonder, their praise and lament, their honest questions, and their quiet acknowledgement of his Lordship. As we read the psalms, we will join with them, and feel our own lives shaped and changed by the Lord Jesus, the One promised in so many of the songs. It's amazing that the psalms were also the words that Jesus himself sang. May the Lord grow *'fruit in season'* in our lives, through reading these psalms.

- - - - - -

Pray

> *'Lord, help us to be people who immerse ourselves in your word – who meditate on it day and night, and delight in it – that our lives might sing your song.'*

The problem of foes

'I call out to the LORD, and he answers me from his holy mountain.'
Psalm 3:4

Read Psalm 3

Throughout the psalms, the writers speak honestly to God about their
problems, including mention of their foes, who are often about to attack
them. They call out to God for refuge and protection. And while we don't
always understand their exact predicaments, we do understand their longing.
Thousands of years later, we do a similar thing – we long for God to supply
immediate rescue, or deliverance from our problems. In Psalm 3, though,
we hear David (who was at the time being pursued by his son Absalom)
ultimately acknowledge something far greater than his need for immediate
help. David sought the Lord, who was a shield around him, and who was
his glory, and who lifted his head high, and who answered him, and who
sustained him in everything. It's the same truth we need to hear today,
whether we're being wrongfully pursued or whether we're making curry
for dinner. The Lord sustains us, the Lord delivers us, not always from our
enemies, but from an eternity spent without him. He delivers us from our
own self-centred ways of thinking. And he does that through his Son, the
Lord Jesus, and his Spirit at work within us. As we understand it again, we
can lie down and sleep, and wake again, because the Lord sustains us.

- - - - - -

Pray

> *'Lord, we thank you. We long for immediate solutions, and yet you have
> given us something better – your presence and promise. Please let it change
> the way we pray today.'*

Remember God's glory

'LORD, our LORD, how majestic is your name in all the earth!'
Psalm 8:1

Read Psalm 8

There are so many amazing reminders in this psalm. Our God is sovereign over the universe. His name is majestic. His glory is above the heavens. He formed all things, and all things praise him! As we consider that, it leads us to one stunning question. *'What is mankind that you are mindful of them, human beings that you care for them?'* (8:4). It's a very good question! Why should God bother with us? And yet the answer is even more amazing . . . because he loves us. God created human beings for his glory. He made us in his image, to know him and to love him, and to care for the intricate creation he formed – all the works of his hands. It's a wonderful answer and mandate. *'You made them rulers over the works of your hands; you put everything under their feet'* (8:6). It should make us shudder with responsibility and awe to think of our God-given task as humans. But the psalm also gives us a glimpse of the Lord Jesus. One day, everything will be placed under *his* feet. Later, the writer of Hebrews quoted from this psalm, reminding us of that truth (Hebrews 2:6). Jesus came in human form, but he will come again to truly rule over all things. We long for that day, and pray for it to come.

- - - - - -

Pray

> *'Lord, we confess that we have not taken our responsibility seriously as human beings. Remind us of the immense calling and the wonder it is to be your child in Christ.'*

He will not abandon me

'With him at my right hand, I shall not be shaken.'
Psalm 16:8b

Read Psalm 16

Every day, we need to sit quietly with the promises of God. What are they? What do we hold onto when life is hard and our knuckles are white? The answer is in this psalm. He will be with us. He will not abandon us to the grave. He will not let us see decay. He is enough for us. Through Jesus, God has defeated death for ever, and he has offered us life eternal. So, because of that, we will not be shaken, even in our hardest moments. I remember reading this psalm when my husband Darren was taken into hospital with a life-threatening heart problem. He needed a 10-hour operation to ablate the extra pathway in his heart. He was only 33, and we had a four-year-old son and a new baby. The doctors weren't sure if they could fix it. But even in the hospital, amidst my awful fears, this psalm spoke to me. He is with us. We will all feel pain and grief, and even terror, but no matter what, God will be with us. He will be our refuge. He won't necessarily take the pain or fear away, but he will be with us. And that's what we actually need, because in life we will experience fear and pain and terror and, through it, Jesus will be present through his Spirit, interceding for us. With him at our right hand, we will not be shaken.

- - - - - -

Pray

'Lord, we thank you that you will never abandon us, and that deep truth causes us to rejoice.'

He has done it!

'My God, my God, why have you forsaken me?'
Psalm 22:1

Read Psalm 22

What an amazing psalm this is! David wrote it one thousand years before Christ . . . and then, as Jesus hung on the cross with his hands and feet pierced by nails, he used these very words as he called out to God in anguish of soul (Matthew 27:46), surrounded by soldiers who gloated over him, and who cast lots for his garments. It's amazing that the whole psalm points ahead to the crucifixion of Jesus, and yet it was also an encouragement to the Jews of the day, and down through the ages. I often wonder whether Jesus knew how profoundly this psalm would be fulfilled in his life as he sang it as a child. But of course, the psalm doesn't finish at the cross with the gloaters, and the bones on display. There is also great rejoicing and celebration and praise – hints of resurrection, and a world responding to God's glorious salvation in Christ (22:26–27). It's a remarkable ending! There is even a sense that, all these years later, every one of us is included in the story. *'Future generations will be told about the Lord. They will proclaim his righteousness, declaring to a people yet unborn: He has done it!'* (22:30–31). As we respond to the grace and victory of God in Christ, we are able to share the message with others. We too can declare God's forgiveness to a people yet unborn!

- - - - - -

Pray

> *'Lord, sometimes we forget. We think the good news is merely for ourselves. Remind us of the wonderful privilege of pouring out your victorious message to those nearby, and far away, and even the ones yet unborn.'*

The Good Shepherd

'The LORD is my shepherd, I lack nothing.'
Psalm 23:1

Read Psalm 23

I haven't grown up on a sheep farm, nor do I have extensive knowledge of the needs of sheep. But I have lived in Nepal for years, and I've watched young barefoot Nepalis clamber over steep terrain to find grass for their small flock of sheep or goats. I've watched them lead their sheep and take great care over each animal, calling them by name and looking after them, as if they matter more than anything else in the world. It makes me appreciate the imagery in this psalm. And I think it must have been profound for the original readers as they also understood not only their kings and prophets to be like shepherds, but also Yahweh himself. Yahweh, who was majestic and sovereign and righteous, was also like a shepherd who cared for them and who comforted them and who led them. *'He makes me lie down in green pastures, he leads me beside quiet waters, he refreshes my soul'* (23:2–3). And Yahweh was even more than a comforting shepherd, he was also a shepherd who would ultimately lead his sheep home, for ever. The Good Shepherd, Jesus, would soon come and defeat evil for all time, and prepare a safe dwelling place for his sheep for ever.

- - - - - -

Pray

> *'Lord, thank you that your care and concern for us occurs in the middle of the dark valleys. And thank you that your promise is of a home for ever. Help us to find rest in that truth today.'*

'Wait for the LORD; be strong and take heart and wait for the LORD.'
Psalm 27:14

Read Psalm 27

There are many times in life when it feels like we're waiting for something, or we're incapable of doing anything ourselves. Perhaps we're waiting for the doctor's call, hoping the diagnosis is not cancer. Perhaps we're caring for someone with mental health issues, hoping they will seek help. Perhaps we're applying for yet another job, hoping to gain employment. It's at those times of waiting that we seek God's face in unique ways, especially when we can't do anything ourselves. In 2006, Darren and I and our boys were living in Nepal and the civil war was getting worse. One day, we had a phone call saying that the rebel group were about to attack our town, and our house was in the firing line. We got in a jeep and moved to the other side of town, away from the danger. The next morning, though, we read Psalm 27. *'Though an army besiege me, my heart will not fear; though war break out against me, even then I will be confident'* (27:3). We couldn't do anything about the civil war, but we could respond well, and wait for the Lord and seek his face. We could consider again where our confidence really lay – not in the absence of war or strife, but in the presence of God in the middle of it, and the amazing opportunity we had every day to gaze at his face, and strengthen each other.

- - - - - -

Pray

> *'Lord, help us to gaze on the beauty of your face, like the psalmist did, to really enjoy your presence, in war and trouble and waiting, always knowing that you care for us.'*

Confession

'When I kept silent, my bones wasted away.'
Psalm 32:3

Read Psalm 32 and 51

It can be easy, as followers of Jesus, to focus on the incredible gift of forgiveness. We know that Jesus died in our place and our sins have been forgiven. They have been removed as far as the east is from the west (Psalm 103:12) and, incredibly, God remembers them no more (Isaiah 43:25). But as part of that forgiveness, confession is important. Even the posture of confession reminds us of who we are before God – unworthy and in need of mercy. It also reminds us of what God is like as the One who is utterly holy, and the giver of all grace and mercy. In these psalms, David did exactly that. He got on his knees and confessed. He must have been full of remorse after his disobedience with Bathsheba, and the resulting deaths of Uriah and Bathsheba's child. But he also acknowledged the heaviness of shame that weighed him down before he confessed to God. It was like his bones wasted away and his strength was sapped. It's a reminder to us. While we might find it easier to cover up our sins, or direct blame to someone else, ultimately it does us no good. We will still feel the heaviness of guilt and shame, like David. *'For day and night your hand was heavy on me; my strength was sapped as in the heat of summer'* (32:4). But when David confessed, his guilt and shame were removed. He knew the Lord's love surrounded him. We too can experience that same release from inner anguish, as we come to God in confession.

- - - - - -

Pray

> *'Lord, we are weighed down by shame. We are inclined to blame. Please hear our prayers today and forgive us our sins.'*

As the deer pants

'My soul thirsts for God, for the living God.'
Psalm 42:2

Read Psalm 42

Some years ago, Darren and I and our boys visited central Australia. It was the middle of summer and we camped in the desert. It was hot! We experienced thirst. We held on to our water bottles like they were the most precious things we owned. It reminded me of this psalm. David also described thirst – but not the kind of thirst that could be quenched by water bottles in the desert. David was thirsty for the living God. He longed to meet with God. His soul cried out for God. Isn't that the most wonderful longing? Our souls do cry out for God and, in reply, God is present. He longs to meet with us. He is knowable. He is not a combination of typed, black words on a white page in a translated Bible. He is a God who hears us and loves us and knows us. He makes our hearts sing. He answers all of our longings. He is not remote. Even when we're struggling, like David was in this psalm, it is God who is our hope for tomorrow. And as David thirsted for the living God, he knew that he would *yet praise him* (42:5,11). David forced himself to remember times in the past when he'd felt closer to God, and he knew that he would feel so again. He told himself to hang on to that hope! And we can learn from him. We too will struggle, and notice our thirst for God, and remember that he is present. We will also be amazed that he promises us a time when all thirst will be quenched for ever.

- - - - - -

Pray

'Lord, we long for you, like the deer pants for water. Please quench our thirst today.'

For the nations

'So that your ways may be known on earth, your salvation among all nations.'

Psalm 67:2

Read Psalm 67

It's interesting that the psalmists move so frequently between personal distress to a much larger concern for the nations. Their personal needs do not overshadow God's plan to bring healing for the nations – the plan he made clear in the beginning when he spoke to Abraham in Genesis 12. This psalm reminds us of his plan. I remember the day we read it in Nepal. The civil war was getting worse and the government had called for elections, which meant that there would be riots and strikes that week. We went to our Nepali church, and one of the leaders read this psalm to begin the service, *'May the peoples praise you, God; may all the peoples praise you. May the nations be glad and sing for joy, for you rule the peoples with equity and guide the nations of the earth'* (v. 3–4). I sat there and thought that praise is good, but it's hard in civil war. Maybe, for us living through riots and attacks, we could just sit quietly and pray. But that day, in our church, everyone stood up and sang to God, loudly! It went on for hours because, in a civil war, God is still God. He is still sovereign; he is still worthy of praise and we still want to praise him. In fact, maybe there's something about war and loss of control that makes us want to praise him even more. Perhaps we also need to learn that deeply, in times of peace as well as in times of war.

- - - - - -

Pray

> *'Lord, you are worthy of praise, and we pray today that the nations everywhere would praise you.'*

Sing to God

'Sing to God, you kingdoms of the earth, sing praise to the Lord.'
Psalm 68:32

Read Psalm 68

Psalm 68 is a beautiful reminder of what God is like. His name is the Lord, and we sing praise to his name, and we are led forth in singing. Why? Because he's a father to the fatherless, and the defender of widows. He sets the lonely in families and leads out the prisoners with singing. That's why we sing! We do not sing to God because everything is fine here, or because we're perfectly well, or happy, or nothing awful has happened this week. We sing to God because he's a father to the fatherless, and he sets the lonely in families. How does he do that? He sent his own Son, the Lord Jesus, to bring us to himself. The psalm reminds us that life *is* often hard and uncomfortable. We grieve and we are lonely. And God sets the lonely in families. In our hardest times, he is like a father to us. And because of that, we can become like a family to those who are lonely or grieving amongst us this week. We can also show grace-filled generosity and hospitality in our churches and communities, because we know the father to the fatherless. Praise be to God!

- - - - - -

Pray

'Lord, we thank you that you care for the lonely and weak, and we ask that as churches we would be like your family for them.'

Lament and the pause before hope

'Will the Lord reject for ever?'
Psalm 77:7

Read Psalm 77

There are days that are hard – when we feel the weight of failure, or sickness, or fear, or profound loss. And on those days, it's right to lament, to groan and to weep. The psalmist does exactly that in Psalm 77. He was in anguish. He felt no comfort at all. His spirit was faint, and he wondered if the Lord would reject him for ever. He even questioned his own heart. But then, slowly, he remembered. It's as if, halfway through the writing, the psalmist paused and breathed out, and then deliberately looked back and remembered God's ways and truth – the evidence in his life, and in the history of Israel. In particular, he remembered the saving miracle of the exodus, in the days of Moses. He said, *'I will remember the deeds of the LORD; yes, I will remember your miracles of long ago. I will consider all your works and meditate on all your mighty deeds. Your ways, God, are holy'* (77:11–13). It was the remembering that led the psalmist to once again consider the character of God. Your ways, God, are holy! It reminds us that even on our hardest days, we can also lift our heads and remember the times when God has acted in the past. We can dwell on his character, and his good purposes through his Son Jesus. He didn't forget us then, and he hasn't forgotten us today.

- - - - - -

Pray

'Lord, we thank you that you understand and you hear our lament. Thank you for this moment to pause and remember your ways and your character. Please move us to hope.'

Number our days

'Teach us to number our days, that we may gain a heart of wisdom.'
Psalm 90:12

Read Psalm 90

One year, Darren and I visited a cemetery in Northern Queensland and we sat beside the grave of a young lady who died at age 31. Her husband had been a missionary in Cooktown, and he also died young. They left behind them a 3-year-old son, and the little boy went to stay with relatives who lived 3,000kms away. He must have been lonely. But years later, the boy married and had three children of his own. One of them was my mother! So I knelt by the grave, and felt thankful . . . for the lives of all those who have gone before us and left a legacy. Much later in the day, I read Psalm 90. *'Teach us to number our days, that we may gain a heart of wisdom'* (90:12). It's an interesting phrase and it made me wonder whether the psalmist was numbering backwards or forwards. If it was backwards, then at that point I'd lived about 18,000 days, but if it was forwards, it was unknown. So what would it mean to number our days forward – to treat each day as a genuine gift from God, rather than a right, or to see each moment as an opportunity and not a burden? How would it change the way we lived if we knew that being alive wasn't something we could assume for next year, or even next week? Our days are limited, and we need the reminder that God holds all of time in his hands.

- - - - - -

Pray

'Lord, we thank you . . . that you are God, from everlasting to everlasting. Help us to see our moments and days in light of your good plans and purposes for the world, wherever we are.'

Let them tell their story

'Then they cried to the LORD in their trouble.'
Psalm 107:6

Read Psalm 107

This is one of my favourite psalms. I love the patterns in it and the repetition. We are called to share our stories of grace! *'Let the redeemed of the LORD tell their story – those he redeemed from the hand of the foe, those he gathered from the lands, from east and west, from north and south'* (107:2–3). It's a wonderful reminder that God is at work everywhere – in every part of the world – east and west, north and south. But also, in every part of the world, we suffer. In this case, the descriptions of suffering include wandering in the desert, hungry and thirsty, and sitting in darkness, and becoming fools, and reeling and staggering, at their wits' end. But in every case, the people cried out to God and he answered them. He saved them from their distress, and they gave thanks to the Lord for his unfailing love. We are part of this grand, expansive description! We can also tell our stories, wherever we are – of God's saving grace in our lives through Jesus. In 2017, I spent time listening to people from Uganda to Kathmandu, Singapore to Colorado, Austria to Northern Iraq tell their stories of coming to faith in Jesus. It was amazing to hear the variety of ways God works in our hearts through Jesus, and answers our deepest longings. So tell your story . . . and honour him for his unfailing love.

- - - - - -

Pray

> *'Lord, we thank you that when we cry out to you, you save us from our distress. Please help us to be people who tell your wonderful, redemptive story, whenever we can.'*

Being known

'You have searched me, LORD, and you know me.'
Psalm 139:1

Read Psalm 139:1–6

Sometimes when we share our faith stories, we tell people about the time when Jesus became a part of our life – the moment when we first responded to him, or acknowledged him as Lord. But this psalm reminds us that even before that time, God knew us. We have always been known by God. Even today, as we read his word, he knows when we sit and rise. He perceives our thoughts from afar. He knows all the things we're worried about, or confused about, or would rather nobody else knew. He discerns our going out and lying down at night. He is familiar with all our ways – all of our questions and pain, all of our criticism and hopes, and the things that make us smile, or laugh, or weep. He knows us, and he can see the world through our eyes when nobody else can. Before a word is on our tongue (or even before it's formed in the language cortex of our brain), God knows it completely. He knows what we'll be thinking in half an hour from now, when we stop reading this psalm. It's more than we can ever fathom. And so often, despite this amazing all-knowing friendship we have with the almighty God, we assume strangeness. He knows us better than we know ourselves, but we go about our days as if he's not present, or as if he's irrelevant, or unacquainted with our concerns.

- - - - - -

Pray

'Lord, let today not be a day of assumed strangeness. Please remind us that you know us, and let the mystery of that cause us to praise you.'

'Where can I go from your Spirit?'
Psalm 139:7

Read Psalm 139:7–12

The first time we left Australia to go and live long-term in Nepal, I was only 24 years old. I hadn't been to Asia before. I hadn't cooked a curry, let alone eaten chilli, or learnt a foreign language. And there we were on the plane, flying to the other side of the world, leaving behind every familiar thing we knew and loved, and we wouldn't be back in Australia for another four years. I remember sitting on the plane and feeling suddenly anxious. Then I pulled out my Bible and read Psalm 139. *'If I rise on the wings of the dawn, if I settle on the far side of the sea, even there your hand will guide me, your right hand will hold me fast'* (139:9–10). It's a needed reminder that there is nowhere we can go, where God is not with us. He hems us in, behind and in front, in our own home and, equally, in the Himalayas. If we go up to the heavens, or the moon, or to Queensland on holidays, or if we move down the street, he'll be with us. If we make our bed in the depths, or in a hospital room, or if we sit for hours at fracture clinic, he'll be with us, in control, unsurprised, loving us, and holding us 'fast'. Isn't that a lovely word? God holds us 'fast' – tightly, not letting go, not getting distracted, not running out of answers, even on the days when our fears threaten to consume us.

- - - - - -

Pray

> *'Lord, thank you that even the darkness will not be dark to you, because you are light and you bring light to everything. Remind us again that there is nowhere we can go without you.'*

Fearfully and wonderfully made

'You knit me together in my mother's womb.'
Psalm 139:13b

Read Psalm 139:13–24

This is the reminder we need. God's works are fearful and wonderful, and we are each one of his works. Years and years ago, he formed us in our mother's womb – back when we were only cells, he made us in the secret place, and he had plans for us . . . and he knew each of them, back then. It's amazing because it tells us that even today, God isn't surprised. He doesn't scratch his head, or wonder what to do with us next. He knows. His works are wonderful and fearful. And it doesn't mean that we won't struggle, needing wheelchairs, and crutches, and hospital beds. We will. But God knit us together, on purpose. He ordained our days, every one of them in his book for a reason . . . that we would know Jesus, and love him, and love the ones in front of us. That we would grow in faith and trust. Amazingly, God knows the best way to grow faith in us. He knows the number of days in which he will do that. And while it's hard to fathom, it's helpful. God is not finished with us yet. So, we sit quietly and praise him, in awe at the vastness of his plans and thoughts. *'Were I to count them, they would outnumber the grains of sand'* (139:18). It also makes us humble. We long for him to search us – to know our hearts and to see if there is any offensive way in us, and to lead us in the way everlasting (139:24).

- - - - - -

Pray

> *'Lord, your ways are beyond us. Thank you that you know us, and that you made us fearfully, for your purposes.'*

Pleading

'LORD, hear my prayer, listen to my cry for mercy.'
Psalm 143:1

Read Psalm 143

Psalm 143 is another reminder that many days are hard. The psalmist himself is feeling pursued and crushed – like he's dwelling in the darkness and going down to the pit. And there are days when we relate to that. Not long ago, one of our lovely friends at church passed away. She was prayerful and faithful and wise. One minute she was sitting next to us in church meetings, singing with us and praying with us, and then the next minute she was in ICU, intubated and ventilated. It was so sudden. Her family and friends were numb with the loss. They knew that they would see her again (and that she's now rejoicing with her Saviour), but the thought of living here without her was too hard. She was such an encouragement! But if there's one thing that grief does, it puts other things back in perspective. It draws us back to the love of God. Like the psalmist, we cry out for mercy, and we plead, and thirst, and admit our aching need. Within all of that, there is a stillness. God is faithful and righteous. His hands made everything. He has redeemed us through his Son, the Lord Jesus. And so we also pray, like the psalmist. *'Let the morning bring me word of your unfailing love, for I have put my trust in you. Show me the way I should go, for to you I entrust my life. Rescue me from my enemies, LORD, for I hide myself in you. Teach me to do your will, for you are my God; may your good Spirit lead me on level ground'* (143:8–10).

- - - - - -

Pray

'Lord, this is our prayer today.'

Wisdom

'Trust in the LORD with all your heart and lean not on your own understanding.'

Proverbs 3:5

Read Proverbs 1:1 – 3:35

There is a time for singing the psalms – for wonderful praise and honest lament and complicated questions and beautiful solace. But there is also a time for pithy sayings – for short bursts of needed wisdom that reflect God's ways and his world. The book of Proverbs gives us that over and over again! But within each proverb, the underlying focus is that *'the fear of the LORD is the beginning of knowledge'* (1:7). If we are to seek knowledge in all its forms and extent, for the sake of knowledge, that might be great, but if it isn't centred on the One who formed all things and sustains all things, then our knowledge will be limited and even harmful. It can turn into decay. So instead, the proverbs remind us to *'Trust in the LORD with all your heart and lean not on your own understanding; in all your ways submit to him, and he will make your paths straight'* (3:5–6). Of course, it feels like a simple thing to do – to trust in the Lord and submit to him every day – and yet it's so hard to do. In a world where other voices clamour for our allegiance daily, what does it mean to immerse ourselves in God's word, to relate to him so deeply that our natural response is to trust him, and to look to him, as the source of all wisdom?

- - - - - -

Pray

'Lord, we admit that our hearts are attuned to every other voice as well as our own needs and understanding. Please change us and mould us as we read your word, and Proverbs in particular.'

Ancient sense

'Does not wisdom call out? Does not understanding raise her voice?'
Proverbs 8:1

Read Proverbs 5:1 – 9:18

It strikes me that the proverbs make such wonderful sense, even in today's world, thousands of years after they were originally written. We too understand the admonishment to drink water from our own well (to not covet what belongs to someone else), and to consider the ways of the ant (who works hard all the time, even without a commander), and to be careful of troublemakers and gossips because they stir up trouble in the community. We know, and have seen, how this advice works out in practice, and we do well to heed it. But there is also a profound reminder in chapter 8. God's wisdom originated at the very beginning – before the mountains were settled in place, and before the sea was given its boundary. Wisdom personified says, *'Then I was constantly at his side. I was filled with delight day after day, rejoicing always in his presence, rejoicing in his whole world and delighting in the human race'* (8:30–31). It reminds us of the glory and delight of creation, and the timeless nature of God who formed everything with his hand. But it also feels like an allusion to the Word itself, to Jesus, who came amongst us and who is described in John's gospel as being *'with God in the beginning'* (John 1:2). What a lovely reminder that within that long span of time, the answers to all of our most puzzling scenarios can be found in a life-giving relationship with God, through Jesus, our true wisdom teacher.

- - - - - -

Pray

> *'Lord, we thank you for your ancient wisdom. Please help us to find life in you again today.'*

Trembling before God

'Blessed is the one who always trembles before God.'
Proverbs 28:14

Read Proverbs 10:1 – 29:27

As humans, we need the reminders in Proverbs, over and over again. Heed discipline and correction (10:17). Don't put your hope in mortals (11:7). Take care with your tongue (10:31). Beware of pride (11:2). If you eat too much honey, you may vomit (25:16). Remember that wealth is worthless (11:4), and that nagging doesn't work very well (21:19). It fascinates me that in every society and generation, we are prone to the same temptations and foolishness, and yet we are also given the same answers. In every situation, the Lord speaks to us through his word . . . and he knows us. *'The crucible for silver and the furnace for gold, but the LORD tests the heart'* (17:3). *'The eyes of the LORD are everywhere, keeping watch on the wicked and the good'* (15:3). *'All a person's ways seem pure to them, but motives are weighed by the LORD'* (16:2). We need this reminder. The Lord knows us. He knows our motives when we easily justify ourselves, or delude ourselves. And it's this reminder (that we are each known by God) that causes us to stop and tremble before him, and to acknowledge his holiness, and to thank him for a clean slate in Christ.

- - - - - -

Pray

> *'Lord, we thank you that you are a God who sees everything, even our own hearts. Forgive us for assuming purity when it hasn't been the case. Forgive us for thinking we were not in need of your forgiveness and grace, through Christ. Forgive us for our delusions.'*

The glory of God

'It is the glory of God to conceal a matter.'
Proverbs 25:2

Read Proverbs 25

One of the difficulties in reading proverbs is the nature of them. They are distilled wisdom. They take generalist concepts and simplify them, often poetically, to make an idea memorable – often remarkably so. For example, when I first read, *'Like a gold ring in a pig's snout is a beautiful woman who shows no discretion'* (11:22), I spent the rest of the day imagining pigs with gold rings in their noses. But later in the day, I read, *'It is the glory of God to conceal a matter; to search out a matter is the glory of kings'* (25:2). Within this world in which we live, surrounded by complex relationships and intrigue and deceit and beauty and science and love and everything in between, there is much that we cannot know or understand. Perhaps God has concealed it for his purposes and glory. As humans, we are wired to want understanding and wisdom, yet we will not know everything. We will want answers to millions of questions, yet we won't find them all. Underneath, this is actually how we want it. We want to worship a God who is bigger than we are; who has not revealed or disclosed everything, and who has the right to conceal a matter, whenever he chooses. In acknowledging that, we leave room for wonder.

- - - - - -

Pray

'Lord, we thank you for this reminder. Help us to stand in awe of you, because you do know everything, and you do hold the most puzzling things in your hand.'

Wonder

'There are three things that are too amazing for me, four that I do not understand.'

Proverbs 30:18

Read Proverbs 30

In Proverbs 30, the reminder from the writer is to look at the world in wonder. Notice stately lions, and busy ants, and strutting roosters, and lizards in king's palaces. Do they belong there? Marvel at the way of an eagle in the sky, and a snake on a rock, and a ship on the high seas, and a man with a young woman. Is it lovely? Practise wonder. Think about locusts. They are so small and they have no king, yet they advance together in ranks. Lizards can be caught with the hand, yet they are found in king's palaces. But the chapter also mentions things that we struggle to understand, like the fool who gets plenty to eat, or the servant who becomes king. It's an upside-down world, full of ambiguity and subtlety, and we are meant to wonder . . . because the wondering reminds us of who we are and who God is. We are small and limited, and we don't know everything. We sin. But we trust in the One who loves us and who holds all things in his hands. The wondering causes us to turn up empty-handed and to say sorry to God for trying to shrink him (and his universe) down to someone, or something, that we could manage or analyse or debate.

- - - - - -

Pray

'Lord, we're sorry . . . please renew wonder in us today.'

Mist

'I have seen all the things that are done under the sun; all of them are meaningless, a chasing after the wind.'
Ecclesiastes 1:14

Read Ecclesiastes 1:1 – 2:26

The teacher whose voice we hear in Ecclesiastes reminds us of something very important. Life is transient and unpredictable and cyclical and fleeting. It disappears quickly, like early morning mist in the valley. It's been like that since the beginning of time. Even when we pretend well, we're not in control, and we're not here for long, and we don't know how many days we have left. So, given the fleeting nature of life, what should we do with our days? What things are meaningful, or useful to do in terms of 'gain'? Is there gain in toil and pleasures and projects and wealth? The writer's questions are apt, of course, because without God there is no gain at all. Instead, there is 'gift'. Everything we have is a gift from God – wisdom, knowledge and satisfaction. And we can choose to live a life defined more by 'gift' than by gain. We can choose to focus on giving from what we have. As we do, we will find meaning in knowing the One who knows the answer to every question. He is in control of our days, and times, including the ones we would never choose. And we know that one day, Jesus will return and make all things clear, even the transient mist in the valley. Until then, we choose to live wisely and faithfully, and to thank him for the simple, beautiful things, like sunshine and streams and wind and trees.

Pray

'Lord, thank you for this reminder. We slip into "gain" so easily. Please breathe your life-giving message of "gift" into us today.'

A time for everything

'There is a time for everything, and a season for every activity under the heavens.'
Ecclesiastes 3:1

Read Ecclesiastes 3:1–22

We all live through hard seasons. One of mine was during our seventh monsoon in Nepal. I was home-schooling our three sons on a Himalayan ridge, through civil war and shoot-on-sight curfews, and monsoonal rain every day. I remember reading Ecclesiastes. *'All streams flow into the sea, yet the sea is never full. To the place the streams come from, there they return again'* (1:7). We had streams everywhere, and there were still 120 days of rain to go! I continued reading. *'There is a time for everything and a season for every activity under the heavens'* (3:1). There I was, hemmed in by rain and civil war, and my closest Nepali friend was dying of a brain tumour. I questioned God. How was he making this time beautiful? In whose eyes was it beautiful? I didn't know, but I read on. *'I know that everything God does will endure for ever; nothing can be added to it and nothing taken from it. God does it so that people will fear him'* (3:14). I stopped there. God works in the world so that we will revere him and respond to him. He longs for that. He's made it possible through Jesus, who will judge all things in the end. And to revere, in the dictionary, means to show profound awe and honour, utmost love and respect. It's a get-on-your-knees-and-weep kind of thing, because that's what God is owed. It's a needed reminder for all of us, in every season.

- - - - - -

Pray

'Lord, we know that every day, in every season, is a fresh chance to respond to you. Help us to revere you today.'

Mind the gap!

'God is in heaven and you are on earth, so let your words be few.'
Ecclesiastes 5:2b

Read Ecclesiastes 4:1 – 5:7

The teacher in Ecclesiastes goes on to question power and oppression and achievement and envy. He concludes that they are all 'chasing after the wind'. And then, what about the lonely person who seems to bear all things on their own? That's very hard. But perhaps the more we see misery and meaninglessness, the more we appreciate the beauty and gift of a friend, *'If either of them falls down, one can help the other up'* (4:10). *'A cord of three strands is not quickly broken'* (4:12b). It's a wonderfully needed reminder. But as well as the gift of friendship, there is the gift of awe – the awe that we need when we approach God. Tremble a bit, says the writer, and guard your steps. Go near to listen, rather than to offer the sacrifice of fools. Why? Because God is in heaven and you are on earth. It's a simple reminder, yet it changes everything. God is in heaven and we are not. So mind the gap . . . and remember there is a gap! The gap causes us to listen reverently and to honour him and praise him as fearful and worthy. But incredibly, God also chose to bridge the gap. He sent his own Son to bear all things so that we could approach him whenever we wanted. It's amazing that on any ordinary day, on the train to the city, or on an arduous walk, or stuck in a traffic jam, we can approach God. We can speak to him, and we can listen to him, and we can give thanks.

- - - - - -

Pray

> *'Lord, we have taken your word and your grace for granted. Renew reverence in us today.'*

Riches

'As goods increase, so do those who consume them.'
Ecclesiastes 5:11

Read Ecclesiastes 5:8 – 6:12

We have a friend who grew up in Benin, West Africa. Her family practised Voodoo worship as protection from the curses. They were also significantly wealthy, due to her father's position in seafaring, and that meant they needed a lot of Voodoo to protect them from the envy (and curses) of their neighbours. But one particular day, my friend's father, Alberic, lost his job. The boat was stolen and the family lost all their power and wealth. It was desolation, in a moment. But at the same time, Alberic was invited to a local church and he happened to hear a sermon on Ecclesiastes. The speaker said that everything in this life, even wealth and power, was transient and meaningless without God. Wealth can be hoarded, but it is never enough. Alberic was amazed. How did the speaker know him? He responded, on the spot, and put his trust in Jesus. Later, every one of the family members came to faith in Jesus as well. They burnt all their Voodoo. Afterwards, Alberic would often quote from Ecclesiastes. *'Everyone comes naked from their mother's womb, and as everyone comes, so they depart'* (5:15). But he knew where true riches lay. He was overwhelmingly thankful for his identity in Christ, and he no longer needed the Voodoo. He also knew the importance of holding riches lightly, and the joy of holding on to Christ with everything he had.

- - - - - -

Pray

> *'Lord, it doesn't matter who we are, we are all occasionally tempted to grip on to the security of our financial position. Please teach us to hold wealth lightly.'*

Enjoy your life

'However many years anyone may live, let them enjoy them all.'
Ecclesiastes 11:8

Read Ecclesiastes 7:1 – 12:14

It seems like a fairly unusual way to sum up complex questions about power and meaning and wealth and vanity, but there it is. Go home and enjoy your life! Taste the cheese on your pizza. Bask in the afternoon sunshine. Find pleasure in the way the cat snuggles on your lap. We will all die, and we don't know when, so we're to hold onto life lightly, to accept its transience and unpredictability, and to enjoy the simple things. *'There is nothing better for a person under the sun than to eat and drink and be glad'* (8:15). *'Enjoy life with your wife, whom you love, all the days of this meaningless life that God has given you under the sun'* (9:9). *'However many years anyone may live, let them enjoy them all'* (11:8). As part of that enjoyment, of course, we are to remember our Creator, to fear him and to keep his commandments . . . *'For God will bring every deed into judgement, including every hidden thing, whether it is good or evil'* (12:14). One day, Jesus will return and, on that day, all the vapour and mist and unknown, perplexing things will be gone for ever! He will bring the healing and justice that the world has been longing for since the earliest of times.

- - - - - -

Pray

> *'Lord, thank you for the way you challenge our false hopes and remind us of transience. Help us to enjoy and celebrate the simple things that you give today.'*

A celebration of love

'Let him kiss me with the kisses of his mouth.'
Song of Songs 1:2

Read Song of Songs 1:1 – 8:14

It seems surprising, and yet wonderful, that the wisdom books in the Bible include this ancient Israelite love poem. It begins unashamedly with a girl longing for her beloved and his kiss: *'Take me away with you – let us hurry!'* (1:4). The poem celebrates the most joyful and vulnerable of human encounters, and the mystery of sexual union – the desire to be fully known and loved, by the one we love. It *is* a wonderful gift from God, and it always has been, since the Garden of Eden when Adam and Eve were made for each other, naked with each other, and fully known. Like them, we are also wired for that kind of giving and receiving of love. We too have felt *'faint with love'* (2:5), desiring to hold and never let go (3:4). We too have basked in a *'season of singing'* (2:12), and yet, there is also an ache. In the poem, the beloved is not always present. He leaves, and there is pain at departure, followed by searching and questions. This too is the reality of love. We live with the effects of sin, and we are flawed and selfish in the way we love each other. Yet, amazingly, the longing for love draws us back to the perfect, unending love of God, made known in Christ. It causes us to long for the day when all human love will be fully restored and redeemed. We can't imagine that day, but we long for it!

- - - - - -

Pray

> *'Lord, we thank you for your beautiful gift of human love, and for the joy of sexual union. Help us to value and honour it today, in all the ways you had in mind.'*

Isaiah's vision

'Hear me, you heavens! Listen, earth! For the LORD has spoken.'
Isaiah 1:2

Read Isaiah 1:1 – 5:30

After reading wisdom literature, turning to the prophets can feel like a change of gear. The prophets were each given compelling messages from God, for specific people groups, in certain time periods. Isaiah, for example, was given a vision from God at the time of the northern and southern kingdoms, regarding the judgement that was still to come. But Isaiah began his message by addressing everything, including the heavens and the earth. It was all under the Lord's governance, and therefore all of it must listen. His message was serious. The people would soon feel the effects of their rebellion against Yahweh. They had been idolatrous and unjust in their dealings, and they would receive judgement. Having read Kings and Chronicles, we know how the story ended, with the destruction of Jerusalem and the exile of the southern kingdom to Babylon. But within that, Isaiah also gave them new and beautiful glimpses of hope and redemption – of a time to come when Yahweh would fulfil his covenant promises. *'Though your sins are like scarlet, they shall be as white as snow'* (1:18). *'He will teach us his ways, so that we may walk in his paths. The law will go out from Zion, the word of the LORD from Jerusalem'* (2:3b). The original reader must have also felt such exhilarating hope! And we also pause, knowing that Jesus ultimately fulfilled this amazing prophecy. For us too we deserved judgement, but our sins that were scarlet have been made as white as snow.

- - - - - -

Pray

> *'Lord, we can hardly believe this message. We thank you for the redeeming life and death of Jesus. We know we are unworthy but we thank you for lives made clean.'*

Isaiah's commission

'And I said, "Here am I. Send me!"'
Isaiah 6:8b

Read Isaiah 6:1–13

The path of Isaiah must have been unenviable in every way. He was asked to give an unwanted message of judgement to Judah leading up to the exile. And yet, as soon as he heard the voice of the Lord saying, *'Whom shall I send?'* Isaiah replied, *'Here am I. Send me!'* (6:8). It seems odd to us that anyone should be keen on such a hard task! Yet, prior to the question, the Lord appeared to Isaiah, high and exalted, seated on the throne. Above the Lord were seraphim, calling out to one another about the Lord's wonderful holiness. As they did, the building shook and the temple filled with smoke! No wonder Isaiah cried, *'Woe to me! . . . I am ruined! For I am a man of unclean lips'* (6:5). In that moment, he became so aware of his own unworthiness. But then, one of the seraphim flew to Isaiah, touched his mouth, and told him that his guilt was taken away and his sin atoned for. Amazing! That's why Isaiah said yes, send me. He was a man raised up for a specific purpose, at a specific time, and he knew without a doubt that his sins were atoned for by a holy God. The Lord humbled Isaiah and revealed his glory to him. But it didn't mean that it was going to be easy. Isaiah was commissioned to give the message of judgement, until every house in Jerusalem lay deserted, and the city was ruined. But Isaiah had something to cling on to. After the destruction of the city, Yahweh said there would be a tiny, 'holy seed' (6:13).

- - - - - -

Pray

'Lord, we ask that you would create in us the same honest response to Jesus. Please, send me.'

Looking ahead to the Messiah

'The virgin will conceive and give birth to a son, and will call him Immanuel.'
Isaiah 7:14

Read Isaiah 7:1 – 12:6

There are many layers of fulfilment within prophetic literature, and it's certainly the case for these passages, written for a pre-exilic people. But we can read them today and hear the thrill and hope of a king to come, to be named 'Immanuel' – God with us. *'The virgin will conceive and give birth to a son, and will call him Immanuel'* (7:14). *'The people walking in darkness have seen a great light'* (9:2). *'For to us a child is born, to us a son is given'* (9:6). The imagery is wonderful – a ruler to come who will be born of a virgin, and bring light to those living in darkness. Finally, that one, all-consuming, penetrating question from Genesis 3 is going to be answered, and the child himself will be called *'Wonderful Counsellor, Mighty God, Everlasting Father, Prince of Peace'* (9:6). Imagine that? It's the trajectory of peace that we've longed for since the time of Judges. It's the true king promised in 2 Samuel, who will reign on David's throne for ever. It's the Lord Jesus himself! And yet, there's even more than that! For the first time in the Bible, Isaiah speaks of a time to come when *'The wolf will live with the lamb, the leopard will lie down with the goat . . . and a little child will lead them'* (11:6). It's God's beautiful plan and purpose for all time. It's the invitation back to the garden – a renewed world under God's care. It should render us speechless.

- - - - - -

Pray

> *'Lord, the thought is too large. We have no words, but we long for your good plan, when Christ will return and bring the kind of peace that we can't even imagine.'*

Tears shed, and wiped away

'On this mountain the LORD Almighty will prepare a feast of rich food for all peoples.'
Isaiah 25:6

Read Isaiah 13:1 – 27:13

Isaiah's vision was for a wonderful, eternal hope through the future messianic kingdom, but it was also one of judgement on the people of Judah and on their enemies. Judah was about to be exiled, and Babylon was to be part of it. But then afterwards, Babylon itself would be destroyed, as would Moab, Damascus, Cush, Egypt, Edom, Arabia, and Tyre. The results were going to be devastating. *'The earth is defiled by its people; they have disobeyed the laws . . . Therefore a curse consumes the earth'* (24:5,6). It sounds a bit like the world as we know it today! But Isaiah kept painting the picture. He never gave in to despair. *'LORD, you are my God; I will exalt you and praise your name, for in perfect faithfulness you have done wonderful things, things planned long ago'* (25:1). Judgement and hope were intertwined, and a previously unimagined reign of peace was also on view. In the time to come, said Isaiah, the Lord would *'prepare a feast of rich food for all peoples . . . he will swallow up death for ever. The sovereign LORD will wipe away the tears from all faces; he will remove his people's disgrace from all the earth'* (25:6,8). It's the first glimpse of eternity! Death is going to be swallowed up! And the Lord himself is going to wipe away the tears from all faces. It's so tender. It's not that our tears are going to dry up by themselves. The Lord will personally wipe them away. That's what he is like, and that's why we sing.

- - - - - -

Pray

> *'Lord, we have been despairing. But we raise our heads today and thank you for the glorious hope to come.'*

The pretence

'But their hearts are far from me.'
Isaiah 29:13

Read Isaiah 28:1 – 35:10

In reading Isaiah's descriptions in this section, it's important to note that his warnings were primarily for the people of Jerusalem. Back in the time of Kings, the people had hardened their hearts and they were about to face judgement in the form of exile to Babylon. It would not be long. But in every sentence directed at Jerusalem, we also recognise our human tendencies. *'These people come near to me with their mouth and honour me with their lips, but their hearts are far from me. Their worship of me is based on merely human rules that they have been taught'* (29:13). We need to pause here. It's also easy for us to pretend in prayer, and to veer towards human rules. It's easy for us to come before God in a self-righteous manner, or to speak vacant, rehearsed lines while thinking about what's for lunch, or trying to impress an audience that isn't God at all. We have perfected pretence! And yet, God knows and cares. Back then, he said, *'Therefore once more I will astound these people with wonder upon wonder; the wisdom of the wise will perish, the intelligence of the intelligent will vanish'* (29:14). And the Lord did astound them! He sent hope and healing, ultimately through his Son Jesus, who not only spoke directly to their hearts but also rose from the dead and broke the power of death for ever – the most astounding wonder of them all.

- - - - - -

Pray

'Lord, we confess that we see ourselves in these lines. We have pretended. We have honoured you with our lips while our hearts were far away. Please call us back today.'

Your God will come

'Strengthen the feeble hands, steady the knees that give way; say to those with fearful hearts, "Be strong, do not fear; your God will come."'
Isaiah 35:3–4

Read Isaiah 35:1 – 39:8

In the centre of the book of Isaiah is the reminder of God's saving work during the time of Hezekiah, as recorded in Kings. We know that Hezekiah spread out his concerns before the Lord, and the Lord answered them, spectacularly. Yahweh saved the city from the Assyrians and added 15 years to Hezekiah's life (2 Kings 20:6). But the postscript of judgement was still there, and it would come in the form of the Babylonians (39:5–8). Judgement and grace do exist side by side. In fact, one without the other wouldn't make any sense. But even within those reminders of judgement, there was a beautiful poetic interlude. Isaiah spoke of a time to come when the parched land would be glad, and the eyes of the blind would be opened, and the Way would be made clear for the redeemed to come home (35:1–10). The remnant would return home! But more than that, the word 'redemption' tells the reader that there will be a cost borne by someone to save the people. I wonder how the people understood it back then. Did they wonder how redemption would occur? Surely the words filled them with hope and joy, even in the time of trial ahead. There would be singing again. *'Gladness and joy will overtake them, and sorrow and sighing will flee away'* (35:10b). We can also hold onto this hope in our own times of sorrow and sighing. We must not fear. The Lord Jesus will come again.

- - - - - -

Pray

> *'Lord, our feeble knees often give way. Please strengthen us to serve you, and to hope and wait until you come again.'*

Wings like eagles

'But those who hope in the LORD will renew their strength. They will soar on wings like eagles.'

Isaiah 40:31

Read Isaiah 40:1 – 44:28

We've probably all dreamed of flying. We've imagined soaring over tall trees and red rooftops. And from that beautifully high perspective, we've pictured our earthly concerns, far below. In this section, Isaiah writes to the remnant, saying that there is something about *'wings like eagles'* that is part of God's promise. There is hope and freedom to come. Historically, by the time of this writing the remnant had returned to the land, and they were finding it hard. They needed to see God's power and character, again. Yahweh was still sovereign. He was still the Creator of the ends of the earth. And those who put their hope in him would renew their strength. They would *'soar on wings like eagles'*. They would *'run and not grow weary'* (40:31). It's a beautiful perspective for a people who were wearily rebuilding their city and doubting God's promises. Yahweh was the Lord who gave them strength, and who had swept away their offences like a cloud, their sins like the morning mist. He said, *'Return to me, for I have redeemed you'* (44:22b). And there, in a sentence, is the heart of God. There are days when we lose perspective, when we visit our friend in hospital, or worry about the bills to pay. God longs for his people. He longs to sweep away our offences. And he has, for all time, through his Son, the servant Jesus. We can return to him, for he has redeemed us.

- - - - - -

Pray

> *'Lord, thank you that we need not be dismayed, for you are our God. We know you will strengthen us and help us. You will uphold us with your righteous right hand.'*

Treasures of darkness

'I form the light and create darkness.'
Isaiah 45:7

Read Isaiah 45:1 – 48:22

A few years ago, Darren and I visited an underground mine. It was a long way into the earth, and unbelievably gloomy. I won't tell you about the smell. But after our eyes adjusted to the darkness, we began to see sapphires. There was a whole row of them, gleaming in the darkness. Perhaps they were more stunning because of the darkness surrounding them. The sight reminded me of these words in Isaiah. The Lord said to the remnant, *'I will give you hidden treasures, riches stored in secret places, so that you may know that I am the LORD, the God of Israel, who summons you by name'* (45:3). It's often the very thing that God does during times of hardship and distress. He shows us again who he is. He helps us to see his beauty and truth and holiness, if we have eyes to see. He reminds us of his servant, Jesus, who brought life-giving salvation through suffering. Back in the time of the remnant, the people were wavering in their trust in Yahweh. Their day-to-day living was hard. They were complaining, and tempted to look to idols. It felt dark. But Yahweh spoke to them, reminding them that he was still the first and the last. His hand laid the foundations of the earth. His right hand spread out the heavens (48:13). And he summoned them, and us, *by name*. It's amazing.

- - - - - -

Pray

'Lord, thank you for the times when the darkness around us points us back to your gleaming holiness. Thank you that you summon us and call us by name.'

The servant of the Lord

'But he was pierced for our transgressions, he was crushed for our iniquities.'

Isaiah 53:5

Read Isaiah 49:1 – 54:17

Up to this point in the Bible, the references to the Messiah are mostly of kingship. The One to come would rule on David's throne. He would redeem and restore his people. He would provide a way home. He would be the true shepherd and the light to the nations. It was all wonderfully hopeful! But now, for the first time, there's a hint that the Messiah will suffer. The servant of the Lord will be beaten and rejected and despised and mocked (49:7 and 50:6). His appearance will be disfigured beyond that of any human being (52:14). He will take up our pain and bear our suffering. He will be pierced for our transgressions (53:5). I wonder what the original hearers thought. Did they fathom the extent of God's sacrifice? Did they wonder why anyone would bear punishment for them? Do we wonder that? Do we tremble at the love of God who took on suffering for us? Isaiah prophesied that the servant would be led like a lamb to the slaughter, yet he would not open his mouth. He would be assigned a grave with the wicked, though there was no deceit in his mouth (53:7,9). But Isaiah's prophecy didn't finish in the tomb. The tender shoot that was good and true and holy, invited our marks onto it (our sins, our pains, our terrible burdens), and then, after it was beaten, rejected and dismissed, the shoot grew into a magnificent tree, and the tree produced wonderful, new, surprising life (53:10–11).

- - - - - -

Pray

'Lord, we thank you for Jesus. We're amazed again that he bore our pain and punishment. We can't fathom it but we thank you for the wounds he bore for us.'

Like rain that nourishes the earth

'Come, all you who are thirsty, come to the waters.'
Isaiah 55:1

Read Isaiah 55:1 – 57:21

There's something lovely about standing in the rain, especially when it hasn't rained for ages. One day, after months of drought, I stood at Sydney harbour in the rain. I felt it on my face and watched it fall on umbrellas, and seagulls, and thirsty plants, and the harbour itself, where those tiny raindrops turned into an ocean. At the same time, I read Isaiah's words. *'As the rain and the snow come down from heaven, and do not return to it without watering the earth and making it bud and flourish, so that it yields seed for the sower and bread for the eater, so is my word that goes out from my mouth: it will not return to me empty, but will accomplish what I desire and achieve the purpose for which I sent it'* (55:10–11). It's an amazing image that we understand . . . because in the same way that the rain nourishes dry earth, so does God's word nourish our souls. Even today, as we immerse ourselves in Isaiah's prophecies, thousands of years after they were originally written, God will accomplish what he desires in us, and in the nations. He will bring about transformation and life – budding and seeding beyond what we can imagine – nourishing the ground, and the generations that will come after us with hope and healing.

- - - - - -

Pray

'Lord, we forget that your word is powerfully alive. We forget that you call us to come to you and to stand in the rain of your truth. Help us to do that today.'

The final fulfilment

'He has sent me to bind up the broken-hearted.'
Isaiah 61:1b

Read Isaiah 58:1 – 66:22

By the end of his prophecies, Isaiah had given the people of Israel a grand vision of eternal hope, and it was magnificent and servant-hearted. As God's people, they would work to maintain justice and do what was right (56:1). They would share their food with the hungry, and provide the wanderers with shelter (58:7). But also, the vision wasn't confined to Israel. Isaiah said the nations would be drawn into God's story, and they would also know their redeemer – the One of whom Isaiah spoke so clearly. *'He has sent me to bind up the broken-hearted, to proclaim freedom for the captives'* (61:1b). It's amazing that hundreds of years later, when Jesus began his ministry, he stood up in the synagogue and read those exact words of Isaiah, saying, *'Today this scripture is fulfilled in your hearing'* (Luke 4:21). And it was. I often wonder about the day when the Lord Jesus will return to the earth to redeem all things. Will he again take the scroll of Isaiah, but instead of reading from chapter 61, will he read from chapter 65? *'See, I will create new heavens and a new earth. The former things will not be remembered, nor will they come to mind . . . Never again will there be in it an infant who lives but a few days, or an old man who does not live out his years'* (65:17,20). Will Jesus then calmly announce to the world, *'Today this scripture is fulfilled in your hearing'*?

- - - - - -

Pray

'Lord, captivate us again with your Son Jesus, and your vision for a renewed world where there will be no need for the sun, for you will be our light.'

Jeremiah's calling

'They will fight against you but will not overcome you, for I am with you and will rescue you.'

Jeremiah 1:19

Read Jeremiah 1:1–19

In a similar way to Isaiah's ministry, Jeremiah also prophesied to the rebellious, southern kingdom of Judah. Like Isaiah, his task was to warn them of their imminent exile. But in contrast to Isaiah, Jeremiah wasn't initially keen. When the Lord told him that he would appoint him as a prophet, Jeremiah replied, *'Alas, Sovereign LORD . . . I do not know how to speak; I am too young'* (1:6). In some ways, it reminds us of Moses. But the Lord said to Jeremiah, *'Do not say, "I am too young." You must go to everyone I send you to and say whatever I command you. Do not be afraid of them, for I am with you'* (1:7–8). It's that same transformative message. Yahweh would be with him. He would put his words in Jeremiah's mouth. He would make him a *'fortified city, an iron pillar and a bronze wall to stand against . . . the kings of Judah'* (1:18). So Jeremiah responded, and went as he was told, and prophesied to the people. But the transformative promise of God's presence didn't mean that it was going to be easy! During the course of Jeremiah's life, he was beaten, accused, put in stocks and prison. He cried out to God in lament. But still, God was with him. And it speaks to us about comfort and ease and ministry. We may prefer ease, but in everything, we hold onto the same promise. God is with us.

- - - - - -

Pray

'Lord, we'd rather it was easy, but we thank you for the promise of your presence with us, in everything, through Jesus.'

Yahweh's anguish

'Does a young woman forget her jewellery, a bride her wedding ornaments? Yet my people have forgotten me, days without number.'
Jeremiah 2:32

Read Jeremiah 2:1 – 3:25

It's easy to think that Yahweh doesn't feel the same kind of anguish that we do as humans. He is holy and utterly good all of the time, so perhaps he doesn't cry or weep or moan like we do. And yet the description of his anguish here is confronting. Yahweh had been rejected by Israel, who had been like a prostitute (or a she-camel on heat), running here and there, craving after every foreign god and lover, and refusing even to blush with shame (2:23; 3:2). It's a striking description. Yahweh was like a husband who had been forgotten and forsaken by his people, and he felt the pain of it. He loved the Israelites. He kept calling them! He said, *'Return, faithless people . . . for I am your husband'* (3:14). He kept giving them another chance to repent, even though he knew they wouldn't. We also need to pause and remember that God experiences anguish when we turn away. Ultimately, of course, he carried the pain of every person and generation, in Christ. But today, I wonder whether it would change our prayers if we reflected on the truth that the Lord feels anguish, and we have contributed to that anguish.

- - - - - -

Pray

> *'Lord, forgive us again for forgetting you and forsaking you. It stuns us that you never forsake us, and you forgive us in Christ.'*

Jeremiah's laments

'Even if Moses and Samuel were to stand before me, my heart would not go out to this people. Send them away from my presence!'

Jeremiah 15:1

Read Jeremiah 11:1 – 16:21

Instead of heeding Jeremiah's warnings and turning back to Yahweh, the people of Judah continued to rebel. They kept turning to false prophets and, finally, there was a point of no return. Yahweh brought judgement in the form of the Babylonians. And Jeremiah lamented. His cries were so honest and personal, full of questions and doubt, and also asking for vengeance on the Israelites who were by then plotting against him personally (11:20). Jeremiah moaned to the point that he wished he'd never been born (15:10). And we relate to him. We are also often weighed down by questions about the world. We may doubt our calling, or wish it were otherwise. But in all of it, we can direct our questions to Yahweh. He understands that we live with doubts, and that our head knowledge doesn't always match our day-to-day experience. In this passage, as Yahweh responded to Jeremiah's laments, Jeremiah was reminded that it was Yahweh himself who would deal with his enemies. It was Yahweh himself who would act justly and righteously, bringing about his plans. It's this understanding of the sovereignty and justice and presence of God that gave Jeremiah the strength to continue. It's the same for us. We also place our confidence in the words of God rather than our own limited experience. He is still present, exercising kindness, justice and righteousness on the face of the earth (9:24).

- - - - - -

Pray

'Lord, we often struggle with doubt. We may know something in our head yet fail to live it. Please give us strength for the task today.'

The potter's house

'Can I not do with you, Israel, as this potter does?'
Jeremiah 18:6

Read Jeremiah 18:1 – 19:15

In the middle of Jeremiah's lament, Yahweh told him to go down to the potter's house, where he would give him a message. Then, when Jeremiah arrived, he saw the potter working at the wheel. And as the potter shaped the pot it suddenly became marred in his hands; so the potter formed it into another pot, *'shaping it as seemed best to him'* (18:4). It's an evocative image. A few years ago, one of our sons learnt pottery at art school, and he told us about it. He found it so immersing, requiring whole body concentration and patience, and yet so often his hand slipped and the pot became marred, so he began again, over and over again. The imagery in this chapter reminds us that the potter has the right to do as he pleases with the pot. It's his pot that he loves! And Yahweh, sovereign and good and loving and timeless, also has the right to do as he pleases with his creation and his people that he loves. *'Like clay in the hand of the potter, so are you in my hand, Israel'* (18:6). Not long after these prophecies, Yahweh allowed the destruction of Jerusalem and the exile of his people to Babylon (2 Kings 24 – 25), forming it into a new pot. Yahweh has the right to do that. He is loving and patient and will always shape the pot in a way that seems good to him.

- - - - - -

Pray

> *'Lord, it's easy to think that we're in control, or even that we're the potter. Teach us from this imagery to trust you more.'*

The plans I have for you

'Also, seek the peace and prosperity of the city to which I have carried you into exile.'
Jeremiah 29:7

Read Jeremiah 25:1 – 29:32

The failure of the kings of Judah was intolerable, and Yahweh allowed the Babylonians to come and destroy their city. But even in exile, the Lord continued to love the Israelites. He still had plans for their future. *'When seventy years are completed for Babylon, I will come to you and fulfil my good promise to bring you back to this place. For I know the plans I have for you . . . plans to prosper you and not to harm you, plans to give you hope and a future'* (29:10–11). In the sweep of the Lord's message to the exiles, the emphasis was on the first *'I know'*. The Lord of the heavens and the earth knows the plans. And in this case, the Lord's plan was to rescue the people in 70 years' time. So, because of that, he said, settle down, build gardens, bless the city, and pray for the city. It's so important! For all of us, it can be tempting to read this letter and imagine 'plans to prosper' each of us, individually. But the letter is about God's rescue of his people from exile in Babylon . . . and his presence and strength and comfort and calling in the meantime. It reminds us that there is another rescue to come. Jesus is coming back. The current exile will come to an end! In the meantime, seek peace, bless the city, and pray for it.

- - - - - -

Pray

'Lord, thank you that your hope and future come through your capacity to forgive. Please help us to wait well, to pray, and to seek peace in the cities you have allowed us to be.'

'So you will be my people, and I will be your God.'
Jeremiah 30:22

Read Jeremiah 30:1 – 33:26

The most wonderful thing about Jeremiah's prophecies is the way he keeps pointing to the promises of God even through the harsh reality of judgement. There will be a new, everlasting covenant! *"'The days are coming,"* *declares the LORD, "when I will make a new covenant with the people of Israel* *and with the people of Judah. It will not be like the covenant I made with their* *ancestors . . . I will put my law in their minds and write it on their hearts. I* *will be their God and they will be my people. No longer will they teach their* *neighbour, or say to one another, 'Know the LORD,' because they will all know* *me, from the least of them to the greatest," declares the LORD. "For I will forgive* *their wickedness and will remember their sins no more"'* (31:31–34). It's the most amazing, relational promise. The law will be written on the people's hearts, instead of tablets of stone, and they will *all* know Yahweh, not just the priests and the prophets! And the one to come, from David's line, will bring this about (33:15). No wonder they were longing for the Messiah. Their hearts must have been stirred by this passage. And we can also read it and feel thankful that because of Christ's sacrifice, we have deep fellowship with Yahweh. He has healed our hearts and brought us back to himself. He remembers our sins no more.

- - - - - -

Pray

> *'Lord, we read this text in a day when it has been fulfilled in Christ. We* > *can't fathom it but we thank you that you remember our sins no more.'*

Feel the pain

'See, LORD, how distressed I am! I am in torment within, and in my heart I am disturbed, for I have been most rebellious.'

Lamentations 1:20

Read Lamentations 1:1 – 5:22

Perhaps it's easy to gloss over our sin and go straight to grateful atonement, or to hide our pain and distress and go straight to superficial optimism. The book of Lamentations reminds us that we don't need to do either. It's okay to vent our emotions and express our pain to God. In the time of the exile, the author gave voice to the distress of the people of Israel, and incredibly, after centuries, their pain was then included in God's word to us, and for generations to come. It's a striking note of desolation, and acknowledgement of sin, and groaning under the Lord's judgement. Yet in the middle of all the protest and confession and submission, the people also discovered an unfailing hope in Yahweh. *'Yet this I call to mind and therefore I have hope: Because of the LORD's great love we are not consumed, for his compassions never fail'* (3:21–22). It reminds us that honest venting can be helpful. It can lead us back to the Lord who is always true to his promises. And if we did not feel our sin, or the effects of it, we would never truly comprehend grace.

- - - - - -

Pray

'Lord, we have also been in distress, we have felt the weight of our sin, and the burdens of this world. We have staggered under the weight of it. Thank you that you hear us today.'

The Lord is not limited

'Yet for a little while I have been a sanctuary for them in the countries where they have gone.'
Ezekiel 11:16b

Read Ezekiel 1:1 – 11:25

It seems so surprising. The book of Ezekiel begins with the word of the Lord coming to Ezekiel by the River Kebar, which was in the land of the Babylonians. The Lord was in the enemy's camp? He had left Israel . . . and appeared to Ezekiel in exile? It seems amazing, not least because of the description of the glory of the Lord – the four creatures, the wheels, the fire, the wings, and the figure on the lapis lazuli throne. Of course, it was awe-inspiring, and Ezekiel fell to the ground at the *appearance of the likeness of the glory of the LORD* (1:28b). And yet the most striking thing seems to be that the Lord was not limited to Israel. He appeared to Ezekiel in Babylon! The people had been exiled to Babylon, but the Lord went to that place, and appeared to Ezekiel. And the vision of the Lord included wheels that moved and turned in any direction – symbolising that he could go wherever he willed (1:15–21). It must have been stunning for them back then. The Lord was with them in exile. He had left the temple. And it's equally stunning to us now. Hundreds of years later, the Lord left heaven and came to earth in the person of Jesus Christ. He is present with us now through his Spirit. He is not stuck! The God we worship is not limited in time, or space, or concept, or anything else within our feeble imaginations. He is glorious.

- - - - - -

Pray

'Lord, thank you for this reminder that we can never truly figure you out, or anticipate your work in this world. Thank you that we can't.'

The Lord is truthful

'The people to whom I am sending you are obstinate and stubborn.'
Ezekiel 2:4

Read Ezekiel 2:1 – 11:13

Sometimes, we invite people to serve in a church community, and we don't tell them the whole story. We don't tell them how hard it might be, or how irascible the people might be! Yet in this narrative, the Lord was strikingly honest with Ezekiel. He told him that the people to whom he was sending him were obstinate and stubborn. They would not listen to him, and their city would soon receive God's wrath for their detestable practises of idol worship and child sacrifice. It's no wonder Ezekiel wasn't keen. But as well as being strikingly honest, the message is also sobering. Yahweh is a jealous God. He stayed true to his covenant promises and curses. Judgement was imminent and Ezekiel began his ministry by embodying that message, using clay, an iron pan and the removal of his hair. It's a strange way to do it, but the outcome was very important. *'Then they will know that I am the LORD'* (7:27b). The people would know who Yahweh was. Previously, at the time of the exodus, it was through miracles and wonders that the Lord was known by his people. And now, it would be through judgement and vindication that Yahweh would be known as holy. Justice and righteousness were as much a part of God's nature as his compassion and miraculous salvation. To know God means to know his utter holiness.

- - - - - -

Pray

'Lord, we would prefer to consider your miracles than your justice. It sits heavily with us. Please help us to know you better today, through the person of Jesus Christ.'

A heart of flesh

'I will gather you from the nations and bring you back from the countries where you have been scattered.'
Ezekiel 11:17

Read Ezekiel 11:14 – 36:38

Earlier in his ministry, Ezekiel shaved his head and scattered his hair, symbolising the judgement that was to come on Israel. But it wasn't the whole story. The Lord said, *'But take a few hairs and tuck them away in the folds of your garment'* (5:3). Even within judgement, there was a salvation plan. And within Ezekiel's prophecies, there was a glorious future hope for Israel. *'I will give them an undivided heart and put a new spirit in them; I will remove from them their heart of stone and give them a heart of flesh'* (11:19). *'I will place over them one shepherd, my servant David, and he will tend them . . . and be their shepherd'* (34:23). *'I will sprinkle clean water on you, and you will be clean'* (36:25). The promises were wonderful, and they pointed to the time after the exile. There would be a shepherd to come, a servant in the line of David. But it wasn't immediate or easy. After their return from exile, the Israelites still struggled. They strayed from the Lord, and their hearts weren't entirely clean. What was Ezekiel speaking of? We know now that Jesus, the true shepherd, returned from the grave and defeated death for ever. The promise is for us! Incredibly, to those who believe, we have been given a heart of flesh. We have been made clean through the Lord Jesus. We have been tended and led as his sheep.

- - - - - -

Pray

'Lord, we are regularly blind to your great mercy. Thank you for your Spirit. Thank you that you give us a heart of flesh, and that you tend us like a shepherd.'

The valley of dry bones

'He asked me, "Son of man, can these bones live?"'
Ezekiel 37:3

Read Ezekiel 37:1 – 48:35

My husband teaches musculoskeletal anatomy at Sydney University. Every day, he helps the students identify bones, ligaments, muscles and tendons. As a spinoff, we have dry bones sitting on our bookshelves at home, just in case he needs another scapula or humerus. So I find the imagery in this passage incredible. Ezekiel was taken to a valley of dry bones, and the Lord asked him whether the bones could live. Then the Lord asked Ezekiel to prophesy to the bones, which he did, and there was a rattling sound! *'The bones came together, bone to bone . . . tendons and flesh appeared on them and skin covered them . . . They came to life and stood up on their feet – a vast army'* (37:7–10). There is nothing more impossible than this. There is nothing more incredible. There is nothing more true to the character of God. He can and does bring life to the driest, emptiest, most forsaken bones. He is the God of the resurrection, of breath and hope and life and wonder. He is Yahweh. He is the One who raised the Lord Jesus from the dead so that we could have life for ever. He is the Lord. And in the text, Ezekiel went on to prophesy about the wonderful, everlasting covenant of peace to come (37:24–28), and the glorious new river of life that would flow from the city (47:1–12), and be described in Revelation 22. And then the final sentence is the most hopeful of them all. *'And the name of the city from that time on will be:* THE LORD IS THERE*'* (48:35b).

- - - - - -

Pray

> *'Lord, your presence is enough. Your holiness matters. Your life-giving work has changed everything. Thank you that you care about dry, forsaken bones.'*

The revealer of mysteries

'But there is a God in heaven who reveals mysteries.'
Daniel 2:28

Read Daniel 1:1 – 2:49

The book of Daniel begins in a similar way to the book of Esther. The people of
Judah were in exile in Babylon, and the king of Babylon sought Jewish people
to enter his service. Among the Jews he chose Daniel, Hananiah, Mishael and
Azariah. After three years of preparation, the king found none equal to them
in matters of wisdom and understanding (1:19–20). In the text, though, it
makes very clear where their gifts came from. *'To these four young men **God**
gave knowledge and understanding of all kinds of literature and learning. And
Daniel could understand visions and dreams of all kinds'* (1:17). Yahweh was
the giver of gifts. Yahweh sustained Daniel when he resolved not to eat royal
food and wine. Yahweh caused the official to show Daniel favour. Yahweh
gave Daniel the interpretation of King Nebuchadnezzar's dream, as well as the
dream itself, which was a mystery to everybody else . . . but our God in heaven
reveals mysteries! And then, in response to the dream interpretation, the king
of Babylon fell prostrate before Daniel, saying, *'Surely your God is the God of
gods and the Lord of kings and a revealer of mysteries'* (2:47). It's amazing. This is
what happens when Yahweh reveals himself, then and now, through the Lord
Jesus. Surprising people acknowledge him, a bit like the Queen of Sheba back
in 1 Kings 10. Yahweh is the giver of gifts. He reveals mysteries, and he reveals
himself in unlikely places, to unlikely people, even you and me!

- - - - - -

Pray

> *'Lord, we easily forget your power to sustain and give wisdom. Thank
> you that in every place and time, you reveal yourself and your everlasting
> kingdom through your Son Jesus.'*

Even if he doesn't rescue

'Look! I see four men walking around in the fire, unbound and unharmed.'
Daniel 3:25

Read Daniel 3:1–30

Like the story of Esther, the account in Daniel moved quickly to a death threat for the Jews. King Nebuchadnezzar ordered everyone to bow down before an image of gold. If they didn't, as in the case of Daniel's three friends, they would be thrown into a blazing furnace. The friends' reply to the king is wonderful. *'King Nebuchadnezzar . . . if we are thrown into the blazing furnace, the God we serve is able to deliver us from it . . . But even if he does not, we want you to know . . . that we will not serve your gods or worship the image of gold you have set up'* (3:16–18). As a result, the three friends were then bound and thrown into the blazing furnace. But, incredibly, they did not burn up. A fourth figure appeared with them and they came out, untouched! It strikes me that the friends knew Yahweh. They knew that he could rescue, and that he might choose not to rescue. Even if he chose not to, they would still worship him. This speaks to us. Yahweh is good and holy and unfathomable. He is able to do as he pleases, and he delights to save us. But whether or not his actions are ones we would choose, we will still worship him. We will still trust his good purposes. In this case, the results were that the foreign king praised the Lord, and enforced a new decree that enabled the Jews to worship Yahweh. Wonderful!

- - - - - -

Pray

> *'Lord, we are in awe of the ways you act to save us from our own sin.*
> *Please help us to worship you today, even if the day doesn't go as we would*
> *choose.'*

A den of lions

**'Three times a day he got down on his knees and prayed, giving thanks
to his God, just as he had done before.'**

Daniel 6:10b

Read Daniel 6:1–28

Daniel grew old, and King Nebuchadnezzar died, as did his son Belshazzar.
After a time, Darius took over and Darius respected Daniel, so he planned
to set Daniel over the entire kingdom. That made the other officials jealous
of Daniel, and they plotted against him. They announced a decree that
anyone who prayed to any god, other than the king, would be thrown into
the lions' den. And Daniel got down on his knees and prayed to Yahweh,
three times a day, *just as he had done before* (6:10). Nothing changed for
Daniel. He had been faithful and prayerful as a young man, serving God
in exile, with all the gifts he had been given. And now he was faithful and
prayerful as an old man, doing what he'd always done before – praying.
As a result, Daniel was thrown into the lions' den (6:16) and the den was
sealed with a stone. But something amazing happened. The next morning,
the king found Daniel unharmed! It's an incredible foretaste of the time to
come when Jesus would also suffer death, and be placed in a tomb sealed by
a stone, and then found alive! But in the time of Daniel, it again brought
forth praise and worship from a foreign king, in a foreign land. Yahweh was
alive and well . . . and working through his faithful people, even in exile.
Daniel was doing what he'd always done, praying.

- - - - - -

Pray

> *'Lord, help us to be people who pray to you when we're young and pray to
> you when we're old, because we trust you and your saving power.'*

Daniel's dreams and visions

'And there before me was one like a son of man.'
Daniel 7:13

Read Daniel 7:1 – 12:13

During Daniel's life in exile, he was given extensive dreams and visions, most of which were puzzling and apocalyptic, revealing the rise and fall of kingdoms and the end times. No wonder Daniel was disturbed by them, especially when he saw times of oppression ahead. But in amongst the times of trouble, there was a vision that must have absolutely stood out to him, and for all time. *'In my vision at night I looked, and there before me was one like a son of man, coming with the clouds of heaven. He approached the Ancient of Days and was led into his presence. He was given authority, glory and sovereign power; all nations and peoples of every language worshipped him. His dominion is an everlasting dominion that will not pass away, and his kingdom is one that will never be destroyed'* (7:13–14). Incredibly, Jesus himself quoted this phrase about himself when he was brought before the Sanhedrin at the trial. *'From now on you will see the Son of Man sitting at the right hand of the Mighty One and coming on the clouds of heaven'* (Matthew 26:64). No wonder the crowds at the trial cried, 'Blasphemy!' They knew that Jesus was saying he was God himself! And yet we hold onto this promise every day. Jesus will rule for ever. We may struggle to interpret apocalyptic literature, but we know that in the end, Christ will rule. He will be given all authority, glory and sovereign power, and his dominion will last for ever.

- - - - - -

Pray

> *'Lord, we're not quite there yet . . . but we hold onto this incredible, undeniable promise that Jesus rules, and he will rule for all time.'*

Press on to know him

'I will heal their waywardness and love them freely, for my anger has turned away from them.'

Hosea 14:4

Read Hosea 1:1 – 14:9

Hosea's writings contain striking reminders for the Israelites back then and for us now. The prophet was writing at a time after the northern kingdom broke away from the south, and prior to the attack by the Assyrians. The Israelites needed to know that the Lord God felt passionately towards them. Yahweh pursued them and longed for them and knew them. He was utterly holy, so he would also call them to account. In fact, Yahweh felt so strongly towards the Israelites that he told Hosea to embody the parable and marry an unfaithful woman in order to show them just how much he loved them. Amazingly, Hosea did as he was told, and the reminders were confronting. But there is a line that stands out. *'Let us press on to acknowledge him'* (6:3). Other translations say, *'Let us press on to know him more and more.'* The encouragement is at the heart of our lives here on earth. Yahweh is knowable! We can actually *know him*, not just talk about knowing him. We can know him 'more and more' – this God whose love *churns* inside him (11:8), whose compassions are aroused (11:8), and whose fierce anger will not be carried out (11:9). It's amazing that 700 years after the life of Hosea, God came himself. The Lord Jesus Christ, God incarnate – embodying love and taking on himself the sins of the whole world, so that God's fierce anger would not be carried out . . . so that we might truly *know him,* more and more each day.

- - - - - -

Pray

'Lord, help us today to press on to know you more and more.
Thank you that we can.'

Rend your hearts

'And everyone who calls on the name of the Lord will be saved.'
Joel 2:32

Read Joel 1:1 – 3:21

It's a repeated theme in Scripture that the Lord knows our hearts. We are able to put on a show of emotion for other people, or even for ourselves, but the Lord knows our hearts and longs for us to be true to him. In this section, the prophet Joel wrote to the people about judgement and repentance and the wonderful hope of the Messiah to come. But in the middle of it all, he said something very personal. *'Rend your heart and not your garments. Return to the Lord your God'* (2:13). Perhaps back then, outward, external repentance was easier. The people could merely tear their garments in a public manner and everyone would think they'd done the expected thing. But how easy was true, inward repentance? How easy is it for us today? Do we sometimes put on a show? The Lord longs for genuine change. In Joel's writing, as well as calling them to repentance, he gave them a new and wonderful promise. *'And afterwards, I will pour out my Spirit on all people. Your sons and daughters will prophesy, your old men will dream dreams, your young men will see visions'* (2:28). It was wonderful! Of course, in Acts 2, Peter quoted these very words at Pentecost, after Jesus had risen from the dead and poured out the Holy Spirit on the believers. The wonderful promise was fulfilled! And we are also filled with the Holy Spirit, so we can come to the Lord, deeply, truly, honestly, knowing that he knows our hearts.

- - - - - -

Pray

> *'Lord, we have pretended in the past. Please help us to come to you honestly today, through the wonderful gift of your Holy Spirit.'*

Reluctance

'Is it right for you to be angry?'
Jonah 4:4

Read Jonah 1:1 – 4:11

The book of Jonah is distinct among the Minor Prophets. Jonah ran away! Instead of bringing a true and compelling word to the people in Nineveh (in Assyria), Jonah ran away. He fled from the Lord, boarding a ship in the opposite direction . . . and then the Lord sent a great wind and a storm. Everyone was afraid; Jonah was identified as the cause and he was thrown overboard. It's striking that the pagan sailors, who didn't know Yahweh, ended up responding to him and making vows to him. Yet the Lord's own prophet, Jonah, continued in his reluctance. Even so, the Lord chose to save him, and use him to convict the Ninevites, who then all believed in Yahweh and repented immediately. It's probably one of the quickest examples of repentance in all of Scripture. Yet, Jonah wasn't happy. He became resentful with the Lord for having compassion on people like them – his enemies! And the Lord's reply is pertinent to all of us. *Is it right for you to be angry?* Is it right for any of us to decide on the boundaries of the Lord's compassion? Jonah still needed another example. If he could care about a small tree that eased his discomfort and then died, does not God care for his creation? Does not God love the people of the world, even our enemies? Does he not love them enough to die for them? Are there people in our lives today for whom we would rather the Lord not show compassion? What might the Lord say to us about those situations?

- - - - - -

Pray

'Lord, convict us again. Show us how deeply you love the people whom we find it hard to love.'

Our sins have been hurled

'And what does the LORD require of you?'
Micah 6:8

Read Micah 1:1 – 7:20

I love verbs. I love the way they create images that we wouldn't otherwise imagine. Micah used verbs like that. He prophesied to the people of Judah prior to the exile, saying that judgement would come. They would soon feel the results of their greed and corruption and worship of other gods. It would be like labour pains! But at the same time, the Lord would send hope and deliverance. He would not stay angry for ever. He would send a Saviour, out of the town of Bethlehem, who would truly shepherd his people, and be their peace (5:2–5). This is such an amazing promise, fulfilled so precisely in the Lord Jesus (Luke 2:4). But there was something else as well, to do with forgiveness. *'Who is a God like you, who pardons sin . . . ? You will again have compassion on us; you will tread our sins underfoot and* **hurl** *all our iniquities into the depths of the sea'* (7:18–19). Somehow, the promised Saviour, born in Bethlehem, would not only shepherd his people, but would also bring about forgiveness. Their sins (and our sins) would be *'hurled'* into the depths of the sea. It's deliberate and intentional. To hurl something means to throw it with great force, or even violence. That's how much Yahweh wants to get rid of our sin for all time, and he has, through the Lord Jesus. We respond with thankfulness, longing to honour God and to do what is good in his eyes, *'To act justly and to love mercy and to walk humbly with your God'* (6:8).

- - - - - -

Pray

> *'Lord, we thank you that you have hurled our sins into the depths of the sea. Please help us to respond with justice and mercy and humility.'*

No grapes on the vines

'Yet I will rejoice in the LORD.'
Habakkuk 3:18

Read Habakkuk 3:17–18

When Darren and I were in our early twenties, we lived and worked in South India for six months, during summer. It was 53 degrees. We could hardly walk from our house to the hospital without passing out. We lay beneath wet towels at night time. As well as that, we couldn't speak anything intelligible to the patients, so we felt useless as well as hot. Why had we gone there? Where was the fruit? I remember on one of those hot days, I read Habakkuk. *'Though the fig-tree does not bud and there are no grapes on the vines, though the olive crop fails and the fields produce no food, though there are no sheep in the sheepfold and no cattle in the stalls, yet I will rejoice in the LORD, I will be joyful in God my Saviour'* (3:17–18). It was helpful! Of course, Habakkuk's situation was entirely different from ours. He was a prophet at the time when the people in the southern kingdom were under threat from the Babylonians. He questioned God about suffering and injustice. He wanted to know why. And then God answered him. In response, Habakkuk prayed, in awe of the Lord. He rejoiced because of who God was, and because of his covenant promises. And so do we. Our rejoicing in God doesn't need to correlate with outward ease or fruitfulness. We rejoice in God because he is good and faithful and true to his redemptive promises, even when it's 53 degrees and the rains haven't come yet.

- - - - - -

Pray

> *'Lord, we stand in awe of your deeds and sovereignty. Help us to rejoice in the Lord Jesus, only and always.'*

Your king comes to you!

'Shout and be glad, Daughter Zion. For I am coming, and I will live among you.'
Zechariah 2:10

Read Zechariah 1:1 – 14:21

Could the people ever have imagined it back then – that the Lord God, Yahweh, would actually come and live among them? Back in the time of the prophet Zechariah, the people had returned to the land, but it was hard work and they couldn't see much evidence of the promise of restoration. Then, Zechariah had a series of strange dreams urging the people to faithful obedience. He said, *'Rejoice greatly, Daughter Zion! Shout, Daughter Jerusalem! See, your king comes to you, righteous and victorious, lowly and riding on a donkey'* (9:9). It was an amazing promise, and it pointed ahead to the day when Jesus would ride through the streets on a donkey (John 12:15). But there was more to it than that. Zechariah also prophesied that the shepherd to come would be struck and the sheep scattered (13:7). Although obscure, Jesus himself quoted Zechariah as he ate the last supper with his disciples. He said, *'This very night you will all fall away on account of me, for it is written, "I will strike the shepherd, and the sheep of the flock will be scattered." But after I have risen, I will go ahead of you into Galilee'* (Matthew 26:31–32). Jesus fulfilled the promises. He was pierced and struck down, but he rose again, changing the history of the world. Back in the time of Zechariah, the people were called to faithful obedience as they waited. It's not that different for us, as we wait for Jesus to return.

- - - - - -

Pray

'Lord, we thank you that you are never surprised or impatient. Help us to cling to your promises and respond with obedience as we wait.'

The best of intentions

'You have wearied the LORD with your words.'
Malachi 2:17

Read Malachi 1:1 – 4:6

Malachi was a prophet in around 400BC. He spoke to the people 100 years after they had returned to the land and, back then, their hopes had been so high. They had rebuilt the temple and responded to the words of Haggai and Zechariah. They had tried to obey Yahweh. But, even with the best of intentions, they couldn't do it. They broke God's covenantal law again and again through intermarrying and through practises of injustice. They even defiled the temple, and they wearied the Lord with their words (2:17). After all that they'd been through and learnt during the exile, they simply couldn't do it. They needed a Saviour. So do we. We also try hard and fail. We weary ourselves, and our Lord, with our words. We have the best of intentions but we can't carry them out. Back then, though, God had an incredible plan and he revealed it to Malachi. *'I will send my messenger, who will prepare the way before me'* (3:1). *'He will turn the hearts of the parents to their children, and the hearts of the children to the parents'* (4:6). From the beginning, God planned to send John the Baptist who would prepare the way for his own Son, the Lord Jesus, who would bring healing and redemption for ever! But back then, the people still had to wait 400 years. Could they do it? Could they hold onto the promise for 400 years without any further word from the Lord? Can we continue to wait now, as we long for Jesus to return? How will that hope change us today?

- - - - - -

Pray

'Lord, our waiting is impatient at times. Help us to be faithful to you in all the times of silence.'

The genealogy, the answer

'And Mary was the mother of Jesus who is called the Messiah.'
Matthew 1:16

Read Matthew 1:1–17

After reading the Minor Prophets for an extended period of time, it feels simply wonderful to arrive at the Gospel of Matthew. Finally! The wait is over! The Messiah is about to come! We can feel the thrill of excitement! Imagine being alive back then, after waiting for that many generations, longing for Yahweh to do something – anything! And then, on an ordinary day, in an ordinary year, a child was born to Mary, who was married to Joseph, who was the son of Jacob, who was in the line of King David himself. It's the answer, finally! It's the One mentioned in 2 Samuel whose throne would be established for ever! And the genealogy sets the scene beautifully, taking us back to the long story of God, including the people and stories we wouldn't expect. Judah was the son of Leah who had weak eyes – Judah who slept with Tamar who had acted as a prostitute. Boaz was the son of Rahab who had been the prostitute and who sheltered Salmon the spy and then married him. Obed was the son of Ruth, a foreigner who had been redeemed by Boaz when she was in personal distress. Solomon was the son of Bathsheba who had been Uriah's wife and then taken by David. It's not a clean family history. But it's the incredible way that God worked through 2,000 years to fulfil his promises and to provide an answer to all of human history. The genealogy itself should make us shudder and sing.

- - - - - -

Pray

'Lord, your ways are beyond us. Thank you for every name in this list. Thank you that because of Jesus, our names are included in your long story that will last for ever.'

Expecting God to answer

'Do not be afraid, Zechariah; your prayer has been heard.'
Luke 1:13

Read Luke 1:1–25

Apparently, priests like Zechariah didn't go into the temple very often. Back then, there were 24 divisions of priests, and Zechariah was in the division of Abijah, so his turn didn't come around very often. But there he was that day – a childless old man, married to a childless old woman – and the *one time* he actually went into the temple, an angel appeared and told him he was going to have a son named John. The son would *'go on before the Lord, in the spirit and power of Elijah, to turn the hearts of the parents to their children and . . . to make ready a people prepared for the Lord'* (1:17). The angel used the exact words of Malachi (3:1). But Zechariah was full of questions. He was old and his wife was well on in years. How would Yahweh give them a child? He didn't need to know. Yahweh had spoken and it was enough. Zechariah would be silent until the baby was born. It strikes me, though, that Zechariah and the others were probably praying for God's answers, through the Messiah, and yet maybe they weren't actually expecting an answer that day. There had been 400 years of silence! But God was not silent or inactive then, and he certainly isn't today. As we pray for his work in the world, and our responses of faithfulness, we can expect him to answer us.

- - - - - -

Pray

> *'Lord, help us to be prayerful and expectant – to remember that you are the Lord who brings about your saving plan, in your world, in your timing.'*

Imagine being Mary

'And he will reign over Jacob's descendants for ever; his kingdom will never end.'

Luke 1:33

Read Luke 1:26–38

Imagine being Mary. She was so young. She hadn't met anyone who'd seen an angel. And there she was, on that ordinary day, and an angel appeared to her and told her that she would have a son. Of course she had questions! How will this be? She hadn't slept with a man. But the angel gave her the most amazing promise about the child she would bear. *'He will be great and will be called the Son of the Most High. The Lord God will give him the throne of his father David, and he will reign over Jacob's descendants for ever; his kingdom will never end'* (1:32–33). Did Mary tremble as she recognised the promise to David? Did she understand that her child would be the One to restore everything? I love the way that within all of that, she got up and did the next thing. She submitted to the Lord's will. She sang. She trusted, and she hurried off to tell Elizabeth. Of course, we know that there was pain and suffering to come for Mary, as well as deep joy, but we hope that that original, astounding promise, given to her by the angel, was the thing that she clung to throughout her life. And we hope that we also cling to the promises of God in *our* worst moments, because we know that the Lord Jesus rose from the dead and his kingdom will never end.

- - - - - -

Pray

> *'Lord, no matter what happens, we know that your kingdom will endure for ever. Help us to be people who put our deepest hope in your promises.'*

No word from God will ever fail

'For no word from God will ever fail.'
Luke 1:37

Read Luke 1:37

The angel told Mary that she would give birth to a son, and he would be called the Son of the Most High. He explained to her that the Holy Spirit would come on her, and the child to be born would be called the Son of God. And then he said something very important. *'For no word from God will ever fail'* (1:37). In other translations it says, *'Nothing is impossible with God.'* And we need that reminder in our ordinary, consuming lives, centuries later. God, who is holy and sovereign and just, will continue to keep his promises. His word and plans will not fail. He has, and will, fulfil every word he has ever spoken. He promised in Malachi to send a messenger, and he did. He promised a Saviour from the town of Bethlehem in Micah, and he brought that about. He promised a king on a donkey in Zechariah, and we know who that was. No word from God will ever fail. Today, of course, we hold onto a myriad of promises since then, especially the one to the disciples after the resurrection, *'This same Jesus, who has been taken from you into heaven, will come back in the same way you have seen him go'* (Acts 1:11). Today, we celebrate the wonderful truth that Jesus came, and we hold on to the truth that he will come again and make all things new. For no word from God will ever fail.

- - - - - -

Pray

> *'Lord, it's easy to get muddled, or to think you might be our private, wish-granting fairy. But your word and plan go far beyond that. None of your promises will ever fail. Help us to lift our eyes today.'*

May your word be fulfilled

"'I am the Lord's servant," Mary answered. "May your word to me be fulfilled.'"

Luke 1:38

Read Luke 1:38–56

Sometimes I wonder what would happen if I prayed like Mary every day, and meant it. *'I am the Lord's servant. May your word to me be fulfilled.'* Of course, Mary's situation was entirely different from ours. She would be the one to carry the child who would be the Son of God and reign for ever. It was an incredible and unique task! And yet, the way she submitted herself to the Lord's will is striking. She believed the angel. She believed that Yahweh could do it, through the Holy Spirit, and she said yes. She hurried off to see Elizabeth and, when she got there, she sang, full of thankfulness to God who was her Saviour. And she knew that the blessing wasn't merely for herself . . . it included *everyone.* The mercy of God would be extended to all *'those who fear him, from generation to generation'* (1:50). Mary's prayer of thanksgiving included us! And as Mary sang, her prayer also echoed phrases from Hannah's prayer, back when Hannah was carrying Samuel (1 Samuel 2). Somehow Yahweh was now doing a far greater thing than in the time of Samuel. This child, Jesus, would be the Saviour! And Mary held her hands open, and said yes.

- - - - - -

Pray

'Lord, we all find it hard to relax our hands and ease our will to yours. Please let your will be fulfilled in our lives today.'

Zechariah responds

'Immediately, his mouth was opened and his tongue set free.'
Luke 1:64

Read Luke 1:57–80

There are so many wonderful stories of restoration in the Bible, including this one about Zechariah. After meeting the angel at the temple, Zechariah went home, silent. Then, after nine months, their child was born and together they named him John. The neighbours must have been surprised. It wasn't a family name. But Zechariah confirmed the decision on a writing tablet, and then his voice returned and he sang! Everybody was filled with awe! The crowd wondered who the child was going to be. But surprisingly, when Zechariah's tongue was set free, the first thing he sang about was not his own son. He must have rejoiced at the birth of his longed-for son, but more than that, he rejoiced at God's answer for the world, his salvation, and his rescue plan. *'Praise be to the Lord, the God of Israel, because he has come to his people and redeemed them'* (1:68). Zechariah's first words were for the Messiah. He knew that his son would be the messenger, and that meant that God *himself* was coming soon. And Zechariah wanted his own son, but he wanted his Saviour even more . . . so he sang praise to Yahweh who had redeemed his people and shown mercy, and who would rescue them. Zechariah had been transformed from disbelieving to praising, from silent to singing, from doubting to trusting, in a moment. That's the power of God, in all of us.

- - - - - -

Pray

'Lord, help us to believe, help us to expect, help us to sing, even on the days when it feels like our tongues are tied, and our faith and understanding is weak . . . because even then, you are Lord.'

Joseph is transformed

'He had in mind to divorce her quietly.'
Matthew 1:19b

Read Matthew 1:18–25

It's noteworthy that even before Jesus was born, God was quietly transforming the lives of the people around him. Mary had been found to be pregnant and Joseph was not the father, so he planned to divorce her quietly. He must have felt the sting and shame of people pointing at them and surmising. But he didn't end up divorcing her, because an angel appeared to him in a dream and told him not to be afraid to marry Mary because the baby had been conceived by the Holy Spirit. The angel said, *'You are to give him the name Jesus, **because he will save his people from their sins'*** (1:21). This child, who began his life surrounded by gossip and pointed fingers, would be the Messiah, the One they'd been waiting for, Immanuel, who would save his people from their sin and shame. It was the answer to every question and burden since Genesis 3, when the whole world became tarnished and askew. Someone was going to reverse the curse! And it fulfilled Isaiah's promise that the virgin would give birth to a son (Isaiah 7:14). But importantly, Joseph did what the Lord commanded him. He took Mary home as his wife and he allowed God to transform his doubting heart. If he didn't, none of the rest of the story would have happened.

- - - - - -

Pray

'Lord, thank you for people everywhere who trust and obey you, even the ones who we think are on the side-lines of the story. May it encourage us to trust you and obey you today.'

The Saviour is born

'And she gave birth to her firstborn, a son.'
Luke 2:7

Read Luke 2:1–7

If we were to write God's story as fiction, I'm not sure we could make it any stranger. *'In those days Caesar Augustus issued a decree that a census should be taken of the entire Roman world'* (2:1). Suddenly, at the exact time when the Son of God would be born, the Roman Emperor ordered everyone to travel to their home town . . . and, as a result, Joseph and Mary went to Bethlehem. Did they wonder about the timing, or complain about the cold? Did they question Yahweh, who could redeem everyone through the gift of his Son, and yet couldn't time it any better? Or did they remember what Micah had said about Bethlehem 700 years earlier (Micah 5:2)? We don't know, but after travelling 130 kilometres, heavily pregnant, Mary and Joseph arrived in Bethlehem, and there was no guest room available, so they settled down with the animals. That's where Mary had the baby – the child who was the Messiah, the Son of God, the Prince of Peace, the promise, the healer, the light, the answer to every unspoken longing and every troubled heart. Mary placed her baby in a feeding trough for the animals, in a cave below ground. The most remarkable thing had just happened – God himself had come to earth, born as a baby, taking on flesh, and he was placed in a manger. It was a long way from Solomon's palace, or the grandeur of heaven. It was the heart of God, lavishly poured out for his people.

- - - - - -

Pray

> *'Lord, we come to you feeling small and moved by your heart of love. Help us to ponder your unlikely story and let it transform our responses today.'*

'So they hurried off and found Mary and Joseph, and the baby.'
Luke 2:16

Read Luke 2:8–20

It's amazing that when Luke recorded the incredible, climactic answer to the whole story of God through the birth of the Lord Jesus . . . he then followed it up with a sentence about shepherds. *And there were shepherds living out in the fields nearby, keeping watch over their flocks'* (2:8). There they were – tired men in worn coats, sitting on a hill, perhaps expecting a yarn, or a hunk of bread. And then suddenly an angel appeared, telling *them* about a Saviour, and great joy, and a wonderful sign for the people! No wonder they ran! No wonder they sang when they found Jesus, lying in a manger. To be honest, I've often wondered about the shepherds. Why *did* God bother telling them as opposed to anyone else? What difference would it have made if he didn't? I love the fact, though, that he did. I love the fact that he filled up the sky with angels . . . to speak to tired men in worn coats. It speaks of such ordinariness. The whole birth narrative is such a wonderful fulfilment of prophecy and yet, at the same time, a window into God's heart. Yahweh revealed his plan to the shepherds and they went running to see the baby – the Saviour of the world – and they responded in praise. God can choose to reveal his plan and purposes to anyone he chooses, whenever he wants, including tired men in worn coats who respond in worship.

- - - - - -

Pray

'Lord, we are in awe of your ways. You humble yourself into the shape of a manger, and you delight to tell your best news to tired men in a field. Thank you that it shows your heart for us.'

Beautiful bystanders

'Simeon took him in his arms and praised God.'
Luke 2:28

Read Luke 2:21–40

When Jesus was born, only a few people seemed to know who he was. As well as the shepherds, there was an old man and an even older woman at the temple. Yahweh revealed to the old man that he wouldn't die before seeing the Messiah, and then the old man actually saw him! He happened to be at the temple steps on the right day, and Mary and Joseph carried Jesus up those steps, and Simeon knew straight away. He reached out and took the baby in his wrinkled arms and he praised God, saying that this child would be the salvation of the nations. He would be a light for the gentiles as well as glory for the people of Israel! He would be the One! Later, Simeon spoke to Mary, *'A sword will pierce your own soul too'* (2:35b). Jesus was only six weeks old, and there was already a glimpse of the suffering to come – the suffering that was needed to bring about the incredible promise for everyone. But I like the way that just at that moment, an old woman came up to Mary and Joseph and she gave thanks. She also knew. She spoke encouraging words to those who were looking forward to the redemption of Jerusalem. It makes me pause and delight in God's provision. Mary and Joseph must have needed her godly encouragement. And 2,000 years later, we can read Anna's words and also be deeply encouraged by God's good plan, for all of us in need of redemption.

- - - - - -

Pray

> *'Lord, we read your word and find ourselves on its pages. We are also in need of redemption. Thank you for your reminders through beautiful bystanders.'*

Magi came and worshipped

'When they saw the star, they were overjoyed.'
Matthew 2:10

Read Matthew 2:1–12

After Jesus was born in Bethlehem, Magi from the East also came to worship him. In reading the account in Matthew, there is much to wonder about – who were the Magi exactly, and where in the East did they come from? Were they Persian tribal priests . . . or star gazers from Arabia? What kind of astronomical event was this that caused such a specific response? And how did the Magi even hear about the king of the Jews? All these years later, the mystery remains. But when King Herod heard about the Magi's search, he was greatly disturbed. He called a secret meeting with them and pretended he was as devout as they were. But he wasn't! Jesus was only a few months old and his life was already a threat, and under threat. But the Magi followed the star and they found the child, and they worshipped him. They brought him gifts. They were so excited! They'd arrived at the right place, at the right time, and they knelt before the king of the Jews – all their fancy clothes in the dust – and they worshipped him. They knew who he was. Then they went home, avoiding Herod, because they'd been warned about him in a dream. The whole account is striking. Strange, unexpected people came. Strange threats occurred. Strange guidance was used. But in everything, worship overflowed. And the Lord Jesus, who would bring hope and healing to the world, was kept safe.

- - - - - -

Pray

> 'Lord, we thank you that your plans are always good and they always prevail. Help us to have a heart of worship and assurance in you today.'

Joseph obeyed

'So he got up, took the child and his mother during the night and left for Egypt.'
Matthew 2:14

Read Matthew 2:13–23

Compared to Mary, Joseph's role in the recorded life of Jesus seems (at first glance) small. He was present in the birth narratives, and then later when the boy Jesus was at the temple, but, after that, Joseph seemed to disappear from the story, causing most commentators to presume that he died early before Jesus' public ministry. But he was a crucial part of the story! In this section, Joseph was given three more dreams during which an angel of the Lord appeared to him. Firstly, the angel told him to get up and take the child and Mary to Egypt because Herod was trying to kill Jesus. Joseph did it (2:14). Then the angel told him to get up and take the child back to Israel because it was now safe. Joseph did it (2:21). Lastly, he was told to avoid Judea because of a current threat. Joseph did it (2:23). He took his small family north, and they settled in Nazareth, in Galilee. It's a wonderful account of simple, unquestioning, faithful obedience. Joseph isn't even recorded as speaking or having a voice. He just did it. In this day and age, when we're surrounded by noise and self-seeking argument and grandiose debate, it's a beautiful contrast. There is a time to quietly obey. And Joseph's simple obedience not only saved the life of Jesus but, through Jesus, life was offered to everyone.

- - - - - -

Pray

'Lord, help us to drink again from the quiet well of simple obedience to you.'

The boy Jesus in the temple

'Didn't you know I had to be in my Father's house?'
Luke 2:49b

Read Luke 2:41–52

It's easy to wonder about the years in between. How did Jesus spend the 30 years in between his move to Galilee as a small child and then his public ministry at age 33? Was he educated by a rabbi, or taught carpentry by his father? Did he care for his younger siblings, or play with the neighbours' kids on the hills nearby? One year, Darren and I visited Nazareth and we wandered around the town, trying to imagine Jesus running up that particular hill, or chasing goats, or playing with objects made from wood. I enjoyed the imagining, but I don't think it filled in any gaps. Instead, Luke tells us that when Jesus was 12 years old, his family went to Jerusalem for the Passover festival, as they always did. That particular year, after the festival was over, Jesus stayed behind in Jerusalem. The family must have worried when they realised he was missing. It took another three days to find him! Yet, Jesus was *'in the temple courts, sitting among the teachers, listening to them and asking them questions'* (2:46). Jesus was in his Father's house, where he was comfortable. And that sentence tells us more than anything. As a child, Jesus knew. He listened, and he grew in wisdom and stature. He found favour with God and man. He knew who he was, and he knew something of what would happen later. So the 30 years passed, as they were meant to pass, in quiet, undocumented preparation.

- - - - - -

Pray

> *'Lord, help us to see that your timing is perfect, and it can pass profitably, even without photos being taken, or moments documented. Please prepare us today for all that will come tomorrow.'*

John the Baptist prepares the way

'But after me comes one who is more powerful than I.'
Matthew 3:11

Read Matthew 3:1–12

In the Old Testament, the Lord often worked through pairs of people. Moses died, and Joshua carried on his task. Elijah was taken up into heaven, and Elisha carried on his life-giving work. Now, there was a new Elijah in the form of John the Baptist. He even looked like Elijah. Back in his day, Elijah wore *'a garment of hair and had a leather belt round his waist'* (2 Kings 1:8), and then John's *'clothes were made of camel's hair, and he had a leather belt round his waist'* (Matthew 3:4). It's striking! It was meant to alert the people that something was about to happen. John would fulfil the words of Isaiah, and be the one calling in the desert, saying, *'Prepare the way for the LORD, make straight the paths of our God'* (Isaiah 40:3). It's exciting! It meant that the Messiah was coming! But it was also very serious. John's task would be difficult, and his message wasn't easy. The people, who were resting on their ancestry, needed to be brought back to genuine repentance, and that was going to be hard. So John spoke to them clearly, and then he said, *'But after me comes one who is more powerful than I, whose sandals I am not worthy to carry. He will baptise you with the Holy Spirit and fire'* (3:11). It's astounding. John knew who he was, and who Jesus was. He wasn't even worthy to carry Jesus' sandals. His ministry was important but he never confused the two. He pointed ahead. We also have the task of pointing to Jesus, and not to ourselves.

- - - - - -

Pray

> *'Lord, you came to offer life, in all its fullness. Please help us to point to you in everything.'*

This is my Son, whom I love

'This is my Son, whom I love; with him I am well pleased.'
Matthew 3:17

Read Matthew 3:13–17

Given that John the Baptist had such a clear sense of who he was, and who Jesus was, it's not surprising that he didn't want to baptise Jesus. *'I need to be baptised by you, and do you come to me?'* (3:14). And yet Jesus, the Son of God, asked to be baptised by John, and John did as he was told. In that moment, Jesus publicly identified himself with our sin and failure, even though he needed no repentance at all. Also in that moment, heaven opened and the Spirit of God descended on Jesus like a dove, and a voice from heaven said, *'This is my Son, whom I love; with him I am well pleased'* (3:17). It's the relational aspect of God, since the beginning of time. It's Yahweh describing his Son, whom he loves. It's Yahweh's own voice after hundreds of years of silence! It's something altogether new and wonderful. It's the Messiah, come at last. And the crowd must have stared. Did they realise what was happening that day? I love the description that Jesus was the One, whom God loves. Back then, Jesus hadn't theoretically 'done' anything yet, but God loved him. He was well pleased with his Son. And it's that love that we also rest in today, because we know that the life and death of Jesus has made it possible.

- - - - - -

Pray

'Lord, it astounds us that your love formed the world for your good pleasure, and that your love redeemed the world. Thank you that your love invites us in today.'

Jesus was tested

'After fasting for forty days and forty nights, he was hungry.'
Matthew 4:2

Read Matthew 4:1–11

As soon as Jesus was baptised and ready for his public ministry, he was immediately led out into the wilderness for 40 days and 40 nights. He ate nothing, and he was hungry, and tempted by the devil. It seems like an unusual way to begin a ministry, or perhaps not something we would choose for ourselves. Yet, this remarkable beginning is an introduction to the whole gospel, and a re-writing of Israelite history. When the tempter gave Jesus an opportunity to turn stones into bread, Jesus quoted from Deuteronomy, *'Man shall not live on bread alone'* (4:4). Jesus was somehow a new and better Moses, trusting in God as his provider, unlike the Israelites who failed Yahweh in the desert. Then, when the tempter suggested that Jesus throw himself off a high point of the temple, he replied, *'Do not put the Lord your God to the test'* (4:7). Jesus again quoted Deuteronomy, completely trusting God as his protector. He would not behave like the Israelites in the desert! Then, when the tempter took Jesus to a high mountain and promised him worldly splendour, he replied, *'Worship the Lord your God, and serve him only'* (4:10). Jesus completely trusted God for his status. And in this one event, Jesus re-scripted all of human history. The Israelites had failed in the desert, but Jesus would not. They had grumbled and disobeyed, but Jesus would trust in Yahweh for everything. And because he did, it means that we too can trust in God as our protector, our provider, and for our status today.

- - - - - -

Pray

'Lord, this is a stunning reminder of who you are, and how much we can trust you. Please help us to do that today.'

Jesus was rejected

'But he walked right through the crowd and went on his way.'
Luke 4:30

Read Luke 4:14–30

In Luke's account, immediately after Jesus was tempted in the wilderness
he began to minister in Capernaum, in the marvellous power of the Spirit.
As he did, people were healed. They began to praise God! The new story of
welcome and invitation was beginning, in a wonderful way! But then, Jesus
went back to his hometown of Nazareth and he visited the synagogue on
the Sabbath. He opened the scroll of Isaiah and read it out loud – about the
One who would proclaim good news to the poor, and set the oppressed free
(Isaiah 61:1–2). He told the people that the Scripture had been fulfilled in
their hearing. It was him! Some of them were surprised. Jesus was saying that
he was the One, who would help the blind to see, and give grace to those
who had lost their way. It was wonderful, and it was extravagant . . . but it
was not wonderful to all who heard him that day. Some of them tried to
kill him by throwing him off a cliff . . . but Jesus walked through the crowd
and went on his way. Was it the pronouncement of his Lordship that riled
the people? Or was it the stories of surprising grace? In his message that day,
Jesus had also mentioned Elijah who helped to feed a foreign widow, and
Elisha who healed the foreign commander. Yahweh had compassion on non-
Israelites! God's new, wonderful story would be thrown wide for everyone.
Could the Jews cope with that thought? Can we? Will we let God's
extravagant grace for the world inform all of our actions and attitudes today?

- - - - - -

Pray

*'Lord, your grace is unsettling and extravagant. If it wasn't, we would not
be welcome. Thank you.'*

The grand story

'The true light that gives light to everyone was coming into the world.'
John 1:9

Read John 1:1–34

I love the way the Gospel of John begins. It's so vast and grand. *'In the beginning was the Word, and the Word was with God, and the Word was God. He was with God in the beginning. Through him all things were made; without him nothing was made that has been made'* (1:1–3). The grand story of God begins with God, and then includes everything and everyone – all of time, all of space, all of humanity. There is nothing outside of God's story! And yet it is also a story that desperately needed light and redemption. So, God sent his own Son who became flesh – the One who was with God in the beginning, and who formed all things. Jesus stepped into the story himself, and he gave light and life to everyone. It's incredible and glorious! And amazingly, the story was never going to be confined to the Jews. *'Yet to all who did receive him, to those who believed in his name, he gave the right to become children of God'* (1:12). Everyone, everywhere, was going to be invited into the grand story . . . because one day, at Bethany, on the other side of the Jordan River, Jesus came – the Lamb of God, the Chosen One, who *'takes away the sin of the world'* (1:29). The answer had arrived! Yahweh had a plan. He was never going to override his promises, or overlook the sin of the people. He was going to show grace, through the life and death and resurrection of his own Son, Jesus.

- - - - - -

Pray

> *'Lord, we thank you that you became flesh. We can't get our heads around it, but the truth is glorious for us.'*

Following him

"'Come," he replied, "and you will see.'"
John 1:39

Read John 1:35–51

When Jesus appeared at Bethany, walking by the Jordan River, people immediately knew who he was. The Spirit came down and revealed it. In response, they followed him, one by one. It began with Andrew, who wanted to find out more. Then Andrew called his brother Simon, and he joined in as well. Then there was Philip, who told Nathanael, *'We have found the one Moses wrote about in the Law . . . Jesus of Nazareth, the son of Joseph'* (1:45). But Nathanael hesitated at first. He wasn't sure whether anything good could come from Nazareth . . . probably not (1:46). And Jesus' reply is the point at which we must pause . . . because Jesus *knew* Nathanael. Of course, Nathanael wanted to know how Jesus knew him, and Jesus said, *'I saw you while you were still under the fig-tree'* (1:48). Nathanael must have been amazed. He immediately bowed down before Jesus, saying, *'Rabbi, you are the Son of God; you are the king of Israel'* (1:49). He couldn't do anything else. He was known. And perhaps it evokes the same response in us. We are all known by Jesus – at the desk, in the car, on the way to work. We are invited to trust him, the one who is the Son of God, and who came from the Father full of grace and truth.

- - - - - -

Pray

> *'Lord, please help us to trust you again, and to respond to the truth that we are part of your grand story, through your Son, the Lord Jesus.'*

That we might believe

'Jesus said to the servants, "Fill the jars with water."'
John 2:7

Read John 2:1–11

Within a few days of Jesus appearing to the people at the Jordan River, something incredible happened. There was a wedding in Cana, Galilee. Jesus and his friends were invited, and at a certain point, the host ran out of wine. On the request of his mother, Jesus turned six jars of ordinary water into the finest wine imaginable. It's the first miracle recorded by John and it was astounding for the host and his guests! But we might wonder . . . of all the things that Jesus could have done first, for humanity, why this? Could he not have chosen something more necessary for our broken state? But no, this was the first sign, as recorded by John, and afterwards the disciples *'believed in him'* (2:11). The miracle revealed Jesus' glory! More than anything, that's what Jesus wanted. He wanted his disciples to be absolutely sure that he was the Son of God, the One who was promised. And it's exactly what Jesus still wants today – that we might be absolutely sure, and *know who he is* – as the Son of God – that we might believe in him – the One who forgives, the One who has authority, the One who is with us. And the reason we can be absolutely sure is that there was a greater sign to come. Jesus yielded his life and, three days later, he rose again. The tomb was empty and death defeated for ever. Even today, we can reflect on the signs and trust him.

- - - - - -

Pray

> *'Lord, help us to notice the signs today – to fix our eyes on the glory and authority of Jesus, and to pause and consider your grand story in which we are amazingly offered grace and salvation.'*

Jesus healed many

'At sunset, the people brought to Jesus all who had various kinds of illness, and laying his hands on each one, he healed them.'
Luke 4:40

Read Luke 4:31–44

I remember the first time Darren and I arrived in South India, and we began to work at the polio clinic. Every day, crowds of people would arrive, needing every kind of assistance – food, medicine, support, rehabilitation. Every day, we would feel overwhelmed and helpless! So whenever I read this passage, I wonder if Jesus felt that way. Luke records that Jesus began at Simon's house in Capernaum. He healed Simon's mother-in-law from a high fever. Then at sunset, he was surrounded by people with various kinds of illness, and he laid hands on each one, healing them. He simply healed them. He showed them who he was! The kingdom of God had come with wonderful, restorative power! And the people were amazed! Even the demons obeyed Jesus, and they shouted, *'You are the Son of God!'* (4:41). But Jesus rebuked them. It wasn't time yet. They must be silent. There was an important timeline and Jesus needed to proclaim the good news of the kingdom of God in the other towns also. But in the middle of all of that, Jesus also needed to pray. *'At daybreak, Jesus went out to a solitary place'* (4:42). He was surrounded by desperate need, and he met the need amazingly (in ways that only the Messiah can), and at daybreak he went to a solitary place and he prayed to his Father. It teaches us, who are by nature so helpless and overwhelmed, to also find a solitary place, and pray.

- - - - - -

Pray

'Lord, we kid ourselves when we think we don't need you. Help us to find a quiet place today, and help us to pray.'

Fishing

'But because you say so, I will let down the nets.'
Luke 5:5b

Read Luke 5:1–11

Some years ago, as a family, we visited the Sea of Galilee. Our first impression was that it wasn't as large as we'd previously imagined. How did the disciples get lost in it? But when we read (in our *Lonely Planet Guide* book) that 'the usually placid lake can be subject to unexpected storms that blow in from the Mediterranean Sea during winter', it made more sense. It was at the Sea of Galilee that Jesus called his disciples and taught them, as recorded by Luke. He commandeered the fishing boat, pulled out from shore, taught the people, and then asked Simon to put out into deep water and let down the nets for a catch. But Simon didn't want to. They had worked hard all night and hadn't caught anything. Surely Simon knew something about fishing? But then the new disciples did as they were told, and they caught such a large number of fish that their nets began to break and their boats began to sink. Simon Peter fell at Jesus' knees and said, *'Go away from me, Lord; I am a sinful man!'* (5:8b). Only hours before this, the catch had been empty, and now the boats were sinking. No wonder Simon trembled. There was no other explanation. Jesus had to be the Lord. And it was too much for Simon. Perhaps the Lordship of Jesus should also cause us to tremble today.

- - - - - -

Pray

> *'Lord, we thank you that you reveal your abundance and Lordship in everything. Please help us to tremble before you, and to find great joy in your invitation to fish for people.'*

The Beatitudes

'Blessed are the poor in spirit, for theirs is the kingdom of heaven.'
Matthew 5:3

Read Matthew 5:1–12

Jesus came to the world to turn everything upside down for humanity. He did that in extraordinary ways – his hands touched the outcasts and he healed them, his voice called the outsiders and they came, his words went to the heart of every person, and his life was poured out as a sacrifice for everyone. As well as that, Jesus challenged every fallen, broken attitude. *'Blessed are the poor in spirit, for theirs is the kingdom of heaven. Blessed are those who mourn, for they will be comforted. Blessed are the meek, for they will inherit the earth'* (5:3–5). In a world where power and wealth and influence were the greatest of merits, Jesus said that's not how God sees it. That's not the kingdom of God. It never has been, and it never will be. I remember reading the Beatitudes with my friend Jalpa in Nepal. She was very poor, living with her family of five in a tiny room. She said in Nepali, 'I know I'm poor. I've always been poor. And now that I'm a Christian, not much has changed for me on the outside. I'm still poor! But everything has changed for me on the inside. I have peace with God now, because of Jesus. That's why I'm blessed.' It was the quietest, truest testimony I'd heard in a long time. Blessed are those who deeply trust in God, more than in their resources, or status, or privilege.

- - - - - -

Pray

> *'Lord, thank you that you came to turn everything upside down. Help us to be people who depend on you, rather than our resources.'*

The salt of the earth

'In the same way, let your light shine before others, that they may see your good deeds and glorify your Father in heaven.'
Matthew 5:16

Read Matthew 5:13–16

There is something wonderful about salt. It spreads. It never acts discriminately. If you put two teaspoons of salt in a curry, it will make the entire meal salty, not just the chicken, or not just the potatoes. It goes everywhere. It is not limited! And when Jesus spoke to the crowd, he said they were to be like salt. He said, *'You are the salt of the earth'* (5:13). Your new hope and life and attitudes (found in Christ) will spread everywhere, to bless the whole world! You can't keep your hope and attitudes to yourself, or just for your family! It spreads! But if the salt loses its saltiness, how can it be made salty again? It is a serious question and message from Jesus. He must have known that it was going to be hard – for his disciples and for us. Like them, we would want to follow Jesus but easily get distracted, or blasé, or fearful. We would become numbed, or lulled into complacency. We would forget the life-giving hope of Jesus, and we would want to blame everyone else. And Jesus said, don't light your lamp and put it under a bowl. Let it shine! Let your hope in Christ be seen by others that they may glorify your Father in heaven. That's what God wants, and that's what we want – that others might come and know the Lord, in all his glory.

- - - - -

Pray

'Lord, forgive us for the times when we have hidden our hope and our faith. Please make us salty again today.'

But I tell you

'If anyone forces you to go one mile, go with them two miles.'
Matthew 5:41

Read Matthew 5:17–42

By the time Jesus began to teach the people, the Israelites had had centuries of trying to follow the Law given by Moses. And even though Moses kept saying to the people back then that it was about their hearts (that they were to love God with everything they had), they simply couldn't do it. For thousands of years, their law-following had deteriorated (in most cases) into greed and injustice and legalism. So then, incredibly, Jesus spoke to the people about a new kingdom – a kingdom where their *hearts* would be transformed under Jesus' rule. It would be altogether different! And they would see that the old Law wasn't being replaced, but instead their hearts were being changed, so that they could love and follow God truly, in every part of life. And the loving would be transformative. Everything they'd heard about murder or adultery or divorce or breaking an oath would be transformed into something wonderfully real and genuine, where hidden motives were exposed, where reconciliation was possible, and where grace was astounding. *'If anyone slaps you on the right cheek, turn to them the other cheek also'* (5:39b). It's confronting! I wonder if the people paused when he said that. Could they do it? Had they seen it done before? They didn't know then, that they were about to witness that very thing, when the Lord Jesus himself would be slapped and beaten and mocked, and he would turn the other cheek. It's only the extravagant grace of Jesus that allows a response of grace in us.

- - - - - -

Pray

'Lord, in an era when we are taught to defend our rights, please speak to us again about our hearts.'

Love your enemies

'But I tell you, love your enemies and pray for those who persecute you.'
Matthew 5:44

Read Matthew 5:43–48

Of all the things that Jesus commanded in his Sermon on the Mount, perhaps this is the hardest. *'Love your enemies and pray for those who persecute you.'* Sometimes, it's hard for us to love our friends and family, let alone our enemies! One of our friends is Kurdish. He grew up in Northern Iraq, and when he was a boy he saw the Iraqi army walk through his street and take the men away, including his father. Years later, when Kuwait was liberated, the Iraqi army moved north and they began shooting at the Kurds from their helicopters. It was horrendous. But sometime after that, our friend found refuge in the hills and he met a Christian man who gave him a Bible. It changed everything in his life, as he responded to Jesus. Perhaps the most striking thing is the way he prays now. When he prays, he prays for all of them the same (in ISIS, in the PKK, amongst the Kurds, the Turks, and the Arabs), that they will truly know God's love and peace. When he prays like that, I know that he has been transformed. He understands the love of Jesus, and that all-encompassing love has enabled him to love. Jesus said, *'But I tell you, love your enemies and pray for those who persecute you, that you may be children of your Father in heaven'* (5:44–45). Then Jesus showed them, and us, how to do it.

- - - - - -

Pray

'Lord, there are times when we have wounded others, and other times when we have been wounded. Please help us to find our solace in you, and to pour out your grace, from that place.'

Live generously

'If you love those who love you, what reward will you get?'
Matthew 5:46

Read Matthew 5:43–48

After Jesus told the crowd on the hill to love their enemies, he said, *'Be perfect, therefore, as your heavenly Father is perfect'* (5:48). That's a difficult command! When I read it, I immediately think about how imperfect I am. But then I wonder whether Jesus was pointing out our lack of perfection so that he could highlight our need for redemption. Or, then again, maybe he was saying (as before) that he would slowly transform our hearts through his Spirit. In *The Message*, the phrase says, *'Live like Kingdom subjects . . . Live generously and graciously toward others, in the way God lives toward you.'* It's helpful to think about. How does God live towards us in a daily way? How does God love us? God's love, at the cross, was everything – it brought about our forgiveness and restoration and the promise of life for ever. And yet God also loves us in a tender, daily way. He prepares our paths, and teaches us, and comforts us, and convicts us. He brings the right friend or prayer partner along, exactly when we need them, even at the hospital, or on the train. He is with us! And he wants us to love others generously and graciously, in the same way that he lives towards us.

- - - - - -

Pray

> *'Lord, your calling to be perfect is something that sounds impossible to us, yet we long to love others in the way you love us. Please help us to live generously and graciously, in all the ways you have in mind.'*

It's not a stage

'Be careful not to practise your righteousness in front of others to be seen by them.'
Matthew 6:1

Read Matthew 6:1–8

The same Kurdish friend of ours who grew up in Northern Iraq and fled during the attacks, eventually found his way to a refugee camp in the hills of Iran. After the initial crisis, he stayed on to help in the refugee camps, and one day he was given a Bible by the camp manager. He said that he'd always wanted to read a Bible, so he began reading Matthew. He got up to chapter 6 and read Jesus' words about prayer, and that's when everything changed for him. Growing up with a Muslim background, he said that he'd always been longing for genuine prayer, rather than something that seemed rote-learned, or for show. So Jesus' words were life-changing for him. *'But when you pray, go into your room, close the door and pray to your Father, who is unseen. Then your Father, who sees what is done in secret, will reward you'* (6:6). Our friend knew it to be true. Then, at the same time as reading this passage, he was invited to join in prayer with the other Christians in the refugee camp. He noticed that they prayed in humble ways, looking to God rather than trying to put on a show. Our friend became convicted that Jesus was Lord, and he himself became a Christian, surrounded by refugee tents and snow. But when he describes his testimony, he says that it was the honest, humble praying that touched him the most.

- - - - - -

Pray

> *'Lord, our motives are often mixed, and we know that it's quite nice to be seen. Help us to rest in the absolute certainty that we are seen and known by you.'*

When you pray

'Our Father in heaven, hallowed be your name . . .'
Matthew 6:9b

Read Matthew 6:5–13

It seems so obvious that we should begin our prayers with acknowledging who God is, the One to whom we speak. He is so glorious and holy and just and merciful . . . and we want to honour him! And yet it's easy to begin our prayers in every other way – with our own concerns and fears, or our desire for a smooth path, or our longing for security. And Jesus said, *'This, then, is how you should pray . . .'* (6:9). Jesus knew that when we begin by acknowledging God and what he has done for us, then everything else will flow naturally. When we remember our Father in heaven, and when we long to honour him, then we will long for his kingdom to come in all its fullness. We know that it will be wonderful! When we understand his nature and his covenant faithfulness, then we will long for his will to be done in the world, and we will trust him to bring that about, and provide what we need. When we remember the depth of his forgiveness for us, through the Lord Jesus, then we will humbly ask him to change our own hearts and grant us the capacity to forgive. We know that he alone can do that! Lastly, when we look at his holiness and purity, then we will ask him to deliver us from temptation, because we know that we are surrounded by it on every side.

- - - - - -

Pray

> *'Lord, we want to honour you today, and so we say, "Father in heaven, hallowed be your name . . ."'*

Forgive and you will be forgiven

'For if you forgive other people when they sin against you, your heavenly Father will also forgive you.'

Matthew 6:14

Read Matthew 6:14–15

In 1999, an Australian missionary named Graham Staines was burnt to death in a vehicle in India, by Hindu extremists, along with his two small sons. That same morning, after Graham's wife Gladys was told the terrible news, she hugged her remaining daughter and said, 'Whoever did this, we will forgive them.' How could she do that, or say that? Could we do that? Years later, when I spoke to Gladys about that time, she said it was unthinkably hard. Forgiveness didn't come easily at all. But, she said, 'As Christians, I don't think we have that option. We've been forgiven. Jesus died for our sins, and he bore the punishment we deserved. We've been shown grace . . . and the more we're overwhelmed by that grace, the more we can forgive.' Gladys and her daughter stayed on in India for another five years, serving the people. For me, hearing Gladys' story, I often wondered how she forgave them, and how she stayed there. But the only possible answer is that she knew Jesus. She sat at the cross. She knew that she had been forgiven, so she could pour it out. And Jesus' words here are so incredibly important. He knew what was coming for himself, and he knew that both receiving and giving forgiveness were crucial tasks for every one of us. He also knew that holding back on forgiveness would be life-sapping, in every way.

- - - - - -

Pray

'Lord, we thank you for the cross, and for your work of grace in our lives. Please help it transform us today, so that we can forgive.'

Store up your treasures in heaven

'For where your treasure is, there your heart will be also.'
Matthew 6:21

Read Matthew 6:19–24

Every part of Jesus' Sermon on the Mount must have been confronting to his hearers back then, as it is today. There they were, sitting on the hillside, perhaps wondering about how Jesus might transform their earthly lives for the better, and he said, *'But store up for yourselves treasures in heaven, where moths and vermin do not destroy, and where thieves do not break in and steal. For where your treasure is, there your heart will be also'* (6:20–21). Did they stop and wonder about their own hearts, and their own treasure? Even for us, it can be hard to know the condition of our hearts. I met a Christian couple recently who previously ran a very successful business. They planned to sell it and retire comfortably. But when they did sell it, the buyer didn't pay, and they lost over four million dollars and went bankrupt. They couldn't even take him to court. When I met them, though, two years had passed and they were renting a small unit, living on the pension. They said they were more prayerful now. They were more responsive to God, and they were happier. They said they didn't realise how tightly they'd been holding onto their treasure before. More than that, in losing their treasure they realised how little it meant. Their story spoke to me about all the things we hold on to, too tightly, without even knowing.

- - - - - -

Pray

'Lord, we know that everything comes from you. Help us to treasure our life with you, and the things that are eternal.'

Do not worry

'But seek first his kingdom and his righteousness, and all these things will be given to you as well.'
Matthew 6:33

Read Matthew 6:25–34

As part of Jesus' revolutionary Sermon on the Mount, he told his disciples not to worry about their lives. Everything was different now. Their heavenly Father cared for them! But it's hard not to worry. A year after Darren and I gave birth to our first child in Nepal, we returned as a family to Australia for a short home leave. During that time we struggled through five miscarriages. It was a long time of tears. After a while, I fell pregnant again, and the medical team told us there were some concerns. We could also lose this baby. I worried, naturally. At the same time, I read Jesus' words about worry, and I reflected on what he meant. Jesus was saying to his disciples that there's a new kingdom coming, and it's a whole new way of thinking and relating to God, where we *can* relate to him – and in this new kingdom, we can talk to him. We can discover how valuable we are as a child of God. We can pray more. And perhaps, the more we pray about our concerns and fears, the more we sense God's holiness and his plans and his sovereignty. He is still Lord, even now, while we cry or worry, and he still has a plan within these worrying times, even when we don't understand any of it. He is still sovereign today, and he still wants us to seek him amidst tears.

- - - - - -

Pray

'Lord, we thank you that in your eyes we are valuable. Help us to seek you in times of fear and worry.'

Be a wise builder

'The rain came down, the streams rose, and the winds blew and beat against that house; yet it did not fall, because it had its foundation on the rock.'
Matthew 7:25

Read Matthew 7:1–28

Most commentators would agree that Jesus summed up his Sermon on the Mount with this final word picture at the end of chapter 7. Be wise. Build your house on the rock. Find your solid foundation on a relationship with God, through Jesus. There's no other way! So, immerse yourself in his teaching. Look to him. And as you do that, you will start to pray in line with God's will, and be careful about judging other people, and you will produce fruit, and you will keep in mind that there are false prophets as well as true ones. And it will be hard. Strong winds will come, and storms, in the form of our own sinfulness and a deeply fallen world. But hold on to Jesus firmly. You are valuable to God, and loved by God, so everything you do and think will start to spring from your identity in Christ, as Jesus continues to be your wisdom teacher. And remember, Jesus has every authority – to judge, and to hold open the narrow door that leads to life. Isn't it amazing that we get to enter through it? Because in that narrow door, there isn't any room for our extra baggage of pride, or accomplishments, or merit, or reputation, or even last week's success story. It won't fit! But we can walk through the narrow door because Jesus holds it open. That's amazing!

- - - - - -

Pray

> 'Lord, some of us have carried baggage for so long that we can't remember how to walk without it. Thank you that you hold open the narrow door to life, for ever.'

The faith of the centurion

'I have not found anyone in Israel with such great faith.'
Matthew 8:10b

Read Matthew 8:5–13

After Jesus finished speaking to the people, he went down the mountainside and large crowds followed him. There was so much need! He then healed a man with leprosy, and later, in Capernaum, he was approached by a Roman centurion. It's a fascinating account because on only two recorded occasions did Jesus comment on the 'great faith' of the person in front of him. One of them was a Canaanite woman who pleaded with him to heal her daughter (Matthew 15:21–28), and the other was this Roman centurion who pleaded with Jesus to heal his paralysed servant. Both of them were outside of the Israelite nation. Both of them trusted that Jesus had power and authority to heal. And in both situations, Jesus did heal, in wonderful ways. He restored them! But as well as that, Matthew tells us that Jesus 'was amazed' at the faith of the centurion. He said he hadn't found anyone in Israel with such 'great faith'. It's interesting because the centurion's faith was certainly remarkable – he believed that Jesus only needed to say a word and it would be done. And it was! But what was most striking to Jesus was that this *outsider* trusted in him when so many of his Jewish audience did not. There is so much encouragement for us in this passage. We are also in the Gentile audience. We were not originally Jews, but we have been welcomed into God's family and the feast to come because of what Jesus has done for us. We too can have faith like the Roman centurion or the Canaanite woman.

- - - - - -

Pray

'Lord, we thank you for your power to heal and bring restoration. And we thank you because you welcomed us.'

The cost of following Jesus

**'Foxes have dens and birds have nests, but the Son of Man has nowhere
to lay his head.'**
Matthew 8:20

Read Matthew 8:18–22

When Jesus spoke to the people, he made it clear that following him wouldn't
be easy. There would be choices to make, and there would be a cost. I think,
these days, we can be tempted to leave out the costly bits. We like to focus on
God's love for us, through Jesus – that lavish, never-ending love – and we can
neglect the truth that if God loves us like that, then our response will always
be serious. It will involve wholehearted, single-minded love. If it doesn't, we
haven't understood the gospel. And wholehearted, single-minded love can be
hard! It can take on so many forms in the course of a lifetime. We might find
ourselves leaving the comforts of home and serving elsewhere in the world,
where the need is greater and the gospel workers are fewer. Or we might
find ourselves teaching under-privileged children in remote areas, or funding
Bible literacy, or pouring our artistic soul into gospel resources that change
lives but don't bring an income. We might spend years providing spare beds
for homeless people in our communities, or to runaway teenagers. We might
find ourselves listening to heartbroken neighbours long into the night, only
to receive backstabbing in the morning. We might be shaped by extravagant
grace, rather than fear and self-absorption. And that will be glorious, but
there will be a cost, and Jesus made sure that his hearers knew exactly what
obedience to the Lord might look like.

- - - - - -

Pray

'Lord, your call to obedience is hard, but there's nowhere else we'd rather go.'

Eating with sinners

'For I have not come to call the righteous, but sinners.'
Matthew 9:13b

Read Matthew 9:9–13

Back in Jesus' time, tax collectors were not highly regarded. Their job was to extract money from the people *for* the Roman invaders, and that didn't make them popular. As well as that, they often did it via corrupt means, which added to the general hatred as well as their wealth! Amazingly, Jesus saw Matthew, the tax collector, sitting at his booth and he asked him to follow him. Equally amazingly, Matthew (who must have heard the incredible stories about Jesus), just got up and followed him. It's a lovely, rapid story of transformation, and we can imagine the celebration that evening at Matthew's house. But the Pharisees didn't understand it at all. Why was Jesus eating with sinners? Jesus said in reply, *'It is not the healthy who need a doctor, but those who are ill . . . For I have not come to call the righteous, but sinners'* (9:12–13). It should make us pause. Are we healthy? Is anyone healthy? Or are we all unwell, needing (and in receipt of) a gracious invitation? Jesus' words were confronting then, but they also remind us never to forget our own state, or to sit in judgement as the Pharisees were doing. The postscript, of course, is that after Jesus called Matthew, and many years after he got up and went, he wrote this gospel that we sit and read today. This is the kind of incredible transformation that Jesus longs to bring about in all of us.

- - - - - -

Pray

'Lord, your invitation of grace is needed by all of us. Please help us to show mercy in response.'

New wineskins

'No, they pour new wine into new wineskins.'
Matthew 9:17b

Read Matthew 9:14–17

When Jesus told the people about the new kingdom that would be altogether different, and that their hearts would be completely changed, the people naturally had questions. How would that fit with their old patterns? What about fasting, for example? Why didn't Jesus' disciples fast? And Jesus said again that their hearts would be utterly transformed. It's the repeated reminder for all of us. When we follow Jesus, every single thing in our life changes – our attitudes and values and choices and priorities and pleasures and concerns – everything changes! We have a friend who lives in outback Australia. In his twenties, he struggled with alcohol and he couldn't keep down a job. But then one night he was assaulted and then airlifted to hospital. While he was in hospital, the Lord spoke powerfully to him, and he became a Christian. When he got home, his entire life changed. The desire to drink left him, and he found ongoing employment. He sorted out his relationships. But it wasn't all easy. Two years after the assault, he was diagnosed with a brain tumour and he went completely blind. But then, someone gave him an audio recording of the Bible, and he found that he could memorise Scripture. He used that gift to share at his church, and encourage his friends for the next 35 years. His life was changed irrevocably, and he kept using his days for God when he could see and, equally, when he couldn't see. It's an encouragement to all of us – to keep letting God transform us, in everything.

- - - - - -

Pray

'Lord, thank you that you give us new wineskins, and you change everything about our lives and hearts. Please keep doing that, even when it's hard.'

Sending out workers

'Ask the Lord of the harvest, therefore, to send out workers into his harvest field.'

Matthew 9:38

Read Matthew 9:35 – 10:42

It's amazing that 2,000 years after Jesus spoke these words, the gospel message has actually spread to almost every language and nation in the world. God has been at work in his harvest field in wonderful ways, drawing people into his kingdom from every nation, one by one, and sometimes in large, exciting people movements. There is so much to give thanks for, but the needs are still very real. Currently, only 30 per cent of the world's population follow the Lord Jesus. And Jesus' words are still relevant. *'The harvest is plentiful but the workers are few. Ask the Lord of the harvest, therefore, to send out workers into his harvest field'* (9:37–38). Back then, when Jesus spoke those words, he had been preaching in all the towns and villages, and he was acutely aware of the needs. *'When he saw the crowds, he had compassion on them, because they were harassed and helpless, like sheep without a shepherd'* (9:36). Jesus' heart was stirred for the people, and part of his response was to send out his twelve disciples. He gave them the authority to heal and speak and drive out impure spirits. It was risky and relational, and wonderful things happened. But Jesus also said it would be hard. His disciples would be betrayed and arrested and falsely accused. It wasn't the most encouraging speech! And yet today, we still respond, we still take up our cross and follow Jesus, because we are utterly convinced that in him is wonderful life, and his message is worth everything.

- - - - - -

Pray

'Lord, we long to follow you, and we ask that the same compassion for the crowds would stir and compel us too.'

Whoever

'Whoever acknowledges me before others, I will also acknowledge before my Father in heaven.'
Matthew 10:32

Read Matthew 10:32

Jesus used the word 'whoever' quite a few times during his public ministry. *'Whoever acknowledges me before others, I will also acknowledge before my Father in heaven'* (10:32). *'Whoever loses their life for me will find it'* (Matthew 16:25b). *'Whoever practices and teaches these commands will be called great in the kingdom of heaven'* (Matthew 5:19b). *'Whoever welcomes one such child in my name welcomes me'* (Matthew 18:5). **Whoever**. Not just the people in the right clothes, or from the right part of Galilee, or speaking the right language, or putting the right amount of coins in the offering bag. Whoever – anyone who believes in Jesus, anyone who puts their trust in him as Saviour and Lord, anyone who acknowledges him before others. And it's the encouragement we need today, because we have also felt like the outsider at times. Maybe we didn't wear the right clothes as a teenager, or listen to the right music, or go to the right social gatherings. Maybe it was worse than that. But today, we can know without a doubt that Jesus died for all of us, the outsiders, so that we would never be the outsider, ever again.

- - - - - -

Pray

> *'Lord, we thank you that your invitation to trust you and follow you was extended to everyone, and to all of us. Thank you that it knew no boundaries of caste or clothes or capacity. Help us to respond again today.'*

Greater than John the Baptist

'Yet whoever is least in the kingdom of heaven is greater than he.'
Matthew 11:11b

Read Matthew 11:1–19

By the time that Jesus was sending out his disciples, John the Baptist was already in prison for denouncing Herod Antipas. It's possible that John really struggled in there, and began to doubt, because he sent word to Jesus saying, *'Are you the one who is to come, or should we expect someone else?'* (11:3). It sounds unexpected, given that John had been so certain of Jesus' identity at the time of his baptism. And yet it must have been hard in prison. Jesus replied to John asking, 'What do you see?' *'The blind receive sight, the lame walk, those who have leprosy are cleansed, the deaf hear, the dead are raised, and the good news is proclaimed to the poor'* (11:5). It was obvious, Jesus said! The answer was in the fruit and the miracles. He was the One described in Isaiah's prophecies! He was the One for whom they'd been waiting for thousands of years! And then Jesus said an even more striking thing to the crowd. *'Among those born of women there has not risen anyone greater than John the Baptist; yet whoever is least in the kingdom of heaven is greater than he'* (11:11). Jesus was referring to all the billions of people who would come after John, and put their complete trust in him, as Lord. He was referring to us. Don't miss out, he said! All these years later, the invitation still stands, remarkably.

- - - - - -

Pray

> *'Lord, in this day and age when we have fears of missing out, we thank you that you assure us that we're part of your kingdom. Help us to respond and be part of your mission for the world.'*

Come to me

'Come to me, all you who are weary and burdened, and I will give you rest.'
Matthew 11:28

Read Matthew 11:28–30

This is one of my favourite invitations in Scripture. Mere moments before, Jesus had confirmed to the crowd that he was the Son of the Father. It was a really big deal! His audience must have been stunned. It was the biggest revelation in the history of the world, and yet the very next thing Jesus said to them was, *'Come to me . . .'* (11:28). Jesus, the Son of the Father, the Lord of all, warmly invited them to come to him and to find rest in him. He didn't say, 'Come to me, all you who are healthy, and sorted, and unashamed . . .' He said, *'Come to me, all you who are **weary and burdened**, and I will give you rest.'* Surely, the crowds back then were as needy and exhausted and lost as we are. And Jesus, the Messiah himself, promised them rest. Amazingly, it's the same word used in Genesis 2. It's the promise of God's rest, and an invitation to share in his fellowship. Jesus, the Son of the Father, who came to invite us, fulfilled the promise not by coming as a great warrior, but he came *'gentle and humble in heart'* (11:29). He invited us to learn from him, and to find rest for our souls, for his yoke is easy and his burden is light. It's the deepest need for all of us, as individuals, and in our world today.

- - - - - -

Pray

> *'Lord, we thank you for your good gift of rest. Help us to find and receive rest in you today, in everything that we're doing, because you carried our burdens to the cross.'*

Lord of the Sabbath

'If any of you has a sheep and it falls into a pit on the Sabbath, will you not take hold of it and lift it out?'

Matthew 12:11

Read Matthew 12:1–14

Everywhere Jesus went, crowds gathered around him, longing to learn from him and follow him. But there were others who tried to trap him. They thought he was a threat, and a blasphemer who needed silencing! In some ways, it was understandable. The Pharisees had been trying to follow the law for a long time, and they knew what would happen if they failed Yahweh. They didn't want another exile! But the tricky thing was that even back in Exodus, the law wasn't given as a duty. It was given in the context of grace, as a way to live out their love for God. It was about their hearts, not about legalism. So Jesus spoke to the Pharisees about mercy. He said don't get so caught up in the rules that you miss the message. The kingdom of God doesn't look like legalistic Sabbath-keeping! And then Jesus went into the synagogue (on the Sabbath) and saw a man with a shrivelled hand, and he healed him! The man was completely restored! It's such a beautiful, visual display of mercy. It's the heart of God. And yet, as a result, the Pharisees were enraged. They went out and plotted how they might kill Jesus, and the opposition to Jesus began to build from that point. But the message is crucial for us today. We must not harbour a spirit that loves ritual more than the Lord himself. We must notice this, in ourselves, daily.

- - - - - -

Pray

'Lord, please change our hearts, especially on the days when it's easy to critique, or judge according to our own personal standards. Restore us today.'

The sign of Jonah

'For as Jonah was three days and three nights in the belly of a huge fish, so the Son of Man will be three days and three nights in the heart of the earth.'
Matthew 12:40

Read Matthew 12:38–45; 16:1–4, 21–28

It's interesting that at the same time as the opposition to Jesus began to build, Jesus himself began to speak more clearly about what was to come. The Pharisees asked for a sign, and he said that none would be given except for the sign of Jonah. We know about Jonah's life. It had been seemingly over, in the belly of a whale, but God brought him back to life, miraculously! Jesus was saying something incredible about his own life, which must have been difficult to fathom back then. How would Jesus be buried in the heart of the earth? But Jesus repeated the phrase later (Matthew 16:1–4) and then even more clearly still. *Jesus began to explain to his disciples that he must go to Jerusalem and suffer many things . . . and that he must be killed and on the third day be raised to life'* (16:21). At the time, Peter took Jesus aside and tried to rebuke him. Peter didn't want anything awful to happen to Jesus! But then, Jesus rebuked Peter, saying that he didn't understand the concerns of God. And it's true, Peter didn't. The suffering of Jesus changed the world. And the great concern of God is that his people might repent and come to him, and be restored. It's been that way since the beginning of time, and it will continue to be, until he comes again.

- - - - - -

Pray

'Lord, we thank you that we have an incredible opportunity to come to you and know you. Help us to be people who love you and love your concerns.'

The extravagant invitation

'Who is my mother, and who are my brothers?'
Matthew 12:48

Read Matthew 12:46–50

We don't read many references to Jesus' family in the gospels, so this section is particularly striking. Jesus was busy inside the house with the crowd, and his mother and brothers stood outside, wanting to speak with him. Someone told Jesus that they were there, and then he replied, *'Who is my mother, and who are my brothers?'* (12:48). At that moment, he pointed at his disciples and he said, *'Here are my mother and my brothers. For whoever does the will of my Father in heaven is my brother and sister and mother'* (12:49–50). Sometimes, I read Jesus' reply and I feel upset for Jesus' mother. How did she feel, being dismissed like that? How would *I* feel? Yet there is an entirely different way to read this encounter. Jesus' purpose on earth was to invite everyone – the lost, the broken, the sick, the empty, the frazzled – every single one of us. If Jesus' invitation, or purpose, or time on earth, had been limited to his immediate family, the invitation would have stalled. But it didn't. Whoever believes in Jesus, whoever trusts him as Lord, whoever does the will of the Father . . . is his brother and sister and mother. This is amazing!

- - - - - -

Pray

> *'Lord, we thank you for your extravagant purpose and invitation. We thank you that it has always been extravagant, since the beginning of time, and we especially thank you that it includes us!'*

The seed on good soil

'This is the one who produces a crop, yielding a hundred, sixty or thirty times what was sown.'
Matthew 13:23b

Read Matthew 13:1–23

The year that we visited Israel as a family, we sat for a while on the hill by the Sea of Galilee. It's covered in crops, even now, 2,000 years later – figs and olives and grapes and all kinds of things that I didn't recognise. It's a very fertile place! So, it's no wonder Jesus spoke to the crowds about seeds and plants and birds and thorns. They were surrounded by crops! And as he spoke, he used word pictures – because that's what the people could see and smell and remember. In this case, they needed to know that the way they *received* the gospel message was important. Some of them would be careless, or superficial in their response to Jesus, or they would let troubles and wealth distract them. So, Jesus told them about the seed on good soil. The seed of the gospel message needs good soil and space for it to grow and become fruitful. Be like the good soil! Don't get consumed by weeds! Weeds can quickly overtake a garden. And in our lives, we can let our diaries and imaginations fill up with things that don't feed our relationship with Jesus. Instead, we must let the seed take root, deeply. We must make choices to listen and trust and obey Jesus . . . and in the years to come, we will see growth in character, and the effects of a rich prayer life, and perhaps even a harvest of people coming to know the Lord Jesus. Wouldn't that be wonderful?

- - - - - -

Pray

'Lord, you said, "Whoever has ears, let them hear." Please let that be us today, so that we can produce abundant fruit for your glory.'

Rules and grace

'But the things that come out of a person's mouth come from the heart.'
Matthew 15:18

Read Matthew 15:1–20; John 15:3

The Pharisees continued to plague Jesus with their questions. What about traditions to do with food and eating. Why don't your disciples wash their hands before they eat? What's going on here? It was understandable, given that they'd spent so long trying to make themselves right with God through sacrifice and strict obedience. Even today, many people live that way. When we stayed in Jerusalem, in a flat belonging to a Jewish lady, she told us that her kitchen was kosher and we must keep it that way – all the meat products and their utensils had to be kept separate from the dairy products and anything they touched. For the first five days, we tried hard, for her sake. We put the breakfast things in the dairy sink, and the dinner things in the meat sink, and we used the right cutlery and pots and dishcloths . . . and I started to feel pretty good about myself. Then, on the sixth night, I accidentally tipped my milky tea into the meat sink. I had broken her rules and I felt the weight of them. But that night Jesus' words seemed louder to me, and his grace so much deeper. *'You are already clean because of the word I have spoken to you'* (John 15:3). It's not what goes into our mouths or the way we use cutlery that makes us defiled, but it's the things that come *from* our hearts. And Jesus has already cleansed our hearts with his sacrificial love.

- - - - - -

Pray

> *'Lord, we are occasionally drawn to rules, and you speak to us about our hearts. Help us to be amazed again today.'*

Who do you say I am?

'"But what about you?" he asked. "Who do you say I am?"'
Matthew 16:15

Read Matthew 16:13–28

A lot of Jesus' teaching was addressed to 'the crowd' in general. He told them stories, and he healed them, and he challenged them with the gospel message, and he called them to account. Mostly it was addressed to a large audience . . . and that means that it's possible to read it and avoid any questions that become too personal. We just disappear into the crowd! But then, on other occasions, Jesus became intensely personal with his disciples. On this occasion, Jesus asked them, *'"Who do people say the Son of Man is?" They replied, "Some say John the Baptist; others say Elijah; and still others, Jeremiah or one of the prophets." "But what about you?" he asked. "Who do you say I am?"'* (16:13–15). It's the question that it comes down to in the end. It has to be intensely personal. Jesus wanted to know whether the individual disciples actually believed in him. Of course, Peter spoke up. *'You are the Messiah, the Son of the living God'* (16:16). And Jesus blessed Peter. Peter was right! Jesus said that only God can reveal such incredible truth. Of course, it's the same intensely personal question that he directs to each of us today. But what about you? Who do you say Jesus is? Do you know he is the Lord?

- - - - - -

Pray

'Lord, we thank you that you revealed yourself to us in an intensely personal way, as individuals. Help us to hold onto your identity, Lordship and truth.'

How many times?

'Then Peter came to Jesus and asked, "Lord, how many times shall I forgive my brother or sister who sins against me? Up to seven times?"'
Matthew 18:21

Read Matthew 18:21–35

I always wonder what Peter had in mind when he asked Jesus the question, *'How many times shall I forgive my brother?'* (18:21). Was he thinking about the times when he'd argued with his brother Andrew, or with his friends? Was he remembering deep hurt, or current offence? And Jesus said, *'Not seven times, but seventy-seven times'* (18:22). Jesus' answer was meant to startle. Other translations say 'seventy times seven'. It's beyond counting. Then, Jesus told them a parable about a king who had a servant who was indebted to him. The servant pleaded with the king, and the king, in his kindness, cancelled the servant's debt and let him go. But then the servant met a fellow servant who owed him much less, and the servant chose not to forgive him! It's such a confronting parable. We wonder about the unforgiving servant. Why couldn't he forgive? And then we realise that we are the same as that servant. We harbour bitterness and we refuse to forgive. They haven't said sorry! And yet we have been forgiven everything. And we hear Jesus' words as he hung on the cross, surrounded by people hurling insults at him, *'Father, forgive them, for they do not know what they are doing'* (Luke 23:34). Jesus spoke to a crowd that was thirsty for accusation and blame and condemnation, while hanging on the cross, and he spoke in love. He cancelled their debt and our debt. We've been let go.

- - - - - -

Pray

'Lord, help us to forgive today, beyond what we think is possible, because we are forgiven.'

Let the children come

'Jesus said, "Let the little children come to me, and do not hinder them, for the kingdom of heaven belongs to such as these."'

Matthew 19:14

Read Matthew 19:13–14

In the gospel accounts, there are not many references to Jesus interacting with children, but the one that stands out, of course, is when the group of children were brought to Jesus. Back then, in the ancient world, children had few rights and little status. They were often shooed away, which is exactly what the disciples did in this instance. But Jesus was indignant. He took the children in his arms and said, *'Let the little children come to me, and do not hinder them, for the kingdom of heaven belongs to such as these'* (19:14). I often wonder about those children afterwards. Did they grow up and stay in Galilee? Was there ever a moment, perhaps five years later, when a few of them were down by the lake, chatting with their friends . . . and the conversation turned to the man Jesus. Did he really rise from the dead, some of them asked, and if he did, what was he really like? Perhaps one of the children piped up in reply, and said, 'If you want to know what that man Jesus was really like . . . he said come. Everybody else turned us away, and he said come. He took us in his arms and blessed us. That's what he was like. And if he can say "come" to us, he can say come to anyone.'

- - - - - -

Pray

> *'Lord, help us to be childlike in the way we trust you and the way we depend on you, and the way we come to you.'*

It's not fair!

'So the last will be first, and the first will be last.'
Matthew 20:16

Read Matthew 20:1–16

As humans, we are wired to notice a lack of fairness. We see it everywhere – in queues, at school, in competitions, and at work. We comment on it. It's not fair! So, it's interesting that Jesus told a parable that seems, at first glance, to be about unfair practice. A landowner hired workers for his vineyard. Some of them were hired at 6am, others at 9am, then at noon, at 3pm, and at 5pm. Yet at the end of the day, the landowner paid them all the same amount. Of course, they began to grumble, but the landowner replied and said, *'I am not being unfair to you, friend. Didn't you agree to work for a denarius? Take your pay and go . . . Don't I have the right to do what I want with my own money?'* (20:13–15). It's a striking story of grace. The landowner went out repeatedly, *himself*, to look for the workers (which was unusual back then), and he invited them in. He cared for them because they had no work and he gave them each a denarius, according to his own generosity. It's striking because it points us to the most incredible, wonderfully fair invitation ever – offered to us all, by God, and made possible through Jesus. Whoever we are, whatever we're doing, or however many years since we heard the gospel, God invites and welcomes us . . . because, in truth, we are all the 'late worker', and we've all been offered extravagant gifts, not wages.

- - - - - -

Pray

> *'Lord, forgive us for being high and mighty about what we deserve, or are owed because, in truth, we deserve nothing. May this story seep into our hearts and change the way we think about grace and fairness.'*

Without delay

'Without delay he called them, and they left their father Zebedee in the boat.'

Mark 1:20

Read Mark 1:1–45

Mark's gospel begins quite abruptly compared to the accounts of Matthew and Luke. It offers no explanation of the birth or early life of Jesus. Instead, it begins immediately with John the Baptist, who came and prepared the way for the One more powerful than him. And then Jesus came from Nazareth. He was baptised, he was tempted, and then he proclaimed the good news. Everything happened so quickly. The time had come! The disciples left their nets and followed him. Without delay, Jesus called them. There was urgency! And then Jesus began to teach, and the *news about him spread quickly over the whole region of Galilee'* (1:28). Every day, something happened 'immediately' or 'at once'. Reading Mark is almost like watching a film on high speed. It's the pared-down, surprising, unfathomable story. God himself came to earth in the person of Jesus Christ of Nazareth, and the crowds came from everywhere (1:45). I love that description. When God is at work, things happen, and the crowds come from everywhere! Jesus was the kind of person that crowds would be drawn to! And the message was one that they desperately needed. *'The Kingdom of God has come near. Repent and believe the good news!'* (1:15). The people urgently needed to respond. And on the days when we think that we have all the time in the world to obey or to respond or to listen to Jesus, we need to read the Gospel of Mark again.

- - - - - -

Pray

> *'Lord, bring us back to a place of urgency, and limited time, and a response to your incredible story today.'*

The power to forgive and heal

'He got up, took his mat and walked out in full view of them all.'
Mark 2:12

Read Mark 2:1–12

The crowds kept coming to see Jesus, and one day there were so many of them that they couldn't fit in the house. Some spilled out into the street, and others squashed up against each other, no doubt wondering what was going on. But then in the middle of it all, a body was lowered down from the roof and landed in front of Jesus. Some people started shouting and saying, 'What are you doing?' But Jesus spoke to the paralysed man. *'Son, your sins are forgiven'* (2:5). No wonder they had questions, *'He's blaspheming! Who can forgive sins but God alone?'* (2:7). Jesus, however, knew what they were thinking, and he said, *'Which is easier: to say to this paralysed man, "Your sins are forgiven," or to say, "Get up, take your mat and walk"? But I want you to know that the Son of Man has authority on earth to forgive sins'* (2:9–10). Jesus had that authority. He told the man to get up, take his mat and go home. And the man did. Those legs that had never moved, came out from under the blankets and the man stood up, and walked out into the sunshine. That day, the unthinkable happened. Jesus proved to the crowd who he was. And every response to Jesus after that moment hinged on it. He was the bringer of hope, the healer, *and* the One who could forgive sins.

- - - - - -

Pray

> *'Lord, your ways are glorious, and full of hope. Help us to be people who trust you, who listen to you, and walk out into the sunshine.'*

The growing seed

'All by itself the soil produces corn – first the stalk, then the ear, then the full grain in the ear.'
Mark 4:28

Read Mark 4:26–29

This is one of my favourite parables, and it is only recorded in Mark. I find myself reading it whenever I feel stuck, or limited, or as if I'm not getting anywhere in regards to fruitfulness as a follower of Jesus. Jesus said to the people, *'This is what the kingdom of God is like. A man scatters seed on the ground. Night and day, whether he sleeps or gets up, the seed sprouts and grows, though he does not know how. All by itself the soil produces corn – first the stalk, then the ear, then the full grain in the ear'* (4:26–28). It's amazing. All by itself the soil produces grain! Whether the man sleeps or gets up, the plant grows! There is mysterious power in seeds, and Jesus was saying, that's what the gospel message is like. The gospel truth is like a wonderful, mysterious seed, full of life . . . and God makes the plant grow. The one who scatters the seed doesn't always need to know where the seeds end up, or how God uses them. The Holy Spirit is at work! And it's amazing that we all scatter seeds of gospel hope every day – through the way we live and love, and share stories, and encourage each other in God's truths. And it's God who makes the plants grow and produce grain, in his time. It's such an encouragement today.

- - - - - -

Pray

'Lord, we have been easily discouraged. Help us to be amazed again at your unseen, mysterious work in the hearts of your people and in your world.'

Do you want to be great?

'Instead, whoever wants to become great among you must be your servant.'
Mark 10:43

Read Mark 9:33–37; 10:35–45

This is a fascinating interaction. When the disciples came to Capernaum, Jesus asked them, *'What were you arguing about on the road?'* (9:33). The disciples kept quiet because they had been arguing about which of them was the greatest. Two things amaze me – that Jesus knew exactly what they were thinking on the road, and secondly, that the disciples were arguing, out loud, about which of them was the greatest. Were they saying, 'I'm better than you?' Or, 'I've been more faithful.' Or, 'He loves me more!' We don't know. But we do know that Jesus said to them, *'Anyone who wants to be first must be the very last, and the servant of all'* (9:35). Jesus' reply is so stunning in a world where the rulers of the age paraded their authority and greatness to anyone who would listen. Later, when James and John asked Jesus for the best seats in glory, Jesus replied that they weren't his to give. He said, *'Whoever wants to become great among you must be your servant'* (10:43). Be humble, be grateful, be like the servant. And in societies where servants are still in existence, the distinguishing thing about them is that they're often *grateful*. Without work, they know they would be on the streets, hungry. It's the same for us. Without the grace and mercy of God, we know that we would be outside the kingdom, perishing. And as we remember that, we grow in gratefulness to God, and we grow in our longing to serve.

- - - - - -

Pray

'Lord, we see the humility of Jesus, and it stuns us. Please make us more like him.'

Receive it like a child

'Truly I tell you, anyone who will not receive the kingdom of God like a little child will never enter it.'

Mark 10:15

Read Mark 10:13–16

When Mark described the children coming to Jesus, he recorded an extra word from Jesus. As well as saying (as recorded in Matthew 19:14), *'Let the little children come to me, and do not hinder them, for the kingdom of God belongs to such as these,'* Jesus also said, *'Truly I tell you, anyone who will not receive the kingdom of God like a little child will never enter it.'* It's a striking sentence. We must receive the kingdom of God like a little child. We must receive it as a gift. Not long ago, Darren and I went to visit our niece on her fifth birthday. We gave her a pink woolly hat with two pompoms on the end. She was so delighted. First, she tucked the pompoms around her neck. Then she danced a bit and watched them jiggle. Then she rubbed them on her cheeks to see how soft they were. She received her gift like a child! She didn't stop and wonder if she was worth it. She didn't expend effort in order to be more loved. She was just loved, and she received her gift with smiling, wonderful delight. It reminds me that we too can receive the kingdom of God like a child.

- - - - - -

Pray

'Lord, we confess that we are often rude or indifferent or ungrateful in response to your gifts. Please help us to receive the kingdom like a child.'

Pouring perfume

'Now which of them will love him more?'
Luke 7:42b

Read Luke 7:36–50

Do you ever wonder about the woman who poured perfume on Jesus' feet? Did she feel small or ashamed as she walked to Simon the Pharisee's house that day? Did she wish things were different? Had she heard much about Jesus? The text says that she arrived with an alabaster jar of perfume. She had heard that Jesus was dining with Simon the Pharisee, and she brought the only gift she could. When she got there, she crouched behind Jesus, at his feet. She wet his feet with her tears, and she kissed them, and she poured perfume all over them until the smell of it filled the corners of the room. Of course, Simon was outraged. Didn't Jesus know what kind of woman she was? Didn't he know what she did?! Yet in response, Jesus told Simon a story about two men. The two men both owed money to a money-lender (and one of them owed more than the other), but both were forgiven. *'Now which of them will love him more?'* It's a needed question, for all of us. The one who had the bigger debt forgiven will love him more! The woman was forgiven much, and she loved much. Simon, on the other hand, didn't seem to acknowledge his need for forgiveness. He was too busy pointing out the need in everyone else. It's an easy thing to do.

- - - - - -

Pray

> *'Lord, we come to you needing grace, like the woman, and like Simon. We want to be people who are overwhelmed with your forgiveness, and who pour out your love in response.'*

Jesus calmed the storm

'He commands even the winds and the water, and they obey him.'
Luke 8:25b

Read Luke 8:22–25

Back in the time of David, or of Solomon, or of Ezra, when the people were anticipating the Messiah and what he would do, I wonder if they imagined storms. Did they picture the kind of Messiah who could speak sternly to the wind? Perhaps they thought the Messiah would bring restoration in the form of healing their land and their relationship with Yahweh, but did they have anything else in mind? When Jesus came, it's simply amazing that he brought restoration in every way. The lost were found, the shameful were forgiven, the crippled were healed . . . and as well as that, Jesus spoke to the chaos of the waves. One day, Jesus and his disciples got in a boat and they went to the other side of the lake. On the way, Jesus fell asleep and, as he did, a squall came up on the lake. The boat was being swamped and the group were in great danger, so the disciples began shouting at Jesus, waking him up! Jesus got up, and he rebuked the wind and the raging waters. He told them to be still, and they were still. The storm obeyed him. Peace and safety were restored. This is the restoring hand and voice of Jesus! This is the restoration that we all need. In fact, the more we sit at the feet of Jesus, the more we will experience restoration of soul and mind – until he returns, or until we go to him.

- - - - - -

Pray

'Lord, we long for your kingdom of restoration. Help us to be a part of it, more and more. And help us to have faith in you on the chaotic days, as well as the calm ones.'

Called by name

'Jesus asked him, "What is your name?"'
Luke 8:30

Read Luke 8:26–39

After Jesus and his disciples reached the other side of the lake, they were officially in Gentile country. There were pigs and caves and a man ravaged by demons. It was an unclean place! Yet Jesus, the holy One of God, had gone there deliberately. And the man he met first was an outcast, and very distressed. Interestingly, the first thing Jesus asked the man was, *'What is your name?'* (8:30). Jesus didn't say, 'What's wrong with you?' Or, 'How long have you been like this?' Or, 'Have you tried talking to the local authorities about this?' He asked him his name. And then, having authority over absolutely everything, Jesus ordered the evil spirits to leave the man, and they did. They went into the pigs and they were drowned in the lake. Afterwards, everybody from the town gathered around the man, and they were terrified! They even asked Jesus to leave. But Jesus spoke to the restored man, and he said, *'Return home and tell how much God has done for you'* (8:39). The man did, and he became the first evangelist to the whole area. It's a wonderful account! In some ways, though, the man represents all of us. We are all unwell, even those of us who think we're quite normal. We're unwell, but we begin to be well as we respond to Jesus. Amazingly, he also knows us, and he calls us by name.

- - - - - -

Pray

> *'Lord, this is remarkable. It moves us to want to be the kind of people who go all over the town and share what you have done for us.'*

The bleeding woman and the dead girl

'But he took her by the hand and said, "My child, get up!"'
Luke 8:54

Read Luke 8:40–56

When Jesus arrived back on the other side of the lake, there was a crowd waiting for him. Amongst the crowd there was a synagogue leader named Jairus, whose 12-year-old daughter was dying. He must have been desperate. So Jesus went to his house, but along the way, the crowds increased, and so did the need. A woman who had been bleeding for 12 years risked everything. She went into the crowd, unclean, and she touched Jesus, and she was completely cured! Jesus said, *'Who touched me?'* (8:45). And the woman came, trembling at his feet – the woman who'd been banished and hidden, admitted in front of everyone that she'd touched him and that she'd been healed. Jesus, in a beautiful moment, called her 'daughter'. It was the only time Jesus called anyone daughter. He said, *'Daughter, your faith has healed you. Go in peace'* (8:48). But then, someone arrived from Jairus' house, saying his daughter had died! It was too late! This is such a breathtaking story! Jesus went to the house anyway (even though the people laughed at him), and he took the girl by the hand (even though she was also unclean) and he said, *'My child, get up!'* (8:54). And she did! This story is full of wonderful hope! It's what happens when a powerful God stands among us. It's meant to be astonishing. It's meant to point us to God's restoration now, as he changes our point of view, and for ever, as he brings in his kingdom, in his timing.

- - - - - -

Pray

'Lord, we want to seek you with the same courage that Jairus and the bleeding woman sought you, and we want to live as people of hope today.'

The transfiguration

'This is my Son, whom I have chosen; listen to him.'
Luke 9:35

Read Luke 9:28–36

After Jesus again predicted his death, Luke records that Jesus took Peter, James and John, and they went up a mountain to pray. While Jesus was praying, the appearance of his face began to change and his clothes became as bright as a flash of lightning! Then, as if that wasn't enough, two men – Moses and Elijah – appeared out of the blue, in glorious splendour, talking with Jesus. It's an amazing link with God's long story. We know that Moses and Elijah both faithfully pointed to Yahweh, and yet they both disappeared from the narrative in strange ways. Moses died in Moab, *'but to this day no one knows where his grave is'* (Deuteronomy 34:6). Even more strangely, Elijah *'went up to heaven in a whirlwind'* (2 Kings 2:11). But then . . . after centuries, both these men suddenly appeared on the mountain, talking with Jesus, and speaking about his departure. Peter saw them and said the first odd thing that came into his head. He suggested they build shelters. But while he was speaking, a cloud covered the mountain, and a voice from the cloud said, *'This is my Son, whom I have chosen; listen to him'* (9:35). It's the same voice that we heard at Jesus' baptism. It's the same identification. This is God's Son! It matters! Listen to him! He is loved and chosen! It couldn't get any clearer, but we also avoid, ignore, and drown out God's voice to us, in Christ.

- - - - - -

Pray

'Lord, help us to learn from Jesus today; help us to be like him, and listen to his life-changing words.'

The Good Samaritan

'Jesus told him, "Go and do likewise."'
Luke 10:37b

Read Luke 10:25–37

There is something about travelling from Jerusalem to Jericho, even these days. The road heads out of Jerusalem's green hills, and then drops 2,500 feet, descending into barren, rugged, desert country. It certainly isn't a place for a picnic! And it was on this lonely road that Jesus placed his story of sacrificial love. There was a man going from Jerusalem to Jericho, he said, who fell into the hands of robbers. Well, of course he did. Jesus' audience knew that road! And the man was stripped and beaten and left half-dead. Then a priest passed by, and kept going. So did a Levite. They did nothing at all to help the man. But a Samaritan man (who was ethnically unclean) stopped and took pity on the anonymous man, bandaging his wounds and caring for him more than could ever be expected. The Samaritan was the neighbour, because he showed mercy and love. That's the new definition of a neighbour! In a society where relationships had always been defined by birth or status, Jesus was saying something completely outrageous. There are no limits on loving our neighbours, he said, or boundaries that define them. This is the new kingdom that we're a part of! And this is the hardest, daily command, to go and do likewise.

- - - - - -

Pray

> 'Lord, we know this familiar story, but we want to respond with the same gut-wrenching need to love, daily, because we know that we've been loved.'

The better thing – Mary and Martha

'Mary has chosen what is better, and it will not be taken away from her.'
Luke 10:42b

Read Luke 10:38–42

It's easy to read this short account of Mary and Martha, and to feel quite challenged, or even defensive on behalf of Martha. When I was parenting three small boys in Nepal, without electricity or a dishwasher, I often felt that way! There was so much to do around the house! And I would think, 'Poor Martha. Someone has to help her!' Of course, we're told by Luke that Martha opened her home to Jesus, which was great, and then she became distracted by the preparations, while Mary did the better thing – she sat at the feet of Jesus. In the bigger sphere of Luke's narrative, Mary was being contrasted with the expert in the law, in the previous verses, who *'stood up to test Jesus'* (10:25). The expert was not approaching Jesus humbly, or wanting to learn, as Mary was. Mary *sat and learnt*. It's wonderful that, as Mary took her place by Jesus' feet (and as Jesus commented on it), he was revealing something brilliantly new and subversive. Mary was sitting in a place that had been traditionally reserved for male disciples. She was now included with them! Jesus said, *'Mary has chosen what is better, and it will not be taken away from her'* (10:42). It's a wonderful reminder for all of us that we are all welcome at the feet of Jesus, regardless of gender or race or expectations. We are all welcome when we come humbly, acknowledging our need.

- - - - - -

Pray

> *'Lord, we thank you that the better place to be is learning from you. Help us to let your words and truth linger in our souls, in all the demanding situations we find ourselves in today.'*

Fear the One

'I tell you, my friends, do not be afraid of those who kill the body and after that can do no more.'

Luke 12:4

Read Luke 12:1–12

We don't often quote these words of Jesus. They're a bit too confronting. Maybe we've become so focused on safety and security that it's difficult to hear what Jesus was saying. Fear the Lord, he said, who has the authority to judge. Don't fear those who can kill the body. Don't let fears over safety rule your life. We have friends who serve in Pakistan. They have raised their four children there, and they're involved in a music ministry which is impacting thousands. It's wonderful, and they need help, but very few people will join them in Pakistan. My friend said, 'We don't want to do foolish things, and we're careful, but there's no guarantee of safety wherever we live. And in fact, Jesus said to fear the One who has the authority to judge. But so often in western society, we're fearful of the things that can destroy our bodies, and we're not fearful of the things that can destroy our souls. Why aren't we terrified of the things that are destroying our souls? Who's really in the most danger?' It's a challenging question. What things are impacting our souls in unhelpful ways today? How can we change their impact? What could we do to change the way we view safety and risk?

- - - - - -

Pray

> 'Lord, we thank you for your promise that as we acknowledge you, you will acknowledge us and give us safety with you for ever. Please let that sit deeply in all those moments when we fear the wrong things.'

Storing up

'Then who will get what you have prepared for yourself?'
Luke 12:20b

Read Luke 12:13–21

There must have been times for Jesus when he knew the crowds weren't really listening, or understanding. On this particular day, Jesus had been teaching about fear and eternal dwellings and being valued more than the sparrows. Then a man piped up and said, *'Teacher, tell my brother to divide the inheritance with me'* (12:13b). It's no wonder Jesus issued a warning about greed! Hadn't the man been listening? But then Jesus told another story. *'The ground of a certain rich man yielded an abundant harvest'* (12:16). And the key to his story is in the second word. The 'ground' yielded an abundant harvest – not the man, nor his clever farming techniques, or abilities. The 'ground' yielded the crop. Everything the man had (and we have) is a gracious gift from God, and yet the man wanted to store it all up for himself. He didn't ask how he could use his extra grain to bless others, he just built bigger and bigger barns, storing it up for a time that never came. The man died in the night, and the birds ate his grain. This is a profound picture for all of us who follow Jesus. Let us overflow with thankfulness, so that the resources we have are poured out generously – our words, our food, our spare bedrooms, our knowledge and skills, and everything we have – to those in need of hope and restoration. Let us be people who know how to bless others, and who live each day with that thought at the very centre.

- - - - - -

Pray

> *'Lord, help us to be on guard against all kinds of greed – especially the kinds of greed that we don't even notice.'*

Watchfulness

'Be dressed ready for service and keep your lamps burning.'
Luke 12:35

Read Luke 12:35–57

When we lived in Nepal during the civil war, our mission agency told us to have a 'go-bag' ready by the front door, full of essential things (like spare clothes, a toothbrush, and our official documents), just in case we had to evacuate the house and escape to India. One day, we did actually use it . . . but more than that, having it by the front door for years changed me. I realised that our time in Nepal was temporary, by necessity. We had to develop deep relationships, and live faithfully, but be ready to go at a moment's notice. We had to loosen our grip on 'things' and hold more tightly onto relationships, and an eternal perspective. We had to be ready to go! And as we lived like that, it made me want that same eternal perspective on our return to Australia. In this passage, Jesus' words to the disciples were of a similar vein. He was saying to them, be ready. The master could come back at any time, so live like it matters. Live faithfully and deliberately. Don't be caught unawares! Keep eternity in mind. He was saying that our time on earth is temporary, by necessity. It's a needed reminder for all of us, because when we go home to be with Jesus, or when he returns, we won't even be taking our go-bag with us. We'll just be going home.

- - - - - -

Pray

'Lord, our hearts are easily distracted. Please remind us to keep watch and be ready for your return today.'

Tiny things

'It is like a mustard seed, which a man took and planted in his garden.'
Luke 13:19

Read Luke 13:18–21

Jesus knows about tiny things. When he spoke to the crowd about the kingdom of God, he immediately compared it to the tiniest thing – a mustard seed. He said, *'What is the kingdom of God like? What shall I compare it to? It is like a mustard seed, which a man took and planted in his garden. It grew and became a tree, and the birds perched in its branches'* (13:18–19). Jesus was saying, we mustn't worry about the size of something, or its fruitfulness. God makes it grow. God is always at work, even when we can't see it, and he brings the growth, and uses the growth, for his purposes. He turns seeds into trees! Near where Darren and I live in the Blue Mountains, there are spectacular limestone caves. They're visited by thousands of tourists each year. But the forming of the caves took thousands of years. Over centuries, tiny drops of water entered the caves through cracks in the limestone, fell to the floor, and left behind tinier amounts of calcite crystal, forming stalagmites and other formations. But it was slow and tiny. At its quickest, a stalagmite grows 1cm every 100 years – one tiny drop after another. It reminds me of the mustard seed, and that life is often slow. It can feel like our walk with God, our ability to trust him, our growth, is really slow. Today it was a tiny drop. But God is at work, building his kingdom through tiny drops and seeds, making it grow. And one day birds will perch in the branches.

- - - - - -

Pray

'Lord, we thank you that you understand tiny things, and you make them grow in your timing.'

The banquet

'But when you give a banquet, invite the poor, the crippled, the lame, the blind, and you will be blessed.'

Luke 14:13–14

Read Luke 14:1–24

By the time Jesus was teaching the crowds about seeds and watchfulness and the kingdom of God, he was on his way to Jerusalem. Luke says that Jesus was full of joy, through the Holy Spirit (Luke 10:21) as he journeyed, no doubt anticipating that his work was nearly done, and he was going home to his Father. No wonder he was excited! Along the way, Jesus also shared meals and banquets. Hospitality was important. On this particular occasion, while Jesus was eating at the house of a prominent Pharisee, he challenged the people about seating and status and invitations. Open the door, wide, he said! Leave behind thoughts of self-promotion or benefit. Take the least important place . . . because God's heart is for the excluded, and it always has been (as we read back in Joshua 6). But in the time of the Pharisees, there was a tendency for their invitations to become exclusive and narrow. They even made new laws over who could attend a banquet. And Jesus was saying invite the poor, the crippled, the lame, the blind, and the ones who can't repay you. Bring them in! *'Go out to the roads and country lanes and compel them to come in, so that my house will be full'* (14:23). I love the use of the word 'compel'. Jesus didn't say, be nice to them if they arrive at your house. He said, go out and *compel* them to come in!

- - - - - -

Pray

> *'Lord, this is still a challenging word for us. We want to be people who have such a love for humanity that we naturally go out and invite . . . and compel them to come in.'*

The father who runs

'But while he was still a long way off, his father saw him and was filled with compassion for him; he ran to his son, threw his arms round him and kissed him.'

Luke 15:20

Read Luke 15:11–31

This has to be the most wonderful parable ever told. Jesus was speaking to the tax collectors and the sinners (who were gathering around him), and at the same time he was speaking to the Pharisees and the teachers of the law (who were muttering against him). Yet somehow, Jesus managed to tell a story that spoke to both groups. He said that there was a man with two sons. One of the sons went away and spent everything – his entire inheritance – and then turned back, and the father ran to him. The father threw his arms around him and kissed him! There was so much celebration and rejoicing! The son who had been lost was found! But the other son grumbled. Why didn't his father ever celebrate over him? The other son poured out his resentment, and he refused to come inside the house. But Jesus was saying, this is what God is like – he's like a father who runs to us, and who rescues and finds and rejoices. He celebrates over us! There is so much rejoicing! But we all have a choice. We can notice the love of the father and respond to him, or we can continue in our resentment and grumbling, looking to our own troubles, or pointing out everybody else's, hardly even aware of grace.

- - - - - -

Pray

> *'Lord, help us realise that you have rescued us, and help us to respond again to your beautiful embrace.'*

The shrewd manager

'You are the ones who justify yourselves in the eyes of others, but God knows your hearts.'
Luke 16:15

Read Luke 16:1–15

Of all Jesus' parables, I find this one the most mysterious. Was Jesus commending dishonesty? Was he encouraging his disciples to use their resources like the world does? Jesus said there was a rich man who had a dishonest manager. The dishonest manager was about to be sacked, so he called in his debtors and he reduced their debts. Then, the master commended him for acting shrewdly. And Jesus said, *'For the people of this world are more shrewd in dealing with their own kind than are the people of the light. I tell you, use worldly wealth to gain friends for yourselves, so that when it is gone, you will be welcomed into eternal dwellings'* (16:8–9). It's not altogether clear but maybe Jesus was referring to being deliberate. There are people in this world who are incredibly invested and deliberate in their use of wealth and resources. They are good at accruing wealth! Can we be as invested and deliberate in our ministry of sharing God's love with our friends, that they too might trust him? Can we be people who accrue friends in heaven? Yet, as well as that, Jesus spoke strongly against the love of money. *'No one can serve two masters . . . You cannot serve both God and Money'* (16:13). It's true. And sometimes we don't even know our hearts. But God does, and he longs to make us more like him in every part of life.

- - - - - -

Pray

'Lord, we are so rich in comparison with many others in the world. Please challenge us to use our worldly wealth and resources for your honour and glory.'

One said thank you

'He threw himself at Jesus' feet and thanked him – and he was a Samaritan.'

Luke 17:16

Read Luke 17:11–19

Jesus continued on his final journey to Jerusalem, and along the way he met ten men who all suffered from leprosy. The ten men called out to Jesus to have pity on them, and he did. He spoke to them, and he sent them on their way, and they were healed! It's amazing! Of the ten, though, only one of them came back. He *threw himself at Jesus' feet and thanked him – and he was a Samaritan* (17:16). It's such a wholehearted response to Jesus, praising him and acknowledging who Jesus was and what he had done for the man. But Jesus noted that only one man came back, and the *only* man who came back and responded wholeheartedly was a Samaritan – a foreigner. What happened to the other nine? Amidst the other parables and teaching in this section, the account highlights the need for response to Jesus, back then and now, today. Have we responded wholeheartedly today? Have we said thank you? Have we fallen at Jesus' feet, praising God in a loud voice, or even a quiet voice? Could we be more deliberate in this regard? I find this naturally hard but, recently, I added in a thankful habit. Whenever I walk around our neighbourhood now, I try to say thank you to God for his mercies, on every corner, or telegraph pole. There are quite a few telegraph poles! It's actually changing the way I innately think. I wonder if there are ways that we can each continue to re-wire thankfulness?

- - - - - -

Pray

'Lord, we are self-absorbed, and it's easy to disregard you, or not respond wholeheartedly. We want to praise you today, exuberantly.'

The ten minas

'So he called ten of his servants and gave them ten minas. "Put this money to work," he said, "until I come back."'
Luke 19:13

Read Luke 19:1–27

Jesus had much to say about resources and wealth and skills, and how we use them. On this particular occasion, he had been chatting with Zacchaeus, the wealthy tax collector. He had even shocked everyone by going to Zacchaeus' house and eating with him! But Zacchaeus responded to Jesus with his life and his wealth, and Jesus announced that salvation had come to his house. In that context, Jesus told the people another parable about resources. Use what you've been given, he said. If you don't, it could be taken away from you. It's a needed reminder for all of us, but we occasionally wonder about *how* we should use our resources. I often think back to the year we visited a homeless centre in Bishkek, Kyrgyzstan. The manager of the centre was a young man with a wide smile and a love for the people, and an extraordinary gift and training in music. Every day, he sat down at the piano and played the most beautiful music in Russian, for the most degraded people in the city. He played worship songs, and the homeless crept into the building, with their black eyes and swollen hands and missing fingers . . . and they joined in the music, and they sang to God, because the young man's soul was pouring out of his hands. It reminded me that it's not our place to prescribe the use of our gifts, it's our place to honour God with everything he's given us.

- - - - - -

Pray

'Lord, we know that everything we have is from you. Please help us to make good use of our gifts today.'

For God so loved

'For God so loved the world that he gave his one and only Son, that whoever believes in him shall not perish but have eternal life.'
John 3:16

Read John 3:1–21

In John's account of Jesus' life and ministry, he included a story about Nicodemus. Nicodemus was a Pharisee, a member of the Jewish ruling council, and he came to Jesus at night . . . which immediately sounds suspicious. Seemingly, Nicodemus had questions about being 'born again'. Surely it's not possible to fit back in a mother's womb? And Jesus' reply contains the gospel message in its simplest, purest form. He said, *'For God so loved the world that he gave his one and only Son, that whoever believes in him shall not perish but have eternal life'* (3:16). There is eternal life on offer, not earthly re-birth. And it's so much better than we can ever imagine! God longs for us to dwell with him for ever. He doesn't want anyone to perish! It's been his plan since the beginning of time, and it's always been motivated by love. Jesus didn't say, 'For God was so frustrated with the world that . . .' or 'For God was so angry with the world that . . .' He said, 'For God so *loved* the world that . . .' And from the beginning, God had the *world* in mind, not just Capernaum, or Galilee, or Israel. He loved the world. He loved the people that we rush past at the train station. He loved the children in remote Himalayan villages. He loved the old men and women in a nursing home. He loved.

- - - - - -

Pray

'Lord, we thank you that it's your love that brings about your plan. Help us to love the ones we normally ignore . . . because you love them, and you want them home.'

Living water

'Then Jesus declared, "I, the one speaking to you – I am he."'
John 4:26

Read John 4:1–42

John's gospel also includes wonderful lengthy stories about individual interactions with Jesus. One day, Jesus was on his way to Galilee and he was tired from the journey, so he stopped at Jacob's well. As he sat there, a Samaritan woman arrived at the well, and Jesus asked her for a drink. He shouldn't have done that! Back then, Jewish rabbis didn't even speak to their wives in public, let alone outcast Samaritan women. And this particular woman was so dubious that she was at the well alone, at midday. But amazingly, in the course of their interaction, Jesus offered her living water. He knew everything about her, he highlighted her issues, and he offered her hope and life for ever. Then, he told her who he was – the Messiah. Incredibly, it was the only time Jesus revealed his Messianic identity to anyone prior to the trial. The person he chose to tell was an unclean, unwanted woman at the well. No wonder she ran! She believed in Jesus, and she wanted to tell everyone. It changed everything for her and, as a result of her witness, many of the Samaritans believed her story. They believed in Jesus too, for themselves (4:39–42). It reminds me that we're all thirsty, and we all feel shame and disgrace. But there's a better answer. Jesus, knowing everything about us, offers us hope and life for ever. And he can, because he paid for our unworthiness on the cross.

- - - - - -

Pray

'Lord, we thank you for your offer of living water. Help us to respond, and to run to the ends of our street, or the next town, to share the good news with people who are just as thirsty as we are.'

Do you want to be well?

'Jesus . . . asked him, "Do you want to get well?"'
John 5:6

Read John 5:1–15

This is another compelling account. Jesus went up to Jerusalem and he passed by the pool of Bethesda. He saw a man lying there who had been an invalid for 38 years. Jesus said to the man, *'Do you want to get well?'* (5:6). As the reader, we think, of course he did! Why wouldn't the man want to be well? Was there something he was getting out of being unwell? But in the middle of our wondering, Jesus did the seemingly simplest thing. He told the man to get up and walk, and the man did – those legs that hadn't walked for 38 years, stood up and walked. It was another compelling sign pointing to who Jesus was. Yet I often think about the question. 'Do you want to be well?' One of our friends has lived with polio all of her life. She told me that reading this passage changed her. As she read it, she questioned whether she could be well in her wheelchair. Could she find wellness and purpose in Christ, while still in her wheelchair? After praying for some time, our friend retrained as a hospital chaplain and she now serves in a large hospital, sharing her faith and hope with the patients. She says she can be well! And the patients listen to her because they know that she understands suffering. What does it mean for each of us, to find wellness and purpose in Christ today?

- - - - - -

Pray

'Lord, thank you for the difficult questions – the uncomfortable ones that get to the heart of all that we hide, or fail to believe. Help us to believe in you today, and to receive your wellness.'

Always at work

'My Father is always at his work to this very day, and I too am working.'
John 5:17

Read John 5:16–18

After Jesus healed the man by the pool, there was an uproar. The day of the healing had been the Sabbath, and work was not allowed. So, the Jewish leaders began to persecute Jesus, and Jesus defended his actions. He said to them, *'My Father is always at his work to this very day, and I too am working'* (5:17). It was a good answer of course, but it infuriated the Jewish leaders even more! Not only was Jesus healing on the Sabbath, but he was calling God his own father! No wonder they tried to kill him. As well as that, though, it's good to notice the truth in this chapter about what it means to work, and to be 'always at work'. Do we imagine God 'always at work'? Recently, I sat on a headland watching the ocean. The waves rolled in, one after another, relentlessly. They didn't stop, pause, or get distracted. They just kept coming, endlessly, always at 'work'. It made me wonder whether God's purposes are a bit like that. He is relentlessly at work. He doesn't stop his work in the world, or pause, or get distracted. He will keep bringing about his purposes, day after day, in every country, and in every people group, and individual, even when we can't see or imagine it. Our heavenly Father is at work in the world today, wave after wave. Let's let that truth influence our decisions and concerns more and more.

- - - - - -

Pray

> *'Lord, we thank you that you are always at work, and we ask that we would live in such a way that reflects your relentless purposes.'*

As long as it is day

'As long as it is day, we must do the works of him who sent me.'
John 9:4

Read John 4:1 – 9:5

The theme of work in John's gospel is continuous and compelling. In chapter 4, after Jesus met the Samaritan woman, he talked about 'work' with his disciples. He said that he himself needed to finish his work (John 4:34). He said that the fields were ripe for harvest, and it was time to work! Then later in chapter 5, Jesus again mentioned the works his Father has given him to finish (5:36). It was important. Jesus knew what he had come to do, and that his time was limited, so he needed to finish the work – that people might believe in him, and that God's glory might be displayed. Then, after feeding 5,000 people, Jesus told his disciples about work. He said, *'Do not work for food that spoils, but for food that endures to eternal life, which the Son of Man will give you'* (6:27). What Jesus had given them that day was bread, but more important was inner life, eternal life – that's what he'd come to give them, and that's what they were to work for! Still later, Jesus said, *'As long as it is day, we must do the works of him who sent me. Night is coming, when no one can work'* (9:4). It's a good reminder for all of us. Out of our faith in Jesus comes *work*, a compelling desire to love and serve the peoples of the world, in all the ways we can, remembering that it's daytime now, and night is coming.

- - - - - -

Pray

> *'Lord, help us to remember that our time here on earth is limited. Help us to believe in you, and to work for food that lasts.'*

He already knew

'He asked this only to test him, for he already had in mind what he was going to do.'
John 6:6

Read John 6:1–15

The story in John 6 is familiar. Jesus had been teaching the crowd on the far shore of the Sea of Galilee, and the day came to an end. There was still a crowd and they were hungry. But there was no food nearby so Jesus asked Philip what they should do. Philip was a local man so he should have known what to do, but he didn't. He said, *'It would take more than half a year's wages to buy enough bread for each one to have a bite!'* (6:7). There were too many of them! But incredibly, just before Philip replied, there is an amazing sentence. *'[Jesus] asked this only to test him, for he already had in mind what he was going to do'* (6:6). Jesus already had in mind what he was going to do! Jesus was not surprised, or without plans. And we need that reminder today, because we are also confronted by the overwhelming needs of the world, and within our streets. Thirty thousand people starve to death every day. There are 150 million orphans, and 3,700 people groups with no current access to the gospel. But even today, Jesus sees our needy world and our streets, and he is not without plans. He already knows what he is going to do, through us, and we trust that he can bring life and hope, abundantly. Incredibly, he invites us to be part of his good plans.

- - - - - -

Pray

'Lord, we thank you that you already have a plan, millions of them. Help us to notice, and to trust you again today and to be part of your good work in the world.'

Jesus walked on the water

'It is I; don't be afraid.'
John 6:20

Read John 6:16–24

It's fascinating that in John's gospel, John doesn't include much of Jesus' teaching about everyday life. Instead, John's gospel is full of signs. He wants the people to know for sure who Jesus is, as the Son of God. He wants them to believe in him! And the believing will change everything. So John recorded signs – healings and miracles and wonderful provision – and in this case, Jesus' complete power over everything. Jesus' disciples were in a boat and it was dark. A storm came up. And then *they saw Jesus approaching the boat, walking on the water; and they were frightened'* (6:19). No wonder they were frightened! Jesus was doing more than telling the waves to be still, he was walking on top of them! And then he said, *'It is I; don't be afraid'* (6:20). It is Jesus. It is enough. It is God's power and sovereignty on wonderful display. It is a vivid reminder of Yahweh parting the waters of the Red Sea (Exodus 14), and then as they entered the land (Joshua 3). It is Jesus! And he is Lord of the waves and the sea. So the disciples took Jesus on board and they immediately reached the shore where they were heading. The disciples thought they were out of Jesus' sight, or concern, but they never were. He never forgot them, or wavered in his commitment to them. And for us, as believers, there are also dark, stormy days. But God is present. He hasn't left us. We are never out of his sight. He says, *'It is I; don't be afraid.'*

- - - - - -

Pray

> *'Lord, we know who you really are. We know your power over everything, and your care for your people. So, help us to calm down today.'*

Unless the Father draws them

'And this is the will of him who sent me, that I shall lose none of all those he has given me, but raise them up at the last day.'
John 6:39

Read John 6:25–71

There are times in our Christian life when we'd love to be able to convince our friends and family that God exists and has a plan for the world through Jesus. We'd love them to believe in Jesus, who deeply cares for them! And yet these words of Jesus remind us that it's God who works in our hearts, to draw us to himself. Jesus said to the disciples, *'No one can come to me unless the Father who sent me draws them, and I will raise them up at the last day'* (6:44). Back then, the disciples needed that reminder, and we need it today. It's God who works in our hearts, in his time. We only come to God because he draws us. In 2017, I came up against this truth over and over again. I spent all year interviewing people who had come to faith in Jesus out of different religious backgrounds. They all described their beliefs (within Hinduism, Buddhism, Islam, the worship of Voodoo and New Age) and they described the questions they had before. But each one of them said they came to a point, while hearing the gospel, that they 'just knew it to be true'. They said, 'I realised Jesus died for me,' and 'I somehow knew it in my heart,' and 'God worked his will in me.' It's amazing. God draws us to himself, in his time, through the living work of Jesus – the bread of life.

- - - - - -

Pray

'Lord, help us to trust you again today, and to see you in the face of your Son, the Lord Jesus.'

Are we spiritually dry?

'Let anyone who is thirsty come to me and drink.'
John 7:37b

Read John 7:1–44

I don't know about you, but I'm not very good at growing indoor plants. They don't seem to get enough of what they need – whether it's sunlight, or water, or attention. Earlier this year, a friend gave me a beautiful, purple orchid. She said, 'You'll be fine. Just spray it with water most days.' I tried . . . but right in front of my eyes, it wilted. The flowers drooped and the leaves went flat. It was clearly longing for water. At about the same time, I was reading this passage in John 7. Jesus was teaching the crowd at the festival in Jerusalem. He stood and said in a loud voice, *'Let anyone who is thirsty come to me and drink. Whoever believes in me, as Scripture has said, rivers of living water will flow from within them'* (7:37–38). It's an amazing promise of the Holy Spirit, which was to be poured out on the believers at Pentecost, and it's also a reminder that Jesus really was the Messiah, the source of life and living water. But it also made me think . . . do we, as humans, give noticeable signs when we need more water, like my plant? Do we become more impatient, or critical, or envious, when we're spiritually dry? Do we seek more control, or lose sight of God's ways? If someone was looking at us, would they say, 'You need more water!' It's wonderful that Jesus gives such a warm invitation – to drink of his life-giving Spirit – *before* our leaves wilt, or our thoughts wander.

- - - - - -

Pray

'Lord, help us to quench our thirst today, with Jesus.'

The good shepherd

'I am the good shepherd; I know my sheep and my sheep know me.'
John 10:14

Read John 10:1–42

It's amazing that in the time of Jesus, the people were still singing the psalms. They'd been singing them for one thousand years, holding on to the deep truth that the Lord was their shepherd and they lacked nothing (Psalm 23:1). And yet some of the Pharisees were confused and misled and critical. So then, Jesus came along and said that he was the gate for the sheep. Anyone who entered through him would be saved (10:9). And then, equally amazingly, he was the *good shepherd*. And the good shepherd would lay down his life for the sheep, deliberately (10:15). It's a profound imagery because we know that sheep, by nature, are so defenceless and vulnerable. They have nothing to protect themselves with, and they don't even have an aggressive nature. They need help! When Jesus spoke about sheep, he had all of that in mind, as well as all the prophecies and the psalms. He knew that the people had been longing for a shepherd for a thousand years. And Jesus said . . . it's me. I'm the good shepherd. Jesus knew them, and called them by name, and led them out, and gave them life. Incredibly, we too can imagine our names on Jesus' lips. We too can feel the strength of his love and commitment. We too are known today and offered life, in all its fullness. We *are* defenceless and vulnerable, in a world of frustration and groaning, but we are designed in such a way that we respond deeply to the voice of Jesus.

- - - - - -

Pray

'Lord, help us to hear your voice and trust you again today, in this groaning world.'

Waiting

'So when he heard that Lazarus was ill, he stayed where he was two more days.'

John 11:6

Read John 11:1–44

We often see waiting as a difficult thing, or a negative time, when our moments are being wasted. But what if they aren't? John records an account where one of Jesus' friends, Lazarus, became very unwell. His sisters were worried about him, and they asked Jesus to come and help. But Jesus didn't go. He waited where he was for two more days, telling his disciples that the illness wouldn't end in death. It was for God's glory, *'so that God's Son may be glorified through it'* (11:4). Then, after two more days, Jesus got up and went to the sisters, saying that Lazarus was dead, and he was glad he wasn't there, so that they might believe (11:14–15). It was for their sake! It seems strange but, once again, Jesus' greatest longing was that his disciples believed in him. And then, of course, when Jesus arrived in Bethany, he met the two sisters on the road and he wept with them. Then he went to the tomb and called Lazarus out, and Lazarus came out, alive! It was an incredible life-giving miracle, and the people believed in him, which was the point! It was for their sake! Perhaps the story is also for our sake, 2,000 years later. Jesus longs for us to believe in him. And sometimes he uses unexpected waiting, or strange delays, to help us to know him, and to grow our faith and belief in him.

- - - - - -

Pray

'Lord, please use our waiting in good ways, that will bring glory and honour to you. And please teach us about waiting, and the way you view moments and days and purpose.'

The resurrection and the life

'Jesus wept.'
John 11:35

Read John 11:1–44

There is a stunning moment in the account about Lazarus. I try not to rush over it. Jesus went to Bethany, and by then Lazarus had been dead for four days. Martha was grieving, and she immediately rushed out to meet Jesus on the road, saying, *'If you had been here, my brother would not have died. But I know that even now God will give you whatever you ask'* (11:21–22). Martha knew who Jesus was. She trusted him. And then, in the middle of all that grieving and pain and waiting, Jesus told Martha the deepest, most unimaginable truth. He said, *'I am the resurrection and the life. The one who believes in me will live, even though they die; and whoever lives by believing in me will never die'* (11:25–26). Jesus spoke the most profound truth in the middle of the deepest pain and waiting and grief. He didn't speak it when everything was going well, or smoothly. He spoke it to Martha in her terrible pain, and she heard it, and she believed it, while grieving. And then Mary arrived, also falling at Jesus' feet, weeping. In response, Jesus wept. It's the **second thing** that happened in the middle of all that grieving and pain and waiting. Jesus wept. Both are worth reading over and over again. In our worst times of waiting and pain, when everything seems impossible and awful, we hold on to the deepest life-giving truths, and we know that Jesus weeps with us.

- - - - - -

Pray

'Lord, we thank you for the reminder to lift our gaze to Jesus in the middle of our pain and waiting. Thank you that you weep with us, and that the story isn't over yet.'

They cried Hosanna!

'Hosanna! Blessed is he who comes in the name of the Lord! Blessed is the king of Israel!'
John 12:13

Read John 12:1–19

The moment when Jesus raised Lazarus from the dead was completely astonishing. And it had huge repercussions, not just for his immediate family (who rejoiced!), but also for the Pharisees, who plotted to kill Jesus. It was time. Jesus was clearly a threat. But amidst their plotting, the Jewish Passover was about to occur and many people travelled to Jerusalem to celebrate. They heard that Jesus was there, the life-giving miracle worker . . . and they went wild! They took palm branches and they went out to meet Jesus, shouting, *'Hosanna! Blessed is he who comes in the name of the Lord!'* (12:13). They knew who Jesus was – the Messiah, the Saviour, the One for whom they'd been longing – the One riding on the donkey, as prophesied in Zechariah 9:9! So they praised him! In Luke's account, though, the Pharisees told Jesus to rebuke his followers. And Jesus said, *'I tell you . . . if they keep quiet, the stones will cry out'* (Luke 19:40). Imagine that? Somehow, the whole creation, including the stones, knew who Jesus was and wanted to praise him. It was time to shout and sing! It's a stunning reminder because even today, the creation knows who Jesus is, and waits for the day when he will be revealed in glory! But in the meantime, we too have a reason to sing, because we know how the story ends.

- - - - - -

Pray

> *'Lord, it's been a while since we let our hearts rejoice in a completely wild, uninhibited way. Please help us to sing today because of who you are, and because of what you have done for us, for ever.'*

Jesus knew

'Unless a grain of wheat falls to the ground and dies, it remains only a single seed.'

John 12:24

Read John 12:20–50

It's amazing that every day, Jesus knew what was coming next – every single day, including the day after the triumphal entry into Jerusalem. Jesus spoke to the crowds and he knew that it was time. His language changed. Instead of saying, 'The time will come,' he said, *'**The hour has come** for the Son of Man to be glorified'* (12:23). The hour had come and Jesus knew it. He was honest and troubled. *'Now my soul is troubled, and what shall I say? "Father, save me from this hour"? No, it was for this very reason I came to this hour. Father, glorify your name!'* (12:27–28). Jesus knew what was coming next, which must have been an unimaginable thought, but he also knew *why* it was coming. I remember the first time we watched the *Jesus* video with our sons. Our 6-year-old was quiet afterwards, and he said, 'It's amazing that Jesus knew everything that was going to happen to him, and *he still did it*.' Jesus still did it. Jesus knew everything that was going to happen to him, and he still did it, because he knew *why*. He knew that when he was lifted up from the earth, he would draw all people to himself. He could see the end of the story. He could see the joy set before him. He could see redemption. He could see his Father. He was accomplishing the grand purpose for the salvation of the world, and he was going home.

- - - - - -

Pray

'Lord, help us to be so immersed in your grand story that we find our eyes fixed on you, in everything – on the joy of knowing you, and on being with you for ever.'

The sheep and the goats

'And he will separate the people one from another as a shepherd separates the sheep from the goats.'
Matthew 25:32

Read Matthew 25:31–46

In the end, Jesus had some serious things to say to the crowd, about choice and response. He knew that he was about to take on the sins of the world, and that God would draw people to himself, but he also knew that salvation was a gift. He knew that the gift had to be received, and he knew about judgement. So he told the people, *'When the Son of Man comes in his glory, and all the angels with him, he will sit on his glorious throne. All the nations will be gathered before him, and he will separate the people one from another as a shepherd separates the sheep from the goats'* (Matthew 25:31–32). Did his hearers understand? Did they long for eternal life, or did they fear judgement? Did they understand that their responses mattered? Do we? Jesus was saying, be ready, the end will come. And in the end, the separation will not be based on merit (or all the clever or kind things we did this week), it will be a free gift. And as we receive that free gift, we will want to respond to God. Our faith in Jesus will be *made evident* through the way we live and show love to God's people, especially to those most in need. *Out* of our love for God, we will respond in loving service. And it will be so natural and obvious that perhaps we won't even remember doing it.

- - - - - -

Pray

> *'Lord, thank you for your wonderful gift of salvation life. Please turn our faith in you into service, in such a way that it becomes the most natural response in the world.'*

Two copper mites

'This poor widow has put in more than all the others.'
Luke 21:3

Read Luke 21:1–37

After Jesus rode into Jerusalem on a donkey, he spent time teaching the crowds in the temple courts. And that same temple site was the place where Abraham prepared to sacrifice Isaac, and where Solomon ordered the cedars of Lebanon, and where the Babylonians came with their destructive forces, and where the second temple was built in 515BC. It was the site where Jesus came as a boy, listened to the teachers and asked questions. But now, in the last week of his life, Jesus came to teach. As he was speaking, he noticed an old widow, bent and worn. She came and placed two small coins in the temple treasury. They were so small they didn't even make a sound. But Jesus noticed. He said, *'Truly I tell you . . . this poor widow has put in more than all the others. All these people gave their gifts out of their wealth; but she out of her poverty put in all she had to live on'* (21:3–4). It's an astounding story. In the last week of his life, Jesus noticed the unremarkable ones – the ones who were normally hidden, including this widow and her generosity. Right till the end, Jesus' message was the same. Love the Lord your God with everything you have, and store up your treasures in heaven.

- - - - - -

Pray

> *'Lord, we often feel like the widow. Our resources may feel small, and we operate as if out of scarcity, but we want you to change our hearts today, so that they reflect your heart, more and more.'*

He washed their feet

**'Now that I, your Lord and Teacher, have washed your feet, you also
should wash one another's feet.'**

John 13:14

Read John 13:1–17

One Easter Thursday, while we were living in Nepal, we met with our local
friends and read John 13 in Nepali. One of the members of the group
decided we should wash each other's feet to help us understand the Bible
passage. April in Nepal is hot and dusty. It's pre-monsoonal, and in the town
where we lived, everybody walked long distances on dirt paths in leather
sandals. You can imagine the state of our feet. And so, as we washed each
other's feet, we pictured Jesus on that Thursday night before the Passover. He
washed the feet of his disciples. He could have chosen to wash their hands,
or their fingernails, or even their handkerchiefs. But he didn't. He bent
down low and he washed their dirty feet, one by one, until the grime came
out from beneath their toenails, and the smell soaked into his hands. And
then he said, *'Now that I, your Lord and Teacher, have washed your feet, you
also should wash one another's feet'* (13:14). It's remarkable in every way. Jesus
served them. He was the Lord of all, and yet he set an example of humble
service. He knew that he had come from God, and was returning to God, so
he served. And he called us to do the same, because when we know who we
really are (as deeply loved by God, and restored and redeemed), then we will
also want to serve each other and the world.

- - - - - -

Pray

*'Lord, help us to remember what it means to serve. We don't find it easy at
all, but we thank you for your example on the night you were betrayed.'*

The last supper

'I have eagerly desired to eat this Passover with you before I suffer.'
Luke 22:15

Read Luke 22:1–23

Jesus must have celebrated the Passover meal every year of his life, with his family, back in Nazareth or in Jerusalem. Perhaps they reclined at the table, and shared their unleavened bread and lamb, and told each other the stories of the exodus when Yahweh passed over the Israelites. Did Jesus rejoice as he heard the stories, year after year, about the blood smeared on the doorposts, and the hand of Yahweh leading them to wonderful freedom? Did he rejoice in the answers that were still to come, and the need for a final, perfect lamb? We don't know. But we read in Luke's account that Jesus told his disciples that he *eagerly desired* to eat the Passover meal with them on that final night, before he suffered (22:15). He eagerly desired it, even though he knew what was to come. We can picture him savouring the richness of the food and the warmth of his friends, in their final meal together. And then, as well as washing their feet and enjoying their company, Jesus said something startling. He took the cup and the bread, and he said, *'This is my body given for you; do this in remembrance of me'* (22:19). It wasn't normally part of the script! The disciples must have wondered. But, incredibly, decades later, Paul quoted the words of Jesus and reminded the Corinthians to partake humbly in the supper (1 Corinthians 11:23–26). And thousands of years later, we also partake humbly and remember the Lord Jesus who became the sacrificial lamb, and shed his blood for us.

- - - - - -

Pray

> *'Lord, we don't deserve your grace. Help us to examine ourselves, daily, and never forget the cost of your sacrifice for us.'*

Life-giving commands and promises

'Very truly I tell you, one of you is going to betray me.'
John 13:21b

Read John 13:18 – 14:31

After Jesus shared the Passover meal with his disciples, he dipped a piece of bread into a dish and passed it to Judas Iscariot, who went out into the night to betray him. There was only a short time to go. The grand story of God was only hours away from its terrible climax, and so Jesus sat down and he talked to his disciples. He told them the most important things again. He said, *'Love one another. As I have loved you, so you must love one another'* (13:34). He said, *'My Father's house has many rooms . . . And if I go and prepare a place for you, I will come back and take you to be with me'* (14:2–3). He said, *'I am the way and the truth and the life. No one comes to the Father except through me'* (14:6). He said, *'Whoever believes in me will do the works I have been doing, and they will do even greater things than these, because I am going to the Father'* (14:12). He said life-changing, subversive, wonderful things! And the disciples didn't understand them all. Thomas and Philip had questions. Peter made wild promises, but Jesus told him he would deny him. So lastly, Jesus spoke of the most wonderful promise of all. He said that he would send the Holy Spirit who would change them, and teach them, and remind them of everything he'd said before (14:26). He would give them peace.

- - - - - -

Pray

> *'Lord, thousands of years later, we hold onto this same promise of your Spirit and your peace. Help us to be people who are so connected to you, and each other, that others are drawn to your grace.'*

Remain in me

'If you remain in me and I in you, you will bear much fruit; apart from me you can do nothing.'
John 15:5

Read John 15:1–17

Jesus and his disciples left the building. They began their final walk to the Garden of Gethsemane and, along the way, Jesus kept teaching them. He knew that there would be hard days ahead. They would be persecuted, and there would be false teachers. So he said to them, *'Remain in me, as I also remain in you. No branch can bear fruit by itself; it must remain in the vine'* (15:4). It's a wonderful analogy, and so profound. Stay connected to the vine! Make your home in me. Abide in me. You're mine. As the Father has loved me, so have I loved you. Now remain in my love. Keep your connection to me, always! It's amazing that Jesus offered them that possibility. They could connect themselves to the living God. That's where the fruit was! Apart from Jesus, they could do nothing! Centuries later, we need that reminder too. We often live scattered, disconnected lives. We move houses or cities or countries. We become easily influenced by the latest lifestyle fads or offers of superannuation or security. Within all of that, we are to remain *in* Jesus. We are to find our deepest sense of belonging and identity and comfort and life in him, so that we can pour ourselves out into the communities around us. As we stay connected to Jesus, then we will also bear much fruit.

- - - - - -

Pray

'Lord, we find it stunning that you invite us into your life. Please help us to remain in you. And Lord, please also prune us as you see fit.'

Jesus prayed for unity

'I pray also for those who will believe in me through their message, that all of them may be one, Father, just as you are in me and I am in you.'
John 17:20–21

Read John 15:18 – 17:26

It's one of the common questions. What would you do if you had six months to live? What would you pray if you had one hour to go? In Jesus' final hour before he was arrested, he chose to pray for his disciples and the world. He had finished speaking to them. He had told them again about the power of the Holy Spirit who would come and convict them of sin, and guide them, and counsel them, and comfort them. He said it would be better if he went away! He promised them that their grief would turn to joy. They would see him again! And then he prayed for them, earnestly. He prayed that God would be glorified in them. He prayed for unity among the believers. He prayed that their unity would be protected. He prayed repeatedly for unity, for them, and for all those who would come after them who would believe in their message. He prayed for us! . . . because he knew that unity among the believers would reveal the glory of God to a watching world. Two thousand years later, we still need this prayer, desperately. Amazingly, God is still longing to answer it.

- - - - - -

Pray

> *'Lord, we confess that we often struggle to find unity with your body of believers around the world, and within our local church families. We stumble and fall and blame and critique. There is so much that divides us. Please remind us of the power of unity in you, to a watching world.'*

Like drops of blood

'Father, if you are willing, take this cup from me.'
Luke 22:42

Read Luke 22:39–46

If you visit the Garden of Gethsemane, even today, you'll see eight gnarled olive trees. They are large and ancient. Three of them have been dated to the time of Jesus. Perhaps they were the silent witnesses to his anguish. Jesus arrived in the garden and he knelt beneath those trees, and his sweat was like drops of blood. Luke says that Jesus went out *as usual* to the Mount of Olives. He often spent evenings on that hill, praying. But it sounds jarring. There wasn't anything 'usual' about what was about to happen that evening, in the history of the universe. And yet Jesus went out as usual to the Mount of Olives, and then he spoke to his disciples, *'Pray that you will not fall into temptation'* (22:40). The disciples meant well, but they couldn't stay awake. Jesus said it twice, the most pressing and urgent reminder. Stay awake! But they couldn't do it. And while they slept, Jesus prayed, *'Father, if you are willing, take this cup from me; yet not my will, but yours be done'* (22:42). Jesus was fragile. He was fully human. He had authority over the crowd, the sea, the demons, the truth, the universe . . . and yet in that moment he was vulnerable, wishing it was otherwise. Perhaps we don't want to see him like that. But Jesus was fully human, as well as fully divine. If he wasn't, he wouldn't have been able to redeem us. And while Jesus cried and felt dread in the garden, he prayed earnestly for the world, and for us.

- - - - - -

Pray

> *'Lord, we come to you quietly, knowing that our own temptation to sleep*
> *is very great. We thank you for the mercy and obedience of Jesus.'*

Condemned

'Jesus, knowing all that was going to happen to him, went out and asked them, "Who is it you want?"'

John 18:4

Read John 18:1 – 19:16

In the Garden of Gethsemane, Jesus gave himself up. Judas arrived with the armed soldiers and Jesus gave himself up. In some ways, Peter's response makes more sense. Peter drew out his sword! But Jesus said to Peter, *'Put your sword away! Shall I not drink the cup the Father has given me?'* (18:11). In his kindness, Jesus healed the man's ear. And then Jesus himself was arrested, tied and bound up, taken to the high priest, questioned, slapped on the face, and taken to Pilate. Pilate tried to extricate Jesus, but the crowd prevailed in the end. *'Crucify! Crucify!'* they said (19:6). And Jesus was flogged. A crown of thorns was twisted together and put on his head, and a purple robe was put on his body. They laughed at him, at God himself. And then Pilate handed Jesus over to be crucified. At this point, it can sound like the angry crowd won. They prevailed. And yet nothing could be further from the truth. In Matthew's account, Jesus said, *'Do you think I cannot call on my Father, and he will at once put at my disposal more than twelve legions of angels?'* (Matthew 26:53). Even in that moment, Jesus had absolute authority. He yielded himself for us, for all the hurt we've caused . . . so that when we get to the end and stand in front of God, Jesus will say, 'I paid for that.' There is no better news in the universe.

- - - - - -

Pray

*'Lord, we thank you for your astounding love. We can hardly bear it.
Please help us to respond today.'*

Peter denied him

'Again Peter denied it, and at that moment a cock began to crow.'
John 18:27

Read John 18:15–18, 25–27

All the way through the gospel story, Peter eagerly followed Jesus. But on occasions, he got into trouble, including at the end when it really mattered. Jesus was arrested and Peter followed at a distance. A servant girl questioned Peter. *'You aren't one of this man's disciples too, are you?'* (18:17). Peter denied it. And then, it happened again. Peter denied Jesus again. Finally, one of the high priest's servants challenged him, *'Didn't I see you with him in the garden?'* (18:26b). Again, Peter denied it . . . and at that moment a cock began to crow, and Peter remembered, and went outside and wept bitterly (Luke 22:62). Within a few short hours, Peter had gone from being an adamant supporter of Jesus, to a friend who couldn't stay awake, to a man with a sword, and then to a person who denied ever knowing him. How could he do that? But the human instinct for self-preservation is so very strong. I remember one day we were caught up in a riot in Nepal. A group of armed men stormed towards us, and we suddenly found ourselves hiding in a nearby shop, hardly knowing how we got there. Perhaps Peter succumbed to fear. Yet afterwards, he wept bitterly. His heart was so soft. And his story wasn't over. Luke recorded that Jesus also said to Peter, *'But I have prayed for you, Simon, that your faith may not fail. And when you have turned back, strengthen your brothers'* (Luke 22:32). Jesus knew even then, that the story wasn't over, and he had much more in mind.

- - - - - -

Pray

'Lord, thank you that you forgive and restore your people, even frightened ones like Peter and us.'

The crucifixion

**'There they crucified him, and with two others – one on each side and
Jesus in the middle.'**
John 19:18

Read John 19:16–37

John tells us that Jesus carried his own cross to the place of the Skull . . . and
that's where they crucified him, between two others. On his cross, Pilate
prepared a notice which read, *'Jesus of Nazareth, the King of the Jews'* (19:19).
Of course, the chief priests complained, but the words stayed written. And
the soldiers took Jesus' clothes, dividing his garments among them, as it
was described in Psalm 22:18 one thousand years earlier. Then, Jesus cried
out in a loud voice *'My God, my God, why have you forsaken me?'* (Matthew
27:46). He used the words in Psalm 22:1. It must have been agony – utter
desolation. It was Jesus' personal cry to his Father as their bond was
ruptured. And in reply to his cry, there was no answer at all. Jesus was bereft.
And we shudder at the terrible cost, as Jesus bore the sins of the world. We
cannot even fathom it. All we can do is hold our hands out and receive it.
Jesus gave up his spirit. The One who had formed breath and life in the
beginning, who had spoken all things into being in the universe . . . gave up
his life, and his breath, for us. And then, they took his body down. Joseph of
Arimathea asked Pilate for it, and he wrapped the dead body in spices and
strips of linen. It had already grown cold and lifeless. And they placed that
dead, tortured body in a new tomb. It was agony. It was over. It was finished.

- - - - - -

Pray

*'Lord, teach us again about the agony you went through for us. Teach us to
hold our hands out and receive it.'*

Jesus forgave me

'Jesus said, "Father, forgive them, for they do not know what they are doing."'

Luke 23:34

Read Luke 23:26–49

There is a well-known singer in Nepal called Karna Das. He grew up in a small village in west Nepal. His mother worked as a cleaner at the leprosy hospital nearby. And from that small beginning, Karna Das went on to become Nepal's best-loved singer and songwriter of all time. He spent years in the United States, and recently he came to Australia to perform at a series of concerts. In the middle of one of his concerts in Australia, someone asked him how he became a Christian. And Karna Das said that he read the Gospel of Luke and he was amazed. 'When Jesus was on the cross,' said Karna Das, 'All the people sneered at him and they mocked him, saying, "Let him save himself if he's the Son of God." But Jesus spoke to the crowd and he said, "Father, forgive them, for they do not know what they are doing."' Karna Das paused, 'That's why I love Jesus. Because Jesus forgave them, and because Jesus forgave me.' He's right. It's the whole, vast, redemptive story of God, captured in three words: Jesus forgave me. After a night and a morning of relentless accusations and beatings and whips through his skin, Jesus looked at the crowd and he said, *'Father, forgive them, for they do not know what they are doing'* (23:34).

- - - - - -

Pray

'Lord, we thank you for the cross. We thank you that wherever we are in the world, in deserts or Himalayan villages, we can come to you each day, and repeat those incredible words: Jesus forgave me.'

The burial

"'Take a guard," Pilate answered. "Go, make the tomb as secure as you know how.'"

Matthew 27:65

Read Matthew 27:45–66

At noon, while Jesus was still hanging on the cross, darkness came over the entire land. The sun simply stopped shining. And then at 3pm, Jesus spoke. *'It is finished.'* He breathed his last breath and he gave up his spirit (John 19:30). In the same moment, the gospel writers tell us that the temple curtain ripped in two, from top to bottom! The curtain that had separated a holy God, Yahweh, from his people for thousands of years, was suddenly torn in two. And there was more! Matthew tells us that the earth shook, the rocks split, and the tombs broke open! The bodies of many holy people were raised to life. It's amazing! Matthew doesn't even wait till Sunday to tell us about the life-giving power of Jesus. Even in the moment of Jesus' death, there was an eruption occurring. God was breaking out of the temple, bursting into the public arena. Resurrection life was suddenly available to Israel and the nations! It was a whole new, liberating story and Jesus hadn't even been buried yet! But Pilate was worried. He'd been told that Jesus said he'd rise to life in three days, so Pilate arranged a guard. He said, *'Make the tomb as secure as you know how'* (27:65). And they did. They placed soldiers on watch, and they sealed the tomb with a large stone, no doubt hoping that the story was completely over.

- - - - - -

Pray

> *'Lord, we are in awe of your ways and your life-giving power. We long for you to transform and resurrect all the parts of our life that are currently consumed by fear or brokenness.'*

Joy

'Jesus said to her, "Mary."'
John 20:16

Read John 20:1–18

There is a wait on Easter Saturday. Back then, it must have been terrible. It was the Sabbath. The women at home were grieving and helpless. They had prepared the spices and there was nothing else they could do (Luke 23:55–56). Yet somehow, the waiting was needed . . . because Sunday and the empty tomb and glorious joy didn't come easily. Jesus bore the agony of the cross and the separation from his Father. He cried out in desolation, his lungs heaved and he stayed there, for us . . . because he knew what was coming next. After the sun turned black, and the earth trembled, and after the curtain ripped in two, and the mourners cried themselves to sleep, there was a very quiet morning. The women rose first. They went to the tomb, carrying the spices, and they turned the last corner and saw that the stone had been rolled away! Mary Magdalene and then the disciples ran inside and fell on the ground . . . because inside that tomb there was nothing at all – just strips of linen and an empty headpiece. Our Lord Jesus had risen from the dead. And on that early Sunday morning he appeared in front of Mary, calling her by name, and then sending her and the other disciples out to tell everyone . . . because death had been defeated for ever, for all time, for us. It was worth the wait of Easter Saturday, and it's worth the wait and the calling now, to share the story until he comes again, until he makes all things new.

- - - - - -

Pray

'Lord, thank you for Easter Sunday and for the very best news in the world. The tomb was empty and death defeated for ever. Help us to praise you with a joy that never ends.'

Thomas doubted

'Then he said to Thomas, "Put your finger here."'
John 20:27

Read John 20:19–31

No matter where we are, we have doubts. We wake up in the night and wonder. What if it isn't true? Thomas was no different. He wanted tangible proof . . . in a world where people didn't normally rise from the dead. By then, the other disciples had already seen the risen Lord Jesus. They had been hiding away in a locked room, worried about the Jewish leaders, and then Jesus appeared to them! He showed them his hands and his side. They were overjoyed! He was alive! But Thomas wasn't there at the time, and he didn't believe the others. He was adamant. He wanted to see for himself! So, exactly a week later, the whole event was repeated. The disciples were gathered again, with the doors locked again, and Jesus appeared among them. But this time, Jesus spoke directly to Thomas. He said, *'Put your finger here; see my hands . . . Stop doubting and believe'* (20:27). And Thomas believed! It's such a lovely account. Jesus knew everything that Thomas was thinking, and he spoke directly and graciously to him. Then, Jesus sent them all out. Those fearful disciples became people who would die for their faith. But there is also a wonderful line at the end. Jesus said, *'Blessed are those who have not seen and yet have believed'* (20:29b). Jesus was referring to all of us who would come afterwards, and who would also prefer tangible proof, but who would hold on to the amazing eyewitness accounts of the disciples. Jesus rose from the dead!

- - - - - -

Pray

> *'Lord, we thank you that you long for us to believe. Thank you for your kindness in bringing us to faith. Help us to look again to your truth within our doubts.'*

Their hearts burned

'Then their eyes were opened and they recognised him.'
Luke 24:31

Read Luke 24:13–35

On the same day that Jesus rose from the dead, he suddenly appeared to two men walking on the road to Emmaus. Why did Jesus choose to appear to these two and not to anybody else? Or did he appear to others as well and it wasn't recorded? Was it a bit like the shepherds? We don't know why God chose to tell them, but we're glad that he did . . . because once again, the spotlight was on two ordinary people, walking along, confused by recent events. Then Jesus, the subject of their grief and confusion, appeared in front of them, and explained everything to them . . . except they were kept from recognising him until they shared a meal, and then their eyes were opened. Amazing! But then, just as suddenly, Jesus disappeared and the two men said to each other, *'Were not our hearts burning within us while he talked with us on the road and explained the Scriptures to us?'* (24:32). Their hearts had been burning! This is what happens when God is at work in our lives, through his word and his Spirit. We simply know it to be true. Our hearts burn within us, with the wonderful knowledge and truth and joy of the living God, whose plans and purposes are wonderful. Like those two men, we also have that deep assurance, every day, as we read the Scriptures and pray to our gracious Lord. Of course, back then, the two men got up and returned at once to Jerusalem, saying to the others, *'It is true! The Lord has risen and has appeared to Simon!'* (24:34).

- - - - - -

Pray

'Lord, please give us the same joy and assurance and wonder and passion, as we read your word today.'

The warm invitation

'Jesus said to them, "Come and have breakfast."'
John 21:12

Read John 21:1–14

After a tumultuous week that included the triumphal entry, the arrest in the garden, the torture of Jesus, the agony of the cross, the fear of reprisal, the wonder of the empty tomb, and the appearance of Jesus . . . the disciples must have felt overwhelmed and exhausted. They went back to fishing. At least it was familiar. But they didn't catch anything at all. Then Jesus appeared to them and told them to throw their net on the right side. They did, and caught so many fish that they couldn't haul them in . . . in exactly the same way as when Jesus first called them to follow him (Luke 5:7). Peter jumped into the water in response! He knew it was Jesus, the Lord! And when they got to the shore, Jesus had prepared a fire of burning coals with some fish on it and some bread. Jesus said to them, *'Come and have breakfast'* (21:12). It's the loveliest invitation in Scripture. It's so warm and ordinary and thoughtful. It's the heart of God. It's Jesus' words to his tired, overwhelmed disciples. Come and have breakfast. It's even reminiscent of Elijah, hiding terrified beneath the broom tree, yet being offered food and comfort by Yahweh (1 Kings 19:5–6). It's the warm invitation to all of us today. Jesus invites us to a life of following him, and it will be hard and costly at times, but we follow a Saviour who knows our needs, and who cares for us in the most ordinary and overwhelming moments.

- - - - - -

Pray

'Lord, you are holy and magnificent, yet your words are also gentle and kind. Thank you for your warm, gracious invitation. Help us to respond in love.'

Restored for a purpose

'Jesus said, "Take care of my sheep."'
John 21:16b

Read John 21:15–25

After Jesus reappeared to his disciples, and after he fed them fish, he spoke to Peter in their first recorded conversation since Peter denied Jesus three times by the fire. Peter must have been acutely aware of his failure and betrayal. He could never be good enough. And Jesus spoke directly to him. He said, *'Do you love me?'* (21:15). He asked Peter the question three times, and Peter said 'yes' three times, publicly. Jesus was giving Peter an opportunity to repent and to say 'yes' three times, instead of 'no' three times. And Peter was restored. But Peter wasn't restored to be comfortable, or to go back to fishing. He was restored for a *purpose*. Jesus told him what was going to happen next. Peter would be the foundational witness, the shepherd of the early church. He was given an incredible task! He was forgiven and commissioned. It reminds us today that God longs to restore each of us. He gives us a chance to privately and publicly repent. He forgives us, and then he restores us for a *purpose*. And that purpose will be different for all of us, but it will flow out of our love for Jesus and our genuine desire to follow him.

- - - - - -

Pray

'Lord, so often we have confused your grace and mercy with our own desire for comfort or ease. Help us to see again that you restore us daily to yourself, and you restore us for a purpose – to serve you and your world.'

Comparison

'When Peter saw him, he asked, "Lord, what about him?"'
John 21:21

Read John 21:20–23

Within each of us, there is an innate human tendency to compare. Maybe it helps us to answer the question: am I doing okay as a wife, or as a friend, or as a student, or as a follower of Jesus? Should I be doing more? Are my children measuring up, compared to hers? For me, even while we were living in Nepal, I would occasionally compare myself to other missionaries, wondering if my language was measuring up, or if I had enough local friends. It wasn't helpful. It took me years to notice these words of Jesus to Peter. Jesus had just commissioned Peter with a specific, unique task. Peter would lead the early church. It was amazing! But when Peter heard it, he wanted to know if John was getting a better deal, *'Lord, what about him?'* (21:21). And Jesus replied to Peter, *'If I want him to remain alive until I return, what is that to you? You must follow me'* (21:22). It's a crucial reminder for all of us. John was going to be the poet and the writer and the seer. Peter was going to be the shepherd and the preacher. They were given different tasks! And whenever we find ourselves in the same situation, maybe Jesus would also say to us, 'Well, if I want him, or her, to do a hundred remarkable things in this church, and even feed the whole neighbourhood, what is that to you? You must follow me!'

- - - - - -

Pray

> *'Lord, thank you for your personal calling to each of us, to follow you on the paths you have prepared for us. Help us to do that with our eyes fixed on you, rather than on somebody else nearby.'*

The great commission

'And surely I am with you always, to the very end of the age.'
Matthew 28:20

Read Matthew 28:16–20

After Jesus rose from the dead, and after he appeared to his disciples over a period of 40 days, he left. He ascended into heaven. He returned to his Father, in glory! But just before he left, he said one more thing to his disciples. *'All authority in heaven and on earth has been given to me. Therefore go and make disciples of all nations, baptising them . . . and teaching them to obey everything I have commanded you'* (28:18–20). It's a stunning reminder that Jesus reigns today. He has been given all authority in heaven and on earth. And because of that (and because his message is true and glorious and life-changing), he told his disciples to go and share it with everyone else in the world. He told them to make disciples. He told them to pass on his message. That was the point since the beginning of time! God wanted everyone to know him – everyone living in high-rise buildings and mud huts and in flood-prone areas in West Bengal . . . and now it was possible because of Jesus. It's an enormous commission! And it's still our commission today. But the commission was also followed by the best promise ever – the same one given to Abraham and Isaac and Moses and David and all the others, and now extended to all those who follow Jesus. Jesus said, *'And surely I am with you always, to the very end of the age'* (28:20).

- - - - - -

Pray

> *'Lord, this stuns us. After all that we have read about your infinite grace . . . you promise to be with us, to the end of the age. We can hardly grasp it. Thank you.'*

Waiting

'Do not leave Jerusalem, but wait for the gift my Father promised.'
Acts 1:4

Read Acts 1:1–26

Jesus said one more thing to his disciples before he left, recorded by Luke in Acts. *'Do not leave Jerusalem, but wait for the gift my Father promised, which you have heard me speak about. For John baptised with water, but in a few days you will be baptised with the Holy Spirit'* (1:4–5). It's an amazing promise, but the disciples wanted to know what it meant. Would the kingdom be restored to Israel? Would they finally be rid of Roman rule? So Jesus told them that the Spirit's coming was for a far greater, wonderfully transformative purpose. *'But you will receive power when the Holy Spirit comes on you; and you will be my witnesses in Jerusalem, and in all Judea and Samaria, and to the ends of the earth'* (1:8). It's the same promise as in Genesis 12! Everyone will hear about Yahweh and be invited in! And the disciples were going to be a part of it! Then Jesus left. He was taken up into heaven, and two angels promised the disciples that he would return in the same way he left. But they were to wait. Amazingly, the disciples did as they were told. They went back to Jerusalem and they waited. They joined together in prayer, and they prepared themselves for the next season by appointing Matthias. They waited. It teaches us that God also has a plan for our seasons, and some of them involve significant preparation in order to more effectively share his gospel message.

- - - - - -

Pray

*'Lord, sometimes your commands are specific. Thank you for the obedience of your disciples, and for reminding us that even **we** can be part of your great commission through the power of your Spirit.'*

The Holy Spirit came

'And everyone who calls on the name of the Lord will be saved.'
Acts 2:21

Read Acts 2:1–47

After their time of waiting, the disciples were together in one place.
*'Suddenly a sound like the blowing of a violent wind came from heaven . . . All
of them were filled with the Holy Spirit and began to speak in other tongues
as the Spirit enabled them'* (2:2,4). What an amazing, visual, audible,
unquestionable event! The Holy Spirit definitely arrived, with great power,
as Jesus had promised! God's fiery presence came to dwell with them! In
response, a large crowd gathered from every nation, and they *all* heard
words spoken in their own language. The great commission to the nations
had begun! *All* the people heard the wonders of God in their own tongues!
Then Peter addressed the crowd. He told them that God had sent his Spirit,
as Joel had prophesied hundreds of years earlier. He explained that Jesus,
the Messiah, had been handed over to death, but God raised him from the
dead. It was impossible for death to keep him down! And now they were
all witnesses to it. Of course, the crowd responded. They were cut to the
heart. They believed in Jesus, repented and were baptised. They received the
Holy Spirit, all 3,000 of them. Everything was brand new! The frightened,
impetuous Peter had become a man of compelling gospel words. The
monoculture crowd had turned into one that included every nation. Jesus'
promise of life and forgiveness had been thrown wide open, and included
everyone. God's story wasn't over! It was just beginning.

- - - - - -

Pray

*'Lord, we easily put our own lens on world events. Help us to trust you
that your promise of life and forgiveness is for all who are "far off". Please
work in their hearts today, and ours.'*

Miracles

'By faith in the name of Jesus, this man whom you see and know was made strong.'

Acts 3:16

Read Acts 3:1–26

Back in the Gospel of John, Jesus said to his disciples, *'Whoever believes in me will do the works I have been doing, and they will do even greater things than these, because I am going to the Father'* (John 14:12). I wonder if the disciples had questions. Surely it would be impossible to do greater things than Jesus? Yet as soon as Jesus went to his Father and sent the Holy Spirit, the disciples began to be part of God's life-giving, restorative work. Peter spoke to a lame beggar, in the name of Jesus, and the man got up and walked! The people nearby praised God too, in wonder. Of course, when Peter responded, he immediately pointed to Jesus. It wasn't him, he said, it was the power and the name of Jesus. The crippled man had put his faith in Jesus! It was part of God's long story, beginning with Abraham and Moses and all the prophets, testifying to Jesus. It was God's amazing answer and plan of restoration! And it's amazing that, today, we too can be part of the long story of God. In the 2,000 years since the death and resurrection of Jesus, there has been a constant, life-giving testimony to Jesus. His own personal ministry was limited to three years, within a small geographical radius, to one people group. Yet today, the testimony of Jesus reaches to the ends of the earth, to every tribe and nation. We are involved in the 'greater things than these'!

- - - - - -

Pray

'Lord, we thank you for your power at work in the world, through your Spirit, for 2,000 years. Please remind us of your marvellous invitation to be involved.'

Trials

'After further threats they let them go.'
Acts 4:21

Read Acts 4:1 – 5:42

There is always tension here on earth, and that tension will continue until Jesus comes again. On the one hand, as soon as the Holy Spirit came there were wonderful miracles and life-giving testimonies to Jesus. The new kingdom was beginning with great power and joy! But it wasn't all easy. Immediately after the healing of the lame beggar, the authorities came and seized Peter and John. They put them in prison and questioned them. Later, they flogged them. There was persecution. Of course, Peter spoke about the wonderful, life-saving power of Jesus. He didn't deny him this time! He said, *'We cannot help speaking about what we have seen and heard'* (4:20). And the disciples kept speaking, boldly, even within the threats and persecution and floggings. They also prayed fervently and shared everything they had, and the number of believers grew and grew. It's an inspiring beginning to the early church! The disciples were obedient and wholehearted, even within serious persecution, and God was wonderfully at work, which was the important thing. I love the words of Gamaliel, a Pharisee, who spoke to the rulers and acknowledged the bigger picture. *'If their purpose or activity is of human origin, it will fail. But if it is from God, you will not be able to stop these men; you will only find yourself fighting against God'* (5:38–39). It's the same as the word to Mary (Luke 1:37). No word from God will ever fail. None of us can fight against God's plan and mission, even today.

- - - - - -

Pray

'Lord, thank you. Please help us to be people who share your truth boldly, because we know who you are and what you have done, and that all your plans will prevail.'

Stephen was stoned

'While they were stoning him, Stephen prayed, "Lord Jesus, receive my spirit."'
Acts 7:59

Read Acts 6:1 – 8:40

The early church continued to grow, as did the persecution. One day, Stephen, who was a faithful servant of Jesus, was seized and brought before the Sanhedrin. He was questioned and falsely accused, and then dragged out of the city and stoned to death. It's a terrible, violent episode. It's so hard to comprehend. Stephen was a good, faithful man. Surely God could have protected him? And yet, there *is* evidence of protection on that awful day. Stephen was given the words to say, as he recounted God's story. He was given comfort and assurance. Even while he was being attacked, he looked to heaven and saw the glory of God, and Jesus standing with him. He was given absolute assurance! Then, as he died, he was given the capacity to forgive. He prayed that the Lord wouldn't hold this sin against them (7:60). Then, Stephen fell asleep and went to be with his Lord. Afterwards, though, we read something wonderful. God used this event to bring about the growth of the church. The persecution of Stephen resulted in the believers being scattered throughout Judea and Samaria. That was a good thing! They had previously been limited to Jerusalem, but now they proclaimed Jesus wherever they went. Philip went to Samaria, and many people were baptised. Later, he went to Gaza, and was led to explain Isaiah's words to an Ethiopian. Every day, the scattering led to belief as far away as Phoenicia, Cyprus and Antioch. And we wonder, would the believers have gone that far afield if they didn't have to?

- - - - - -

Pray

'Lord, we are humbled by your story. Please help us to share your gospel in all the places that you have surprisingly scattered us.'

Saul was converted

'At once he began to preach in the synagogues that Jesus is the Son of God.'

Acts 9:20

Read Acts 9:1–32

At the heart of the persecution of the early church was a man named Saul who went from house to house, dragging off the believers and putting them in prison (8:3). It was awful. But then something happened. Saul was nearing Damascus, and a light from heaven flashed around him. He fell to the ground and a voice said to him, *'Saul, Saul, why do you persecute me?'* (9:4). That's a fairly direct approach from God! Saul believed. He went into the city, blind. And Ananias was given a vision and told to speak to Saul. It was important. Saul was going to be God's chosen instrument to the Gentiles. He was going to be transformed from the persecutor, to the persecuted. He was going to be a crucial part of the testimony to Jesus! Ananias prayed for Saul and the scales fell from Saul's eyes, and he got up and was baptised. Immediately, Saul began to preach about Jesus in the synagogues (9:20). Everyone was astonished! Wasn't this Saul? What if he hadn't really changed? I find the narrative fascinating. Two years ago, I met a man from Uganda who also used to persecute believers, until he had an amazing conversion on a city street. He was convinced of the gospel and he immediately began preaching about Jesus. The sacrifice for him was significant, but it was also a sign that God was unequivocally at work, even today.

- - - - - -

Pray

'Lord, we thank you for your saving purposes and the way you accomplished the next stage through Paul. Please show us that there are a million stories after Paul, and we can be one of them.'

'I now realise how true it is that God does not show favouritism.'
Acts 10:34

Read Acts 10:1 – 11:30

Even today there is a house in Joppa which is said to have belonged to Simon the Tanner. Peter was staying in that house when Cornelius asked him to come to Caesarea. The amazing thing is that Peter wouldn't normally have gone. He was a strict Jew. He wouldn't have gone into a Gentile home! But immediately prior to the servant's arrival, Peter went to the roof of that house and God gave him a vision, telling him not to call anything impure that God had called clean. So Peter went and he met with the Gentile family, and they all became convinced that God's plan included them. They believed and received the Holy Spirit. And Peter said, *'I now realise how true it is that God does not show favouritism but accepts from every nation the one who fears him and does what is right'* (10:34–35). This is a key moment in Scripture. If Peter hadn't gone to the Gentile home that day, the whole sweep of God's plan would have stalled. But it didn't! God wouldn't let it! From the beginning, Yahweh had the nations in mind. And that night, the Lord poured the Holy Spirit on the Gentiles (10:45). Perhaps it's hard for us to imagine how shocking it must have been for the Jews. They had spent centuries being reminded that they were set *apart* as God's people. But now everyone was being invited in! Everyone was being granted the repentance that led to life. Everyone was welcome!

- - - - - -

Pray

'Lord, even today, we're tempted to show favouritism. Please remind us that that was never a part of your plan, or heart. Please grant us again your wonderful lens on the world.'

God's patience

'For about forty years [God] endured their conduct in the wilderness.'
Acts 13:18

Read Acts 12:1 – 13:52

There are many days when we wonder about God's patience. When will Jesus return? What is he doing? How long must we wait? Surely, 2,000 years is long enough, given the state of the world? But it's helpful to read the summaries of God's story in Acts. When Paul was in Antioch, he explained the gospel again to the people. He told them about God's saving power in the exodus, and his wonderful promises through David, fulfilled in Jesus. He told them that God was their provider and the one who had sustained them. But there is a sentence in the middle that is worth re-reading. *'For about forty years [God]* **endured** *their conduct in the wilderness'* (13:18). Yahweh endured their conduct. He endures. He waited while the people felt the effect of their disobedience. He endured them. Perhaps there are also times when God 'endures' our conduct. He waits, as we learn and grow. He feels it and bears it and endures it . . . while at the same time he keeps speaking, and promising, and loving, and drawing his people to himself through Jesus. And he will keep doing that, around the world, until Jesus returns in glory. There will be a day when the waiting and the enduring will finally be over.

- - - - - -

Pray

'Lord, we thank you for your endurance, and your incredible message that everyone who believes in you is set free from sin. Please help us to respond again today.'

The yoke we can't bear

'No! We believe it is through the grace of our Lord Jesus that we are saved.'
Acts 15:11

Read Acts 14:1 – 15:41

Throughout Acts, there are wonderful stories of conversion and growth in the early church as God was at work. But it wasn't all simple. One day, Paul and Barnabas were in Lystra where they healed a lame man. The crowd decided the gods had come and wanted to worship them. Paul and Barnabas were horrified! They said, *'We too are only human, like you'* (14:15). They pointed back to the living God, who was the maker of everything. But then, the same crowd became influenced by Jews from Antioch, and they decided to stone Paul and Barnabas, on the same day! It went from one extreme to the other. Paul and Barnabas survived, but then there was another problem. Back in Jerusalem, some of the Jews decided that the new Gentile believers needed to follow Jewish law and be circumcised. Paul and Barnabas were once again horrified! Fortunately, Peter spoke up about the law. No one had ever been able to bear the yoke of the law. It was through the grace of the Lord Jesus that they had been saved (15:11). The Gentiles were encouraged to leave behind their pagan temple sacrifices, but they didn't need to adopt ethnically Jewish customs. They were saved by grace. It's the same for us. We've been saved by the grace of God. We are human and sinful, but we are forgiven, and so we extend grace to others who seek the Lord.

- - - - - -

Pray

'Lord, your ways are foreign to us. We're naturally drawn to rules, and yet you want to change our hearts so that generous, sacrificial life flows. Please keep doing that, even when we appear stubborn or proud.'

The gospel spreads surprisingly

'God did this so that they would seek him and perhaps reach out for him and find him, though he is not far from any one of us.'
Acts 17:27

Read Acts 16:1 – 17:34

By the power of the Holy Spirit, the gospel continued to spread. Churches appeared in new, surprising places, and they grew in number and faith. The believers were deeply encouraged. But once again, God's ways didn't seem altogether predictable or smooth. Paul and Barnabas were flogged and thrown in prison, their feet in stocks. While in stocks, though, they sang and prayed, and at midnight there was a violent earthquake. The prison was shaken and the doors flew open! The jailer woke up and was terrified, but Paul and Barnabas stayed inside (even though the doors were wide open), and they shared the gospel with the jailer. He and his family came to faith and were filled with joy. It's an incredible story. God cares about the jailer, and Paul knew that. He shared the gospel wherever he went, in ways that the people could understand, in prison and then later on, equally, at the Areopagus, with well-schooled philosophers. In that case, Paul saw an altar to an 'unknown God', and he told them that their 'unknown God' could indeed be known! The God who had made the world was not far from any of them! Even within the well-schooled group, people responded. They repented and believed, like the jailer (17:34). It's an encouragement to us today. God is still building his church in surprising ways, in prisons and in places of great learning. We can trust him and participate.

- - - - - -

Pray

'Lord, we thank you that even today we can seek you and find you, wherever we are. Please surprise us today with your mission for the world.'

Run the race

**'My only aim is to finish the race and complete the task the Lord Jesus
has given me.'**
Acts 20:24

Read Acts 19:1 – 28:31

There is a well-known fun run in Sydney. It attracts 80,000 people and
every time I run it, I enjoy the buzz of that many people, and the sounds
of our feet on pavement, and the singers on the side-lines encouraging us.
One year, I noticed an old man. He was running the race for his thirtieth
time. He was bent over and shuffling, but he was not giving up. In reading
Acts, Paul often seems like that to me. He was misunderstood, maligned,
arrested and tortured, but he was not giving up. He was shipwrecked and
imprisoned, but he kept going, absolutely sure of the gospel of Jesus Christ.
And towards the end he wrote, *'I consider my life worth nothing to me; my
only aim is to finish the race and complete the task the Lord Jesus has given
me – the task of testifying to the good news of God's grace'* (20:24). Paul knew
why God had put him on earth – to share the message of Jesus with the
Gentiles. And it's true that we each have different tasks, and different ways
of running, and different challenges. But we're each called to serve faithfully,
in all our different ways, until he takes us home. Some days it feels long, or
our legs feel weak, or our toes go numb, but the finish line is up ahead and
there are singers along the way encouraging us. In fact, we could be a singer
today and remind each other to finish the race.

- - - - - -

Pray

*'Lord, we thank you for the days ahead, and for the singers, and for your
glorious task. Help us to delight in it today.'*

Made acceptable

'For all have sinned and fall short of the glory of God.'
Romans 3:23

Read Romans 1:1 – 4:25

Towards the end of Paul's life, he wrote a letter to the church in Rome. It became one of the most influential letters ever written! Back then, the church in Rome was relatively small, perhaps 200 believers, meeting in houses, dwarfed by the Roman Empire. So Paul wrote to remind them of the hope and unity of the gospel. He did it passionately. He said that God has always been wonderfully knowable through his glorious creation. Yet his people turned away. From the beginning until now, there has been distortion in every way – distorted desires, evil, greed, depravity. Nothing and no one is exempt. But God, who is perfectly good and righteous, sent his Son, the Lord Jesus, to liberate the world – to rescue guilty humanity and to restore the groaning creation. It's wonderful news! Everyone who calls on the name of Jesus will be set free! It's still a needed message today. We have failed God and others. We stand in need of his mercy and grace . . . and yet we often recoil from the idea of judgement. Why do we deserve judgement? Surely we have the right to do as we choose? But if we believe in God, who is infinitely good and righteous, then he is also, by his very nature, a hater of evil. If he didn't hate evil, then he wouldn't be good. But he also provided an answer. He took the curse on himself, in Christ, so that when we come to him in faith and repentance, he accepts us.

- - - - - -

Pray

'Lord, we thank you that you are bigger than the sun and the sea . . . and you move towards us in kindness and mercy. Please speak to our stubbornness today.'

A life overflowing with hope

'Not only so, but we also glory in our sufferings.'
Romans 5:3

Read Romans 5:1–20

The best news of Christianity is that, through Christ, we have been made right with God. We are forgiven and offered peace and hope. We experience reconciliation with God and each other. We are filled with the Holy Spirit, who works to change us and grow us. But it won't be easy, in this groaning world. So, Paul wrote about suffering. We will all suffer, he said. Yet somehow, even in suffering, God produces perseverance and character and hope. I have friends who remind me of this regularly. One of their children was born with a significant disability and then another child died at birth. So, when they talk about hope, it's not superficial or easy. They have had to adjust their life goals. But they know that, even now, God is at work within them, to build character and hope. They agree with Paul that *'suffering produces perseverance; perseverance, character; and character, hope. And hope does not put **us** to shame, because God's love has been poured out into **our** hearts'* (5:3–5). God longs to produce character and hope in all of us. But my friends would point to the pronouns in this section. In our individualistic society, it's easy to think 'me' and 'I', but Paul used the words 'us' and 'we'. We need each other to grow hope and character. There will be days when we will struggle with despair . . . and we will need each other to tell us the gospel again. We will need each other to *show* us the gospel again, and to share that wonderful hope.

- - - - - -

Pray

'Lord, we thank you for the overflowing hope we have in you. Please help us to be people of hope for each other.'

Being transformed

'What shall we say, then? Shall we go on sinning, so that grace may increase?'

Romans 6:1

Read Romans 6:1 – 7:25

The first part of Paul's letter to the Romans is a wonderful reminder that no one is righteous (none of us at all), but through faith in Jesus Christ we can receive full redemption. Jesus has paid for our sins! And because of that truth, we have full assurance that we are forgiven and accepted. We can breathe out! We can rest in his glorious gift of salvation. We can sing and shout! But perhaps, occasionally, there is a temptation to think that in breathing out, and in wonderful rest, the whole story is finished. Everything is restored and sorted, so we can tuck ourselves away in a cosy corner and wait for the Lord Jesus to return. Or, alternatively, we can do some of the quiet, hidden things that we are tempted to do, because no one is watching, and we're already forgiven. Paul says, no. He reminds his readers that God is at work to transform us, by his Spirit, every single day, for his glory. That's his heart. He wants to make us more and more like himself. Paul later writes to his readers, *'For those God foreknew he also predestined to be **conformed** to the image of his Son'* (8:29). It's the long, inevitable process of change, for all of us, as believers. And we thank God that he does it through his Spirit.

- - - - - -

Pray

'Lord, it would be easier if we were already changed, but we know that the work is daily. Please do your good work in us today.'

No condemnation

'Therefore, there is now no condemnation for those who are in Christ Jesus.'

Romans 8:1

Read Romans 8:1–17

We have a lovely neighbour who grew up on an island in Vanuatu. Her parents were missionaries there. She describes the beaches and the shells, and the way her local friends would share their canoes and paw-paws. But when she was 9 years old, she was sent away to boarding school in Australia. It was an awful day. She stood on the jetty, crying and clinging to her parents. But nothing could be done. They were upset as well, but it was the 1950s and feelings weren't always expressed well then. So, for years afterwards, our friend thought she was being sent away because she wasn't good enough. She then spent years trying to be good enough, to be better, to please her parents, even well into her adult life. That sense of never being 'good enough' seeped into her soul. Until one day when she read Romans 8:1. *'Therefore, there is now no condemnation for those who are in Christ Jesus'* (8:1). She read it over and over again. She wept. She couldn't believe it. It was true, she wasn't good enough for a holy God, but he had made her good enough through his own Son, the Lord Jesus. He had absorbed into himself all that wasn't good enough, and he had given her grace and life. It's the same truth for each of us today.

- - - - - -

Pray

'Lord, we confess that it's easy to forget, or assume that your grace didn't cost you anything. Please make us thankful today that you have taken our shame. We are no longer condemned.'

The Spirit helps us to pray

'We do not know what we ought to pray for, but the Spirit himself intercedes for us through wordless groans.'
Romans 8:26b

Read Romans 8:18–27

Every day we're aware of the groaning of this world. Loved ones are missing, relationships are strained, work is toilsome and frustrating, the earth is not flourishing, and misunderstanding and injustice is rife. This is exactly why Jesus came. We desperately need his grace and mercy and restorative power. Amazingly, within that, his Spirit helps us to groan and to pray, sometimes wordlessly. One year in Nepal, we became friends with a Sri Lankan family who had moved there long-term for Sam and his wife, Deshi, to teach at the university. They had two small children, and on their second day in the country they found out their accommodation had been mixed up and they had nowhere to stay. It was very stressful, after the long flight, the sleeplessness, the luggage, and without any Nepali language to sort it out. So we prayed. We took it in turns, both Darren and I coming up with various solutions during prayer. Then Sam prayed, 'Lord, when I am most distressed, help me to bring glory to you.' That was all he prayed . . . nothing about a solution or a place to stay, or even a request . . . just one thing, 'help me to bring glory to you'. And in that moment we all paused and looked to God in ways that we didn't normally. Since that day, Sam's prayer has stayed with me as a prayer for emergencies, but also for the ordinary, groaning moments in between.

- - - - - -

Pray

'Lord, when I am most distressed, help me to bring glory to you.'

Nothing can separate us

'And we know that in all things God works for the good of those who love him, who have been called according to his purpose.'
Romans 8:28

Read Romans 8:28–39

It's easy to read Paul's words and feel a sense of disconnection. They're true. God does *'work for the good of those who love him'* (8:28), but we find it hard to fathom. How is this 'good'? What does God mean by 'good'? Is it the same thing as 'nothing *irredeemable* can happen to those who love him'? What about murder and trauma and abuse? How is God working for good then? Certainly, if we were to quote these words to someone who was profoundly grieving, they might not wish to speak to us again. But we need to remember that when Paul wrote to the Roman believers (who were under persecution from Nero), he didn't use sentences in isolation. He also wrote with the full assurance that God's love is present, in everything, even during the hardest times. *'Who shall separate us from the love of Christ? Shall trouble or hardship or persecution or famine or nakedness or danger or sword? . . . No, in all these things we are more than conquerors through him who loved us. For I am convinced that neither death nor life, neither angels nor demons, neither the present nor the future, nor any powers, neither height nor depth, nor anything else in all creation, will be able to separate us from the love of God that is in Christ Jesus our Lord'* (8:35,37–39).

- - - - - -

Pray

> *'Lord, there are so many things we don't understand. We struggle. But we hold tightly to the truth that nothing can separate us from your love. And we thank you that you help us to bear it.'*

God's sovereign choice

'I will have mercy on whom I have mercy.'
Romans 9:15

Read Romans 9:1 – 11:36

We've all asked the question. What about God's sovereign choice? Why does he call some and not others? Is it fair? What about my family? And back in the time of Paul, the questions were also numerous. What about the Jews, God's covenant people, who had lived by the law yet not responded to Jesus? What would happen to them? And Paul reminded the Romans of Yahweh's words to Moses in Exodus 33:19. He said that God, being God, is able to do as he wills. He will have mercy on those for whom he has mercy (9:15). He can form pots for special use, and pots for common use. It's true, of course, both then and now . . . but it's still hard to comprehend from our human viewpoint. So Paul repeated the most important thing. He said that anyone who calls on the name of Jesus will be saved (10:9). And in order for people to call, they must hear the message! They need others to go to them, to share the gospel of grace. Indeed, *'How beautiful are the feet of those who bring good news!'* (10:15b). And in everything, we are to trust God's character. He is good. It is beyond our understanding but, in the end, he will be good. He will not give up on his people. His paths are beyond tracing out, but we wouldn't have it any other way. We trust him. And we can come to him in prayer.

- - - - - -

Pray

> *'Lord, there are many people whom we love. We'd love you to work your purposes in their lives, and bring them to faith. So, we hold them up to you again in prayer.'*

Keep your spiritual fervour

'Never be lacking in zeal, but keep your spiritual fervour, serving the Lord.'
Romans 12:11

Read Romans 12:1 – 13:10

In wrapping up his letter to the Romans, Paul reminded the believers to continue to be transformed by the Holy Spirit. He told them to love, and to serve together as a unified body. He said to pour out their gifts cheerfully, and to honour one another above themselves. He reminded them to be generous, and joyful, and patient, and prayerful. He said they must forgive each other, even when it seemed impossible, because it was up to God to judge. And through all of that, he said one important thing. *'Never be lacking in zeal, but keep your spiritual fervour, serving the Lord'* (12:11). That can be a hard command for any of us over long periods. How do we maintain our spiritual fervour and keep on loving God, and each other, for decades and decades? One of our friends is a musician. He plays multiple musical instruments and he is surrounded by music at work. But he told us that he really needs to go to church to sing. He can, and does, sing worship songs at home by himself, but he really needs to sing with other people at church. He needs to hear *them sing truth back to him.* That's what keeps his spiritual fervour. And for each of us, it will be different. But we are all able to encourage each other – to sing truth back to each other, to share our stories of faith, and to point to what God is doing in the world. Never be lacking in zeal, but keep your spiritual fervour.

- - - - - -

Pray

> *'Lord, some of us have loved you for a really long time, but we want to keep growing in zeal and fervour, for you.'*

Consider the time

'And do this, understanding the present time.'
Romans 13:11

Read Romans 13:11–14

Paul understood 'time' in the same way that Jesus did. It was limited! So when Paul wrote to the Romans about loving one another, and serving together, and submitting to the authorities, he also reminded them that there was urgency. He said, *'And do this, understanding the present time: the hour has already come for you to wake up from your slumber, because our salvation is nearer now than when we first believed. The night is nearly over; the day is almost here'* (13:11–12). For Paul, and for the rest of us, our days are limited and unknown. So, it's helpful to pause and consider. What is different in our lives this year compared to last year? Are there different people in front of us, to serve and to love? Do we have access to different gospel opportunities or resources this year? Are we aware of the needs around us, and in the world? Recent statistics tell us that 60 per cent of the world's Christians now live in Africa, Asia and Latin America. That's wonderful, but it also means that the needs are changing. There is less need for expatriate church planters, and there is more need to encourage and support local expressions of the gospel. There is more need to be engaged in holistic development, and to advocate for the millions of displaced people groups, and to support the persecuted church. We too can 'consider the time' and notice today's needs in the world – for prayer and advocacy and the millions of ways to share the gospel in our streets today.

- - - - - -

Pray

> *'Lord, your timeline is not known to us, but we ask that your gospel mission would be compelling today, and tomorrow, and next year, and until you come again.'*

Avoid passing judgement

'Instead, make up your mind not to put any stumbling-block or obstacle in the way of a brother or sister.'
Romans 14:13

Read Romans 14:1 – 15:33

It's easy to critique someone, or to notice their different behaviours, and decide they're wrong. Back when Paul was writing to the Romans, some of the believers were observing Jewish food laws and the Sabbath, and others were not, so there was judgement within their cultural differences. But Paul said, no! It's not the most important thing. We're all part of God's family, he said, through grace. So, accept each other. Don't quarrel over disputable matters. *'Who are you to judge someone else's servant? To their own master, servants stand or fall. And they will stand, for the Lord is able to make them stand'* (14:4). It's an important reminder for us today, when the list of non-essential things has grown very long indeed. But the non-essentials don't define who's in or out of God's family. He will judge in the end, and we will each stand before him. So, we act in love. We edify. We build up. We try not to put stumbling-blocks in each other's way. We notice when we have those tendencies! And we pray. *'May our dependably steady and warmly personal God develop maturity in you so that you get along with each other as well as Jesus gets along with us all. Then we'll be a choir – not our voices only, but our very lives singing in harmony in a stunning anthem to the God and Father of our Master Jesus!'* (15:5–7 MSG).

- - - - - -

Pray

'Lord, we love the imagery of your choir. Please help us to sing with each other, even when it doesn't come easily at all.'

It's not a popularity contest

'God chose the lowly things of this world and the despised things – and the things that are not – to nullify the things that are, so that no one may boast before him.'

1 Corinthians 1:28–29

Read 1 Corinthians 1:1 – 4:21

Before writing to the believers in Rome, Paul also wrote to the Corinthians. And back then, there were specific, known problems in the Corinthian church, so Paul addressed them, one by one, beginning with the leadership issues. Don't follow human beings, as if the answers lie in them, he said. They are servants of *Christ*! Follow Christ, who was crucified for you! And it's a tendency that we still have today. We all want to follow godly leaders. We want their wisdom and guidance. That's good. But we must remember, every day, that our leaders are also weak. In fact, good leaders will acknowledge their own weakness and point to Christ's wonderful strength in everything. We recently attended the funeral of an older man who pastored a number of churches in Australia over a period of 45 years. None of the churches were large. There were no amazing success stories in the world's eyes. But at his funeral, everyone said the same thing. He was honest and humble. He pointed to Jesus in everything, even in his failures. And because he did that, he helped us to do that too.

- - - - - -

Pray

'Lord, we have been quick to idolise leaders, as well as to judge them . . . and neither serves your purposes. Please turn our hearts back to you, and please help us to be people who humbly point to you in everything.'

Run in such a way

'But we do it to get a crown that will last for ever.'
1 Corinthians 9:25b

Read 1 Corinthians 5:1 – 10:33

There were other problems in the Corinthian church. Being situated near the port, the believers were easily influenced by passing traders and the ways of the world. There was sexual immorality, and disagreement over food sacrificed to idols. Paul said to them, you've been shown grace. You've been given life, so honour God with your bodies. You are temples of the Holy Spirit! Sexual purity is not an optional extra. The Lord has come to dwell with us! But in everything, he said, don't be enslaved or distracted. The time is short. So, *'Run in such a way as to get the prize. Everyone who competes in the games goes into strict training. They do it to get a crown that will not last; but we do it to get a crown that will last for ever'* (9:24b–25). It's a helpful imagery. Years ago, I used to watch Darren compete in triathlons. After the swim, he'd get out of the water, leap on the bike, throw his helmet on, hardly pausing, eyes on the finish line. Run in such a way as to get the prize. Don't be distracted by things that won't last. There will always be temptations and questions, and some days they will feel overwhelming. We may not feel like running at all. But even on those days, we can look to Jesus. We can believe that he is the Son of God, and that he died and rose for us. Run in such a way as to get the prize.

- - - - - -

Pray

> *'Lord, you know our weaknesses and distractions. Please fill us with your Spirit so that we can look to you, and run in such a way to get the prize.'*

Planting roses

'Now if the foot should say, "Because I am not a hand, I do not belong to the body," it would not for that reason stop being part of the body.'

1 Corinthians 12:15

Read 1 Corinthians 12:1–31

There was another problem in the Corinthian church. They had become disorderly in worship. There was no unity, and this caused some to become confused. So Paul told them about the body. Be the body of Christ, he said. Serve together. God has designed each of us differently . . . so that we can serve him, together. And we need that reminder, daily, because it's so easy to think that our part is unimportant or too small. Recently I met an old man who used to work on the railways, digging. He never married or drove a car, but he was very good at digging. So when he came to our church, 14 years ago (when he was 78!), he dug a garden out the front of the church. Then, he took the train to Penrith (one hour away), walked to the plant market and bought beautiful roses. He carried them home, one by one, on the train, and he planted them in front of our church. These days, people walk past our church and they enjoy the roses. They walk in the doors and they hear about Jesus. The roses are part of it! We are all part of the body of Christ, serving together with the gifts we've been given, that Christ might be glorified and the body of Christ built up. It's an incredible privilege.

- - - - - -

Pray

'Lord, on the days when we grumble or want each other's gifts, please remind us that you have placed the parts in the body, every one of them, exactly as you wanted them to be.'

Love in the ordinary

'And now these three remain: faith, hope and love. But the greatest of these is love.'

1 Corinthians 13:13

Read 1 Corinthians 13:1–13

It's wonderful that as Paul responded to the Corinthians, his central theme was *love*. Without love, he said, everything else was useless, even tongues, prophecy, faith, giving, and knowledge. Everything was useless without love. Indeed, love was the key to the entire gospel, and it should compel each of us in our service and witness. If it doesn't compel us, we can stop now! Of course, love is hard work. It's particularly hard work in families and in close communities. Perhaps it's because our closest relationships take place in all the ordinary, stressful moments, when we can't find the keys, and the car won't start, and the tax returns are due. It can be hard to keep choosing kindness and patience and trust. But that's the calling. Paul wrote, *'Love . . . always protects, always trusts, always hopes, always perseveres. Love never fails'* (13:6–8). Love compels us to say sorry, and thank you, and please. Love forces us to put pride and fear aside, and to truly notice each other, and to listen well, and to understand, even when the car won't start, and we can't find the keys. Even then, cherish. And in everything, remember that we're not in heaven yet. It's hard here, but there will come a day when we will be fully known, and we will see God face to face. That's amazing! Even in that glorious day to come, it's love that will remain.

- - - - - -

Pray

'Lord, we long for that day to come, and we are in awe of your ways. We know that we won't even need hope or faith then, because you will be with us, but we will always need and experience love. Thank you.'

Therefore, stand firm

> **'Listen, I tell you a mystery: we will not all sleep, but we will all be changed – in a flash, in the twinkling of an eye, at the last trumpet.'**
>
> 1 Corinthians 15:51–52

Read 1 Corinthians 15:1–58

This is a wonderful passage! It's my 'go-to' part of the Bible when I want to remember the most important things. Paul wrote to the Corinthian believers about the resurrection. It's true, he said. It's our glorious hope. Christ died for our sins. He was buried, and *raised* on the third day, according to the Scriptures. Then, he appeared to Cephas, and to the 12, and to more than 500 of the believers. Jesus definitely rose from the dead! And it really matters, because if Christ *hadn't* been raised, then our faith would be useless. We might as well stay in bed. But he has been raised! And we hold on to that hope. Death has been swallowed up in victory! We will be made alive in Christ! I love the way that Paul concludes this passage. He uses lots of amazing words to describe the end, and the reign of God, and our resurrection bodies, and the splendour of it all – that we can hardly fathom. And then he says one more thing, *'Therefore, my dear brothers and sisters, stand firm. Let nothing move you. Always give yourselves fully to the work of the Lord, because you know that your labour in the Lord is not in vain'* (15:58). When we hold onto the biggest, most important, eternal, fabulous things, it will help us to serve and to love him in the mundane, ordinary things. It will help us to stand firm.

- - - - - -

Pray

> *'Lord, we can hardly imagine the splendour of heaven and being with you. Raise our vision again, so that every day we stand firm.'*

The God of all comfort

'Praise be to the God and Father of our Lord Jesus Christ, the Father of compassion and the God of all comfort.'

2 Corinthians 1:3

Read 2 Corinthians 1:1–11

Paul wrote a second letter to the Corinthian believers, and in the intervening time there had been a significant misunderstanding. Some of the believers had challenged Paul's integrity and authority as an apostle, and he had responded with a visit and further teaching. By the time of his second letter, though, there had been reconciliation. And so, Paul began his letter with a description of the God of all comfort. God is a God who comforts us in all our troubles, he said, so that we can comfort others with the comfort we've received from him. Paul himself had known deep discomfort and anguish. He'd been through troubles in Asia, far beyond his ability to endure, so that he despaired of life itself. He'd felt the 'sentence of death'. But then he wrote, *'But this happened that we might not rely on ourselves but on God, who raises the dead'* (1:9b). It's an astounding truth, worth reading over and over again. This happened (this sentence of death) that we might not rely on ourselves, but on God who raises the dead. Our God is a God of comfort, and we experience it most profoundly when we ache. In those moments we learn to rely on him more than we do at other times. And we are gently equipped to comfort others.

- - - - - -

Pray

> *'Lord, we thank you for your comfort. We rely on you, and we long to share your comfort with those who need it today.'*

Fix your eyes on the eternal

> **'Therefore we do not lose heart. Though outwardly we are wasting away, yet inwardly we are being renewed day by day.'**
> **2 Corinthians 4:16**

Read 2 Corinthians 4:1–18

After writing about comfort, Paul then addressed the problem with the Corinthians. He told them that his word was reliable. He could be trusted because his focus was on *God.* It's *God* whose word is reliable, whose promises are sure, whose Spirit is the guarantee, and whose effect in the world is a fragrant aroma. It's not Paul! And because of that, Paul was able to keep going. He didn't lose heart (4:1). He knew that he was frail and weak, like a lump of baked dirt. But it was good, because it showed that the all-surpassing power was from God, and not from him (4:7). It's also an amazing truth for us. Our human weakness (and even our suffering) somehow magnifies the power of Christ's resurrection and his victory over death. We don't understand it, but we follow a Saviour who suffered deeply for us, and who renews us daily. Paul reminded his readers that their troubles and weaknesses could actually help them to see that the world is fleeting. It could renew in them an increased longing for what is to come. *'So we fix our eyes not on what is seen, but on what is unseen, since what is seen is temporary, but what is unseen is eternal'* (4:18). I find the word 'fix' helpful. Don't occasionally glance over in that direction, but *fix* your eyes on the unseen. Deliberately look at what God is doing now, and what he will do for ever.

- - - - - -

Pray

> *'Lord, we confess that sometimes we just wallow in our troubles. Please use them to transform us, and to change the things we pray and long for.'*

A generous life

'Each of you should give what you have decided in your heart to give, not reluctantly or under compulsion, for God loves a cheerful giver.'
2 Corinthians 9:7

Read 2 Corinthians 8:1 – 9:15

The believers, back in Paul's day, were often financially dependent on each other. It was a good system because times of need were frequent and support was required. However, by the time of Paul's second letter, the Corinthians had neglected their normal generosity. So Paul reminded them to give. But he didn't write it as a command. He said it was the opposite of a command. Giving was a natural, heart-felt response to a generous God – an earnest desire to bless others because of the grace we have received from the Lord Jesus. It's a natural eagerness, he said, a willingness to provide and help, not because we have to, but because we want to. *'For if the willingness is there, the gift is acceptable according to what one has, not according to what one does not have'* (8:12). It's also a helpful reminder for us today. We live in a noisy, consumer-based society that directs our attention to what we don't have (or we think we need), rather than what we already have. And we sorely need the reminder to look at what we already have. How can we use it today? How can we live generously? How can we give, willingly and cheerfully, without resentment or even that niggling sense of duty?

- - - - - -

Pray

> *'Lord, you gave up everything for us. You became poor. And yet we often operate out of a scarcity mindset. Please change our hearts today, so that we long to give more than we long to keep.'*

Weakness

'My grace is sufficient for you, for my power is made perfect in weakness.'

2 Corinthians 12:9

Read 2 Corinthians 11:16 – 12:21

In Paul's encouragement of the Corinthians, he was honest about himself. He said he was weak. He was unimpressive. He struggled with a terrible, undescribed suffering. And in a world where prideful boasting had turned into an art form, it must have been striking. Paul wasn't saying that his suffering was easy. He pleaded for it to be taken away. Yet somehow, he 'delighted' in weakness. He was content, even within that terrible suffering, because the weaker he became, the stronger he felt in Christ. And it's true that we are all weak. We will grow weaker as we age! We will continue to be weak until Jesus returns. One year, I met a Korean dentist serving in Central Asia. He had been there for 18 years, doing community health work and establishing dental clinics and training local dentists. He had left an amazing legacy. But he said to me, 'I've been so weak.' He then described his brain haemorrhage and the treatment it required. After that, he was assaulted and robbed. Then he had a serious car accident, and his daughter needed two brain operations back in Korea. After they returned to Central Asia, they lived through three revolutions in their city. All their clinics were looted. 'But,' he said to me, 'it's shown me that this is not my work. This is God's work and it's in my weakness that he displays his immeasurable strength, over and over again.'

- - - - - -

Pray

'Lord, we don't understand it, but we acknowledge again, and cling to your immeasurable strength within our shared weakness.'

The fruit

'But the fruit of the Spirit is love, joy, peace, forbearance, kindness, goodness, faithfulness, gentleness and self-control.'
Galatians 5:22–23

Read Galatians 1:1 – 6:18

The debate over the law was an ongoing issue in the early church. So Paul wrote to the Galatians and said, no. Justification by the works of the law was no gospel at all. It would mean that *'Christ died for nothing!'* (2:21). Instead, Paul told them about the Spirit, who would slowly change them and guide them, and produce fruit in their lives – love, joy, peace, forbearance, kindness, goodness, faithfulness, gentleness and self-control. It's a wonderfully long list! Today, we rest on that same promise. God will work in us through his Spirit. He will help us to live for him, and to obey the words of Jesus, *'Love your neighbour as yourself'* (5:14b). It will be hard, but it will be God's work in us, to change our normal habits and desires, and to make us people who love him and each other. But Paul didn't mean that we do nothing. He told the believers to be intentional, to restore each other gently, to watch themselves, to test their own actions, to carry each other's burdens, and to not become weary in doing good (6:1–6). There was so much that they could do to cultivate fruit, at the same time as recognising that the fruit was a work of the Spirit. It's a wonderful truth for us today. If we see an increase in fruit, we praise God, and if we need more, we run to him . . . which may be the more common response!

- - - - - -

Pray

'Lord, we thank you for your Spirit who transforms us and helps us to love. But there are so many other desires that consume us, so please help us to run to you for more.'

Lavished

'In him we have redemption through his blood, the forgiveness of sins, in accordance with the riches of God's grace that he lavished on us.'

Ephesians 1:7–8

Read Ephesians 1:1–14

Paul wrote a letter to the Ephesians while he was under house arrest, handcuffed to a Roman guard. It was about AD60, and back then the temple of Artemis (in Ephesus) was dominant, and the church gathering was small . . . so Paul wrote to them. But he didn't begin his letter small. He began it by reminding them of God's vast, sweeping, sovereign plans for the world through Jesus. *'Praise be to the God and Father of our Lord Jesus Christ, who has blessed us in the heavenly realms with every spiritual blessing in Christ . . . In him we have redemption through his blood, the forgiveness of sins, in accordance with the riches of God's grace that he lavished on us'* (1:3,7–8). It's a wonderful reminder! God has 'lavished' grace on us. He didn't dribble it through the cracks of a boarded-up window. God lavished grace on us extravagantly, not holding back. And as believers, we have been chosen and marked with a seal, the promised Holy Spirit. So, every day, we must let that reality infiltrate our lives. Back then, the believers may have felt dwarfed by the temple of Artemis. Today, we may feel dwarfed by the gods of greed and injustice and consumerism and self-absorption, even in our own hearts. Paul would say to us, think big again. Remember God's saving, sovereign work, through Jesus, that he's bringing about right now . . . for the world and for your neighbours.

- - - - - -

Pray

'Lord, we confess that we have been discouraged. Please renew in us your perspective on the world, and help us receive the grace that you have lavished on us.'

Know him better

'I keep asking that the God of our Lord Jesus Christ, the glorious Father, may give you the Spirit of wisdom and revelation, so that you may know him better.'
Ephesians 1:17

Read Ephesians 1:15–23

After Paul reminded the Ephesians of their part in the vast, redeeming story of God, he thanked God for them, and he prayed for them. *'I keep asking that the God of our Lord Jesus Christ, the glorious Father, may give you the Spirit of wisdom and revelation, so that you may **know him better**'* (1:17). I always pause there. That's what God wants, then and now. He wants us to *know him better.* Know him better this year, on every late train, or in every meeting that goes on too long, within misunderstanding, or misplaced debate, or when the budget doesn't stretch. Know him better today, tomorrow, and next year. Know him better, within unanswerable questions. Because as we do, our perspective will slowly change. Perhaps we'll have a heightened sense that we're part of something grand and purposeful. Perhaps we'll be less caught up in things that are trifling. Perhaps we'll long to pour out our gifts in generous, sacrificial, non-begrudging ways. Perhaps we'll tend more towards hope than cynicism. Perhaps we'll be less concerned with the approval of others, and more concerned with the words of Jesus. Perhaps we'll get our hands dirtier with the people whom we currently walk past. And as we know God better, each day, we'll definitely pray more for others, that they too will know him better in everything.

- - - - - -

Pray

> *'Lord, we do long to know you better today, and this year. Please replace our cynicism with hope, and our weariness with wonder, as we gaze on your plan in Christ.'*

Together

'And I pray that you, being rooted and established in love, may have power, together with all the Lord's holy people, to grasp how wide and long and high and deep is the love of Christ.'
Ephesians 3:17b–18

Read Ephesians 3:14–21

Paul continued to write to the Ephesians and to pray for them. He said, *'I kneel before the Father, from whom every family in heaven and on earth derives its name'* (3:14–15). It's an amazing acknowledgement. Our God, to whom we bring praise, is the creator of every person, in every rainforest and desert and pacific island and mountainous region, and generation past and present. He knows every person in every airport, and school, and hospital, and trade centre, and football stadium, and shopping complex. Every family in heaven and on earth derives its name from him. And Paul wanted the believers to *know God*, and to grasp how wide and long and high and deep was his love. He wanted them to grasp it as individuals, and also ***'together with all the Lord's holy people'*** (3:18). It's true that we can understand God's love on our own. We can stay at home and listen to a podcast, or watch a church service on TV. But it is also good to gather with a range of believers – old and young, men and women, people of different languages and cultures – because as we gather together, we will grasp it *better*. We will be reminded of God's largeness and sovereignty, together. We will be less likely to put God in a small box of our own making. Grasp the love of Christ, together.

- - - - - -

Pray

'Lord, we are thankful for your body around the world, because we know that we grasp your love better in community than alone. Please help us to continue to gather.'

Bear with one another

'Be completely humble and gentle; be patient, bearing with one another in love.'

Ephesians 4:2

Read Ephesians 4:1 – 5:20

It's true that as we gather in church communities, we will have disagreements. We will not see eye to eye on everything. And back when Paul was writing to the Ephesians, the Jew/Gentile divide was a major issue. So Paul urged them to live a life worthy of the calling they had received. He said, *'Be completely humble and gentle; be patient, bearing with one another in love. Make every effort to keep the unity of the Spirit through the bond of peace'* (4:2–3). He didn't say it was going to be easy, or to smile sweetly all the time. He said, *bear* with one another. He said, make every effort. He said, work hard at unity in Christ, and don't be surprised when it takes energy and commitment. It *will* be hard! But as we bear with one another and work hard at unity, there will be moments when we will see disagreement as a gift. Perhaps times of disagreement will provide opportunities to communicate more clearly, or to listen better, or to go deeper in our understanding of each other and human nature. Disagreements may provide opportunities for grace and forgiveness and truthful words. And every time, being a body is worth it. God's design is wonderful. He has formed us with different gifts and passions, deliberately, so that the body of Christ may be built up and his people equipped. It's a wonderful design.

- - - - - -

Pray

'Lord, we confess times when we have harboured anger and blame. We have wallowed in pride and fear. Please forgive us again and help us to live out of your fullness, not our lack.'

Stand firm and pray

'Therefore put on the full armour of God . . .'
Ephesians 6:13

Read Ephesians 5:21 – 6:20

At the end of his letter, Paul told the believers that unity would transform Christian households. Submission and love and respect would be at the centre, out of reverence for Christ. Then he said, *'Finally, be strong in the Lord and in his mighty power. Put on the full armour of God, so that you can take your stand against the devil's schemes . . . and after you have done everything . . . stand'* (6:10–11,13). He said put on three things – the belt of truth, the breastplate of righteousness, and shoes ready with the gospel of *peace*. And take up three things – the shield of faith, the helmet of salvation, and the sword of the Spirit. And stand. Help each other. Don't break rank or give up. Stand for the truth and beauty and goodness of the gospel. There is a dark world of spiritual forces out there, and we must not be ignorant of its power. Even staying angry can give the devil a foothold. But we can pray, on all occasions, with all kinds of prayers and requests, for all the Lord's people. Last year I spent time with a dear friend during the last week of her life. She was very ill, confined to a hospital bed. But next to her bed and the bottle of morphine were some prayer notes for God's work in the world. She had one week to live and she was still praying, and fixing her eyes on God's vast plans and purposes for the world. Pray on all occasions!

- - - - - -

Pray

'Lord, we want to be people who stand firm and who pray on all occasions. Thank you that your glorious gospel and your Spirit enable us to do exactly that, wherever we are.'

It's his work

'Being confident of this, that he who began a good work in you will carry it on to completion until the day of Christ Jesus.'

Philippians 1:6

Read Philippians 1:1–11

There are times when we feel stuck in a muddy swamp. Perhaps we're worried about our family, or the future, or our finances, or something we can't even name. Whenever I feel like that, I re-read Paul's letter to the Philippians. He wrote to thank them for their generous financial gift to him, and for their partnership in the gospel. He had been deeply encouraged by them, even while he was in prison. And then he said that he was confident *'that he who began a good work in you will carry it on to completion until the day of Christ Jesus'* (1:6). Paul was absolutely confident that it was God's work within the believers that had produced such beautiful generosity and faithfulness. And because God had begun that good work in them, God would complete it. It's the same for each of us, 2,000 years later. God saved us through the Lord Jesus. He's working in us now, through his Holy Spirit, and he will carry it to completion until the day of Christ Jesus – until we go to him, or until he returns and makes all things new. He knows what's ahead until then. It's his work, through the Holy Spirit, even when we're feeling unable, or stuck in a muddy swamp.

- - - - - -

Pray

'Lord, we thank you for this reminder that you will complete your work in us. Please let it sink in deeply when we think it's all up to us.'

Even in chains

**'Now I want you to know, brothers and sisters, that what has happened
to me has actually served to advance the gospel.'**

Philippians 1:12

Read Philippians 1:12–30

It's amazing that Paul saw every event in the light of the spread of the
gospel, even his time in prison and his possible execution. He wrote to the
Philippians and said that being in prison had served to advance the gospel
in two ways – firstly that there were more people who had heard the gospel,
and secondly, that the local believers were now more confident in speaking
about Jesus because Paul was in prison. It's an interesting phenomenon.
I guess it's also possible that the local believers could have become more
scared. What if they ended up in prison as well? But no, they had become
more confident. They must have thought that if Paul could withstand trials
and death threats, then they could grow in confidence in Christ as well. If
Paul could testify that salvation was only found in Jesus, then they could
also trust Jesus. It's the same phenomenon that we see around us today. If
our friends, or church members, leave home (and western comforts) to serve
in a medical mission in Cambodia or Afghanistan or Bolivia, then we feel
the same encouragement to take risks for the gospel. If someone near us
regularly prioritises reading the Bible over other pursuits, then we will also
be encouraged in that direction. We too want to love and trust Jesus, as we
are surrounded by people who live out that longing.

- - - - - -

Pray

*'Lord, help us to be people who live out our love for Jesus in everything. And
may we, by your grace, become people who encourage others to do the same.'*

Humility

'Therefore God exalted him to the highest place and gave him the name that is above every name.'

Philippians 2:9

Read Philippians 2:1–30

At the very centre of Paul's letter to the Philippians is an astoundingly beautiful poem. Paul pointed to the glorious Lord Jesus, who was, in nature, equal with God, yet emptied himself to become human. Jesus didn't grasp onto his heavenly glory, but he made himself nothing and became a servant, even obedient to death on a Roman cross. It was a horrific and humiliating death. But it wasn't the end of the story. *'Therefore God exalted him to the highest place and gave him the name that is above every name, that at the name of Jesus every knee should bow, in heaven and on earth and under the earth, and every tongue acknowledge that Jesus Christ is Lord, to the glory of God the Father'* (2:9–11). Right now today, Jesus reigns on the throne above everything and everyone. One day, every knee will bow before him, and every tongue will acknowledge his name! And Paul wrote to the believers in Philippi, telling them to imitate the humility of Jesus. Notice his self-sacrificial love. Be someone who pours out your heart and soul on behalf of others, that they too might love Jesus. Be someone who doesn't care about personal glory. Be someone who keeps your own ego in check and remembers what's important. We need this reminder today!

- - - - - -

Pray

'Lord, we want our small stories to be caught up in your grand story of humble self-sacrifice. We want to grumble less. We want to work on our pride and vanity, and point more to Christ.'

The Lord is near

'Do not be anxious about anything, but in every situation, by prayer and petition, with thanksgiving, present your requests to God.'
Philippians 4:6

Read Philippians 3:1 – 4:9

I only noticed it recently. Immediately before Paul's admonition to the Philippians to *'not be anxious about anything'*, he wrote four words. He said, *'The Lord is near'* (4:5). And, at the time of writing, the Philippians were genuinely fearful. They were undergoing serious persecution from the authorities. But Paul said, don't give in to fear. The Lord is near. You can tell everything to God, and he will hear you, and he will give you peace. But his peace won't be one marked by the absence of fear or worries. It will not be an easy peace. It will be the peace of knowing that God is near, right in the middle of our worries. It will be the peace that he gives which transcends all understanding. He will guard our hearts and minds. And it will come even more, as we focus on what is good and lovely, and when we are thankful, even in the midst of overwhelming hardship. One of my friends has a difficult home life. She is honest about her challenges. But when we pray together, the first thing she does is acknowledge God, and then she gives thanks, deliberately, specifically, and with great variety. She says that she does it, in part, out of self-discipline. It's easy to complain about things. But thanksgiving is an act that slowly changes our hearts and realigns us as followers of Jesus.

- - - - - -

Pray

'Lord, we thank you for all that you give us today – limbs that move, and books to read, and mouths that smile, and friends who remind us that you are near, even in our troubles and fears . . . and it's enough.'

Being content

'I have learned the secret of being content in any and every situation, whether well fed or hungry, whether living in plenty or in want.'
Philippians 4:12

Read Philippians 4:10–23

It can be hard to learn contentment, especially when we live in places where we're surrounded by things that are readily available and feel like necessities. Sometimes it's easier when they're not available! One day, while we were living in Nepal, we visited an Indian family who had arrived there 12 months earlier. They hadn't brought many of their material possessions with them, so when we sat down for a meal, they had four plates and four forks – for all nine of us – and we shared them. For dessert Muriel made custard, but she had no bowls, so she washed out some old tuna tins and she put a blob of custard in each tuna tin and we shared the four spoons amongst nine of us – and it was delicious. Later, I read Paul's words to the Philippians. *'I have learned the secret of being content in any and every situation, whether well fed or hungry, whether living in plenty or in want'* (4:12). Paul had actually *learned* it. He had discovered, perhaps, that we suffer from discontent when we face deprivation, but also, in a more complicated way, when we face abundance. The secret, wherever we are, is the depth of our contentment in God and our dependence on him, the only One who gives us true strength (4:13).

- - - - - -

Pray

> *'Lord, help us to be content today, even when surrounded by abundance, or by peers who have the relationships or resources that we easily long for. Convict us again and strengthen us in you.'*

> **'Whatever you do, work at it with all your heart, as working for the Lord, not for human masters.'**
>
> Colossians 3:23

Read Colossians 1:1 – 3:25

When Paul wrote to the believers in Colossae, he reminded them that their faith in Jesus would change everything. It was all encompassing. They had been reconciled to God through Christ! They had been made holy in his sight, without blemish and free from accusation . . . so, because of that, they were to continue to live in Christ (2:6), and to set their hearts on things above (3:1), and to forgive each other as they had been forgiven (3:13). In fact, *everything* they did and thought was now in the light of Christ's sacrifice. He said, *'Whatever you do, whether in word or deed, do it all in the name of the Lord Jesus, giving thanks to God the Father through him'* (3:17). I find it a challenging reminder. Whatever you do – at work, and on your days off, and when cleaning the sink, or buying more rice, or using social media, or when no one is watching – do it all in the name of the Lord Jesus. It's a hard reminder! Later, Paul extended the words to children and parents, slaves and masters, everyone. *'Whatever you do, work at it with your whole heart, as working for the Lord, not for human masters . . . It is the Lord Christ you are serving'* (3:23–24). In our compartmentalised, western life, where work and home life and church are often separate, we need this reminder that following our risen Lord Jesus will transform everything, daily.

- - - - - -

Pray

> *'Lord, we need you to speak to us again about the parts of life we keep hidden or complain about. Please transform us so that whatever we do is in the light of your healing love for us.'*

Sing!

'Let the message of Christ dwell among you richly as you teach and admonish one another with all wisdom through psalms, hymns and songs from the Spirit, singing to God with gratitude in your hearts.'
Colossians 3:16

Read Colossians 3:15–17

Amidst Paul's reminders to the Colossians to live wholeheartedly for Christ, he also told them to sing. In fact, he told them to teach others through song. Don't just sing alone, he said, but sing together. And this is a theme throughout Scripture. When the Israelites crossed the Red Sea, they sang! When Hannah gave birth to Samuel, she sang! After hundreds of years, when the Israelites returned to the land, they sang! When the Lord Jesus was born in Bethlehem, the angels sang! In Revelation, the ongoing imagery is of multitudes singing! But it makes me wonder, what are our songs of hope now? Do we always acknowledge the great privilege of singing in communities and in churches? Of course, there are places in the world where Christians aren't allowed to meet publicly to sing. And there are also times when singing is restricted, for example, during a pandemic. But I remember reading the story of an older Christian couple in North Korea. They loved to sing, but they couldn't do it publicly, so whenever they could, they walked into the mountains, pretending they were searching for herbs. Then they found a deep cave and they walked in as far as they could, and when they were sure that no one could hear them, they sang to God, as loudly as they could, because they needed to sing.

- - - - - -

Pray

'Lord, we sometimes take singing your praises for granted. Help us to sing today, with gratitude in our hearts.'

More and more

'Now we ask you and urge you in the Lord Jesus to do this more and more.'

1 Thessalonians 4:1b

Read 1 Thessalonians 4:1–12

After Paul visited Thessalonica, early in his ministry, the church there grew rapidly. It was a wonderful response to the gospel – lots of keen, new believers who longed to follow Jesus faithfully, even amidst what became intense persecution. So Paul wrote to encourage them. He thanked God for their faithfulness. He acknowledged that they were living to please God, and then he said, *'Now we ask you and urge you in the Lord Jesus to do this more and more'* (4:1). It's an important phrase, for them and for us now, whether we've been believers for decades or whether we came to know Jesus last week. The Thessalonian believers still had years of life ahead of them, and Paul wanted them to live for Christ *'more and more'*. He didn't tell them to simply maintain their current devotion. He said, do this *'more and more'* ! Then later, when Paul commented on their great love for each other (and for all of God's family throughout Macedonia), he repeated the same phrase. *'Yet we urge you, brothers and sisters, to do so more and more'* (4:10). Don't love each other 'less and less' as time goes on. Love each other *'more and more'* ! I wonder what someone would say, observing our lives. Are we loving God and each other more and more? What would it look like if we were?

- - - - - -

Pray

'Lord, you began a good work in us. You grew faith in us, you transformed us through your Spirit. Please do that more and more (not less and less) as time goes by.'

The Lord himself will come

'For the Lord himself will come down from heaven.'
1 Thessalonians 4:16

Read 1 Thessalonians 4:13 – 5:11

Part way up the Mount of Olives, even today, there is a large graveyard with many tombs. When we visited some years ago, we stopped to look at the tombs. A local man noticed our interest and he tried to explain it to us. 'The prophets are all buried there,' he said. 'Haggai and Malachi and Zechariah. They all want to be in the best spot when the Messiah comes back.' Then the man went on his way. Our boys wanted to know if there would be a queue when Jesus returns. We replied that nobody is really sure. But later on that day, we read Paul's letter to the Thessalonians. Paul told the believers that they mustn't grieve over their loved ones who die, like people without hope. *'For we believe that Jesus died and rose again, and so we believe that God will bring with Jesus those who have fallen asleep in him . . . For the Lord himself will come down from heaven, with a loud command, with the voice of the archangel and with the trumpet call of God, and the dead in Christ will rise first. After that, we who are still alive and are left will be caught up together with them in the clouds to meet the Lord in the air. And so we will be with the Lord for ever'* (4:14,16–17). It's a wonderful promise! Of course, we don't understand God's timeline, or the miraculous nature of his coming, but we hold onto those last nine words. *'And so we will be with the Lord for ever.'*

- - - - - -

Pray

'Lord, thank you for your wonderful, death-defying hope. Please let it infiltrate the weariness or ordinariness of today.'

Be a witness to the world

'This is good, and pleases God our Saviour, who wants all people to be saved.'

1 Timothy 2:3–4

Read 1 Timothy 2:1 – 2:15

Reading the Bible can be hard work. There is context and authorship and purpose to consider, as well as the way it fits within the span of Scripture, and the promises of God in Christ. And then we must work hard to apply it to our different world today. When Paul wrote to Timothy, he had a specific problem in mind within the Ephesian church. There were corrupt teachers leading both men and women astray. The men were involved in angry disputes, and the women were excessive in their adornment, as well as trying to teach poor theology. Paul addressed the specific issues via Timothy. But there is a verse that stands out in the paragraph prior. Paul was urging the community to pray for those in authority, and then he said, *'This is good, and pleases God our Saviour, who wants all people to be saved and to come to a knowledge of the truth'* (2:3–4). Every day, in every time and place, that's what God wants. He wants all people to be saved through his Son, the Lord Jesus. And he wants the church to be an effective witness to that end – not embroiled in disputes or leadership coups or unfortunate distractions. So Paul gave specific commands regarding the distractions, but in each case his words were so that *'people everywhere could be saved'*. It teaches us that this is still God's heart, and we will worship and witness with that goal in mind, and pray that nothing will hinder God's purposes.

- - - - - -

Pray

> *'Lord, we are easily diverted and distracted by conflict and questions we can't answer. Please remind us today of your biggest desire for the world.'*

Leadership

'Here is a trustworthy saying: whoever aspires to be an overseer desires a noble task.'

1 Timothy 3:1

Read 1 Timothy 3:1 – 6:21

I've been involved in churches all my life, but for the last five years, my husband and I have been on the leadership team at our local church. We've found it complex and challenging. There have been numerous confidential, pastoral issues that are never as simple as they look from the outside. Enormous wisdom and prayerfulness are required. So back when Paul was writing to Timothy, he told him that leaders should be chosen carefully. Given how hard it was going to be, choose well! Of course, looking at Paul's list, the immediate response is that nobody is qualified. And that's true. But Paul then pointed to Jesus. He is our only source of true godliness, and a good leader will realise that, in everything. Paul went on to give more specific recommendations to Timothy regarding widows, who were a vulnerable group. But it wasn't simple, he said. There were widows who were abusing the system of generosity and who weren't needy at all. I find this an encouraging reminder. Back then, and now, there will be complicated needs within any church community, all requiring different responses. It won't be simple! If nothing else, it sends us back to our knees to pray to our sovereign Lord for our church families and loved ones, realising that we don't have the answers, and we often feel helpless. But being on our knees in front of our sovereign Lord is a very good place to be.

- - - - - -

Pray

'Lord, we recognise that our human gatherings are wonderful but also very complicated. We are all needy and dependent on you. Help us to come to you, and trust for your purposes in each human life.'

All Scripture is God-breathed

'All Scripture is God-breathed and is useful for teaching, rebuking, correcting and training in righteousness.'
2 Timothy 3:16

Read 2 Timothy 2:1 – 4:8

There is an interesting statement in Paul's second letter to Timothy. He was near to death himself and he wrote to Timothy, *'But mark this: there will be terrible times in the last days. People will be lovers of themselves, lovers of money, boastful, proud, abusive, disobedient to their parents, ungrateful'* (3:1–2). The list was long and awful. Reading it in today's world could make us suspect that's exactly how it is right now. People seem to be 'lovers of themselves'. Or, have we always been like that and social media is making it more obvious? Did readers of the Bible 100 years ago, or 500 years ago, read Paul's words and look around them and think that they were in the last days? We don't know. But once again, in Paul's last letter before he died, he pointed to God's faithfulness. God's word was good and true, so he said, cling on to it! It has the wisdom we all need. It is God's story, for now and for ever. It is God-breathed! And there will always be human tendency to hear what we want to hear (4:4), but even then, Paul said, stay immersed in the Scriptures. Understand that they are inspired by the Holy Spirit, and useful in *every* part of life, and for every age, including today.

- - - - - -

Pray

'Lord, we often neglect your word. Thank you that even today you speak life through it, to each of us, in all the ways we need to hear right now.'

Welcome him!

'Yet I prefer to appeal to you on the basis of love.'
Philemon v. 9

Read Philemon

This is a fascinatingly short and striking letter from Paul to Philemon. Paul wrote it while he was in prison, but it's the backstory that's important. Apparently, Paul's friend Philemon used to own a slave named Onesimus, but Onesimus wronged Philemon, and then found his way to Paul in prison, and then became a believer through those new interactions. So Paul wanted to send Onesimus back to Philemon as a brother. He wanted Philemon to forgive him, and to welcome him as a fellow believer in Christ. At the time, it must have been an unheard-of request. How could Philemon possibly welcome his slave Onesimus as a social equal? Yet that is the power of the gospel. The love and grace of Christ has transcended every single boundary. Jesus has reconciled us to himself and to each other . . . and therefore we forgive, and are reconciled, even when it seems unheard of. I also love the way Paul urged Philemon to forgive and restore. He didn't 'command' him to reconcile, even though he could have; he appealed to him on the basis of love – *'although in Christ I could be bold and order you to do what you ought to do, yet I prefer to appeal to you **on the basis of love**'* (v. 8–9). And that's the same urging for each of us. We have been marvellously loved and restored in Christ, and so, on that basis, we love and welcome.

- - - - - -

Pray

'Lord, we thank you for your marvellous love. Please speak to us today if there is someone with whom we need to be reconciled. Thank you that you will help us to do it.'

Confidence

'Let us then approach God's throne of grace with confidence.'
Hebrews 4:16

Read Hebrews 1:1 – 7:28

Confidence is an important thing to have. The dictionary says that confidence is 'a feeling of certainty that we can handle something'. The writer of Hebrews mentions confidence quite a lot. He says have confidence in Christ. He doesn't say, have confidence because you did some exercise on the weekend, or you stayed up late studying. He says have confidence in Christ. Jesus is our great high priest. Jesus has entered the most holy place and offered himself as a sacrifice for us . . . and so, because of his sacrifice, we can have confidence to draw near to God, and speak to him today. The original Hebrew readers must have been amazed too! They knew their Old Testament Scriptures well, so they knew how incredible it was that Jesus had done away with the need for sacrifice. They could approach God with confidence. And then, more than that, the writer explained to them that, even now, Jesus lives to intercede for them. *'Therefore he is able to save completely those who come to God through him, because he always lives to intercede for them'* (7:25). And it's true for us as well, today. Jesus suffered, yet stayed obedient. He was tempted in every way, yet he remained true. And now he *intercedes for us*. He understands suffering and trials, and he prays for us. Therefore we can have confidence!

- - - - - -

Pray

'Lord, thank you for Jesus, that he was sinless from the beginning yet learned obedience through suffering. Thank you that he is interceding for us today.'

Expect the Bible to speak

**'For the word of God is alive and active. Sharper than any double-edged
sword, it penetrates even to dividing soul and spirit, joints and
marrow.'**

Hebrews 4:12

Read Hebrews 4:12–13

Sometimes, when we've been followers of Jesus for a long time, we can
grow accustomed to his words in the Bible. We're unsurprised when he
tells us to love our enemies, or do good to those who hurt us. But what if
we were to read the Bible today, as if we were reading it for the first time?
Recently I talked with a man from Iran who grew up in a Muslim family
and who spent his childhood reciting the Quran. As a late teenager, he went
to study in India, and he began to listen to Christian radio. Then he signed
up for a Bible correspondence course and he read the gospels for the first
time. He said to me, 'I fell in love with Jesus straight away. I read Matthew
and I'd never heard of anyone like Jesus, *and I loved him*.' Listening to this
man describe meeting Jesus in the Bible for the first time and loving him,
reminded me of the power of God's word as described in Hebrews 4. *'For
the word of God is alive and active. Sharper than any double-edged sword, it
penetrates even to dividing soul and spirit, joints and marrow; it judges the
thoughts and attitudes of the heart'* (4:12). The word of God is living and
active. It speaks richly to our hearts. And we too can respond, in fresh ways,
to the love of Jesus today.

- - - - - -

Pray

> *'Lord, your word to us is alive and penetrating. Please help us respond
> today, and trust you in new ways.'*

Don't give up meeting together

'And let us consider how we may spur one another on towards love and good deeds, not giving up meeting together, as some are in the habit of doing, but encouraging one another.'

Hebrews 10:24–25

Read Hebrews 10:1–35

All the way through this letter, the writer to the Hebrews kept telling the Jewish readers that it was serious. The sacrifice of Jesus was the one, all-time answer, and they must not miss out on their opportunity to be reconciled to God. They must trust him! As they did, they were to spur one another on towards love and good deeds. They were to keep meeting together, and encouraging each other. They were to stay close! They needed each other! In April 2015, Nepal suffered its worst earthquake since 1934. More than 9,000 people died and 23,000 people were injured. My husband Darren went in response to the tragedy and he served at Dhulikhel Hospital, alongside our Nepali friends. The hospital was inundated with patients, many of whom had been trapped for days under concrete. It was tragic, but it also brought out incredibly generous service and care for each other. In that time of need, everyone cooked rice for each other, and stayed close. In Kathmandu, it was interesting to see that the old houses that survived were the ones that were butted up against each other, almost leaning on each other. They survived, holding each other up. It's a good reminder for us. We must stay close to each other. We must not give up meeting together. It's more than a healthy saying. It's survival, as we walk with Christ.

- - - - - -

Pray

'Lord, we thank you for the other believers that you have put in our lives. Help us to stay close, and to spur them on too.'

In just a little while

'For, in just a little while, he who is coming will come and will not delay.'

Hebrews 10:37

Read Hebrews 10:36–39

There are so many truths tucked away in Scripture. When the writer to the Hebrews was urging his readers to persevere, even through suffering, he picked up some phrases from Isaiah and Habakkuk, and he said to them, *'For, in just a little while, he who is coming will come and will not delay'* (10:37). In just a little while. Not long! When I read that verse, I imagine thousands of people reading the same promise, down through the ages, in hundreds of languages, in deserts and rainforests and cities. *'For, in just a little while, he who is coming will come and will not delay.'* 'To delay' means to postpone, or to put off, to defer. God will not do that. Jesus is coming back, and he will make all things new. There will be no more tears, or funerals, or pain, or fear. God himself will be with us. And because of that promise, we can keep going and persevere, even when it feels hard, or when we don't understand anything. Even then, we won't give up; we will put our confidence in Jesus, who died for us, and who brought about the promise for ever. He wrote a new covenant on our hearts! Even today, in the middle of our most pressing struggles, we can say to ourselves, *'In just a little while, he who is coming will come and will not delay.'*

- - - - - -

Pray

> *'Lord, we thank you for your promises, and we thank you that you will come and not delay. Please let that truth grow faith in us today.'*

By faith, even though

> **'By faith, Abraham, when called to go to a place he would later receive as his inheritance, obeyed and went, even though he did not know where he was going.'**
>
> **Hebrews 11:8**

Read Hebrews 11:1–40

I love the repetition in chapter 11 of Hebrews. It's a remarkable account. The writer was pointing the readers to the Ancients of faith, who had held on to the promises of God down through the ages. As we noticed previously, some of these apparent 'heroes', like Gideon, Barak and Samson, were not always wholly devoted or inspiring. Most of them made dreadful mistakes. Yet they were included in this list because they held onto the promises of God, *even though* they couldn't see it. By faith Abraham went, *even though* he didn't know where he was going. By faith he offered up Isaac, *even though* God had said the promise would come through him. By faith, Abel still speaks *even though* he is dead. In strange and wonderful ways, God is still at work, *even though* it seems impossible! And the Ancients of faith trusted God, *even though* they couldn't see it. They didn't receive what was promised in their lifetime, but they held tightly on to God. And the writer lists their stories again, for the Hebrews in the first century and for us today, to help us to do the same thing. Hold on!

- - - - - -

Pray

> *'Lord, we want to have a faith like that – that holds on to you, through droughts and storms and grief and unfair dismissals and a world gone completely awry – because you have promised us a city, with foundations.'*

Like foreigners and strangers

'They did not receive the things promised; they only saw them and welcomed them from a distance, admitting that they were foreigners and strangers on earth.'

Hebrews 11:13

Read Hebrews 11:13–16

When we first moved to Nepal, it was the first time that we'd lived outside of Australia. We couldn't speak the language, or buy bananas, or read the signs, or answer the lady at church, or understand what anyone was saying. It was very difficult. We were the foreigners! And sometimes we longed to return to the country we had left. But at the same time, we regularly read Hebrews 11. The Ancients were still living by faith when they died. They were still aliens and strangers, not looking backwards, but looking for a better country, a country of their own – a heavenly one – that God was preparing for them. And maybe that's what we're all doing as believers in Jesus, whether we're living in the Himalayas, or Sydney, or Alice Springs, or London. Whether we're comfortable or not, surrounded by buffalo or flowers, there's a deeper longing for the city to come, where we will never be the outsider again. And we hold on to that promise in every place. Perhaps the challenge for those of us who currently live in our passport countries, or homes, is to actually remember that being a foreigner is our true state on this earth, as we wait for the city to come that God is preparing for us.

- - - - - -

Pray

> 'Lord, we thank you for the reminder that no matter how comfortable we might be right now, this is not our true home. You are preparing a city for us. May our hope in you bring deep delight and commitment to the community where you have placed us.'

A great cloud of witnesses

'Therefore, since we are surrounded by such a great cloud of
witnesses . . .'

Hebrews 12:1

Read Hebrews 12:1–29

Role models are important – people who we can look up to, and who can
show us different ways of growing older, and expressing wonderful faith in
Jesus. I met a couple in outback Australia who were both 89 years old. They've
been fostering needy children for 60 years. In that time, they have raised more
than 60 children, most of whom have had irreparable brain damage due to
foetal alcohol syndrome. Even today, they have a foster child living with them
who is two years old and who never seems to stay still. I asked them how
they found time to do anything, and Verle said, 'Well, I read my Bible in the
middle of the night. That's when I have my quiet time.' They were such an
encouragement to me! They were faithfully using their gifts at 89, running the
race with perseverance, and fixing their eyes on Jesus. And they encouraged
me to do the same. Wherever we are, we are also surrounded by a great cloud
of witnesses throughout history and in our communities today. We too are
blessed by their encouragement to keep going, and to also fix our eyes on Jesus
who endured the cross and sat down at the right hand of God. The reminder
to the Hebrews is equally helpful for us today, *'Consider him who endured such
opposition from sinners, so that you will not grow weary and lose heart'* (12:3).

- - - - - -

Pray

*'Lord, we remember your grand, long story, and all the people who have lived
before us, faithfully, with their eyes fixed on you. Help us to also run the race
with perseverance, behind them, in all the ways you have gifted us to do so.'*

Faith and deeds

'Show me your faith without deeds, and I will show you my faith by my deeds.'

James 2:18b

Read James 1:1 – 2:26

In another wonderfully transformative story, James, the half-brother of Jesus, became one of the leaders of the early church in Jerusalem, after Peter. During that time, he wrote this summary letter to the followers of Jesus, and it was full of wise, practical advice, not unlike some of Proverbs. Be quick to listen, he said, slow to speak, and slow to become angry. Keep a tight rein on your tongue. (It can be ferocious!) Look after orphans and widows in their distress. Don't show favouritism. But mostly, James said that a genuine faith in Jesus would produce good deeds. Faith would be obvious in a person's life, by their actions. He even mentioned Rahab (Joshua 2). Of course, James knew that believers wouldn't be *saved* by their good deeds, or judged by them, but a true faith in Jesus would produce them. Indeed, James felt so strongly about it that he said that faith without deeds was dead (2:17). It's a strong sentence. But James grew up with Jesus, and he saw how Jesus lived his life. How could he *not* have been transformed? He saw that Jesus' words led to healing action within a needy, fractured society, plagued by all the things that we continue to be plagued by. And today, genuine faith in Jesus will also produce love towards a myriad of people who may never be able to repay us, and, indeed, we won't even mind.

- - - - - -

Pray

> *'Lord, your gospel is one of action, yet we so often spend our time on worthless debate over trivialities. Forgive us and transform us today, on behalf of the ones you love.'*

Hold the plan loosely

'Why, you do not even know what will happen tomorrow.'
James 4:14

Read James 3:1 – 4:17

Some of us are natural planners. We like to create extensive timelines and to-do lists, and detailed goals for the next five years or so. Sometimes it works out well, but at other times, the whole thing derails. Accidents, sickness, misunderstanding, delayed flights, pregnancy, job loss, stock market crashes, and worse. Then we say, 'What's going on?' James might reply to us, *'Why, you do not even know what will happen tomorrow. What is your life? You are a mist that appears for a little while and then vanishes. Instead, you ought to say, "If it is the Lord's will, we will live and do this or that"'* (4:14–15). James would remind us that it's an attitude of the heart. In everything, even our most excellent plans, we submit to the Lord, who is sovereign and good and often surprising. He has his own plans, and he brings them about in his own timing, for his purposes. Sometimes they may even involve deep suffering, or seeming inefficiency. I recently talked with a couple who served in Bolivia as missionaries. They prepared for a long time, and when they arrived they had a season of fruitfulness, until their child was born with special needs and they had to return to Australia prematurely. Why did that happen? We don't know. We trust in the One who does know, and we live with an attitude that makes good, godly plans, but then holds them very lightly.

- - - - - -

Pray

'Lord, your plans are good. Teach us to prepare well, and to pray often, but hold our plans lightly, in submission to your will.'

The prayer of faith

'The prayer of a righteous person is powerful and effective.'
James 5:16b

Read James 5:1–20

I love James' call to prayer at the end of his letter. It was so important! He said, if you're in trouble, pray. If you're sick, pray. If you're caught in sin or temptation, pray. If you're happy, pray . . . and praise the Lord! And don't just pray on your own, or with your family at mealtimes, pray with your leaders, and pray with your friends; pray all the time, pray with oil, pray with anyone you can. Because . . . *'The prayer of a righteous person is powerful and effective'* (5:16b). Perhaps one of the reasons we don't pray as much as we could today, is because we don't know what or how to pray. What words should we use? I recently met a Christian lady in her eighties. She told me that she has less energy now, so she doesn't go out much. But she can pray, and she prays at night when she can't sleep. (She doesn't sleep well, so she prays a lot!) But then she said to me, 'I don't always know what to pray. So I just go through my list of all the people and things on my mind, one at a time, and I think of them, and I say, "Lord, have your way."' She looked at me apologetically and said, 'It's not a very good prayer, I suppose.' I said, 'It's one of the best prayers I've ever heard' . . . because when we say, 'Lord, have your way', it orientates us back to God, who knows more than we do, who loves more than we do, and whose sovereignty brings about good answers for his people and his world.

- - - - - -

Pray

'Lord, have your way today.'

A living hope

'Though you have not seen him, you love him.'
1 Peter 1:8

Read 1 Peter 1:1–25

It's remarkable to trace Peter's life through the Scriptures. At the beginning, he was an ordinary fisherman called to follow Jesus. Along the way, he asked questions and passionately trusted and blurted out the wrong things; he even denied Jesus at the end. But Jesus restored and commissioned him. Peter became the rock of the early church, giving powerful sermons that testified to Jesus, and caused thousands to turn to the Lord in faith. Right through the book of Acts, there are wonderful glimpses of Peter's life of faith and service as he continued to obey his Lord and lead the church. And then at the end of his life, Peter put together this letter with a co-worker, addressed to the Gentile believers *'scattered throughout the provinces'* (1:1). I love that beginning! It almost includes us. And then Peter immediately praised God. He spoke of God's great mercy and his saving plan through Christ. He marvelled at the inheritance that awaits every believer, and he thanked God for the living hope that was so evident amongst the new, scattered believers. *'Though you have not seen him, you love him; and even though you do not see him now, you believe in him and are filled with an inexpressible and glorious joy'* (1:8). It's an amazing acknowledgement. Unlike Peter, the new, scattered believers hadn't seen Jesus in person, yet they believed in him implicitly. They loved him, and they were filled with an inexpressible and glorious joy. We are, in fact, included in them! We too have not seen Jesus, yet we believe in him and we love him.

- - - - - -

Pray

'Lord, we are filled with joy because we know you and we put our hope in you.'

Like newborn babies

'Like newborn babies, crave pure spiritual milk.'
1 Peter 2:2

Read 1 Peter 2:1–25

Darren and I are part of a mid-week group that reads the Bible together. We love it. It's the kind of group that welcomes you in your slippers, or lets you cry if you need to. Some years ago, one of the other couples had twins. Back then, the rest of us had grown children or teenagers, so we were quite besotted with the babies. One night when the twins were still tiny, they came to our group and we passed them around, and we fed and burped them. After a while, we thought they were ready for a sleep, but then they both suddenly arched their heads and cried loudly, in unison. They needed more milk. At the same time, we happened to be reading this passage from 1 Peter 2. *'Like newborn babies, **crave** pure spiritual milk . . .'* Sometimes, extra imagery is not required! There were the babies in front of us, with their instinctive needs and cravings and head turnings. It made me think about how, so often, I don't crave spiritual milk in the same natural, eager way. I read the Bible because I have to, or to prepare for a talk. What would it mean for us to crave God's word all day long, like a newborn baby arches her head and cries till she gets what she needs . . . or until we get what we really need – time alone with our Saviour, food from his word, hope for our souls, perspective for our muddled-up lives.

- - - - - -

Pray

'Lord, we thank you for your word that nourishes us today, and all year.'

Be prepared to give an answer

'Always be prepared to give an answer to everyone who asks you.'
1 Peter 3:15

Read 1 Peter 3:1–22

Peter went on to remind the new, scattered believers that life would be hard as Christians. They would be persecuted. But they were to hold onto their wonderful hope in Christ. In addition, Peter said, *'Always be prepared to give an answer to everyone who asks you to give the reason for the hope that you have'* (3:15). It's a good reminder for us too, because questions can come anytime. Darren and I were at the beach one day with our boys and dog. The boys and Darren were playing on the sand, and I remained on the grass with the dog, because in Australia you're not meant to have dogs on beaches. I was feeling a bit grumbly (wishing I was with them), but then along came a girl who wanted to pat our dog. Then she asked me what I did on Sundays. I said we go to church. She said, 'Oh, you're the third person!' In the previous two days she had met two different strangers who had answered her genuine questions about faith and Jesus. She desperately wanted to know if Christianity was true or not, so that morning she had said to God, 'God, if you're real, please bring along a third person who will tell me about Jesus, and then I will believe.' And he did. He brought her to me on the grass (even though I was grumbly), and then he brought her to faith in Jesus.

- - - - - -

Pray

'Lord, please show us that being prepared to give an answer about the hope we have is the most natural thing we can do, because we get to talk about you.'

A thousand years are like a day

'But do not forget this one thing, dear friends: with the Lord a day is like a thousand years, and a thousand years are like a day.'
2 Peter 3:8

Read 2 Peter 1:1 – 3:18

By the time Peter wrote his second letter to the scattered Gentile believers, he was imprisoned in Rome, and he didn't have long to live. He would soon be executed, so he wrote down all the important things for the believers to remember. God had given them (and us) everything they needed for a godly, productive life (1:3), and through God's incredible divine power, they could make daily choices to honour him in their relationships. As well as that, Peter urged the believers to be careful of false teachers (who caused trouble), and then Peter said the most striking thing, *'But do not forget this one thing, dear friends: with the Lord a day is like a thousand years, and a thousand years are like a day. The Lord is not slow in keeping his promise, as some understand slowness. Instead, he is patient with you, not wanting anyone to perish, but everyone to come to repentance'* (3:8–9). It's a magnificent reminder. Back then, the people were questioning the truth of Jesus' return and asking, 'Where is he?' Peter said, hold on. Jesus will come when you least expect it. And his timeline is not ours. We can hardly fathom it, but the reason for God's wait is his patience. He loves his people. He dearly wants every generation to have a chance to know him, and to respond. He waits.

- - - - - -

Pray

'Lord, we thank you for your ongoing, incredible patience, and we ask that you would work in the hearts of those you love, and grow a faith in them.'

That which our hands have touched

'We have seen it and testify to it.'
1 John 1:2

Read 1 John 1:1–10

Most scholars agree that the same 'John' who wrote the Gospel of John, also penned three letters to a group of house churches in Ephesus. He was an old man by the time of writing, and he wanted to pass on the truths of what he'd heard and seen. He was an eyewitness to Jesus! And that was important because, in any situation, we would prefer to see and touch something ourselves to believe it. The more extraordinary it is, the more we want to touch it! We have friends who lived in Asia for three years. During that time, they left their 20-year-old daughter back in the UK. But one Mother's Day, Emma decided to surprise her family. She flew from London to their city (without telling anyone) and she found her way into their living room. When they came home from church, there she was, popping out from behind a lounge chair. They all stared. One of her siblings burst into tears, thinking she was a ghost. Another sibling reached out her hand to check. Was she real? Can I touch her? That's exactly why John wrote to the believers. He said, *'That which was from the beginning, which we have heard, which we have seen with our eyes, which we have looked at **and our hands have touched** – this we proclaim concerning the Word of life'* (1:1). John knew that in every generation since then, we would want the assurance that Jesus was real . . . and so John said, yes, you can believe in him, we touched him.

- - - - - -

Pray

> *'Lord, we thank you for the eyewitnesses to your glory, like John, but we thank you even more that we can believe in your truth today.'*

Do not love the world

'If anyone loves the world, love for the Father is not in them.'
1 John 2:15b

Read 1 John 2:1–27

We can pretend that we don't, but perhaps we do love 'the world', or at least certain, beautiful aspects of it. There are many lovely things to enjoy! And we know that God's creation is good, at the same time as being broken and in need of restoration. But John wrote to the believers and said, *'Do not love the world or anything in the world. If anyone loves the world, love for the Father is not in them. For everything in the world – the lust of the flesh, the lust of the eyes, and the pride of life – comes not from the Father but from the world'* (2:15–16). John was reminding the believers that human desires are easily distorted. It's true that all of our hearts are idol factories, and we must often stop and ask ourselves the hard questions. Are my hands so gripped (onto that good thing/house/job/status) that my knuckles have gone white? Could I let it go if I needed to? Do I let my thoughts and imagination linger in unhelpful places? Is pride a force in my life that affects my closest relationships in a negative way? Has my focus shifted lately, so that my love for Jesus has become peripheral, or even forgotten? These are, of course, hard questions to ask of ourselves, which is why we benefit from a family of faith who may gently ask them of us. When we have a family of faith like that, we can be thankful!

- - - - - -

Pray

> *'Lord, we know that our hearts can be deceptive, or self-defensive. Please show us what it means to love your world, in a healing, restorative way, rather than in an obsessive, self-seeking way.'*

A child of God

'See what great love the Father has lavished on us, that we should be called children of God!'

1 John 3:1

Read 1 John 2:28 – 3:24

Identity is a funny thing. Over the years, it changes, or we change the way we describe ourselves to others. Sometimes we're a student, or a physio, or a writer, or a parent, or an engineer, or a volunteer. It's nice to have a neat description. For many years, Darren and I were 'missionaries' serving in Nepal. Our photos were on church noticeboards back in Australia, and on people's fridges. But when we returned to Australia, our photos came off the fridges. A lady from church asked whether they could take our pictures off the noticeboard. I said, 'Yes, that's fine.' But then I wondered. Maybe it's not fine, because if I'm not a missionary in Nepal anymore, then maybe I don't know who I am. Later, I read this letter from John. He urged his readers to remember who they really were, in Christ. They were forgiven. They were children of God. It was amazing! *'See what great love the Father has lavished on us, that we should be **called children of God**! And that is what we are!'* (1 John 3:1). John used exclamation marks! That is what we are! Being a child of God is our deepest, truest, constant identity. And perhaps, whenever we hand in the nametag, or the ID, or the car-parking space . . . we learn that truth again in new ways. Who are you? You're a child of God, and loved by him. And that's enough.

- - - - - -

Pray

'Lord, we admit that we like labels, and there are times when we feel the lack of them. Remind us in every moment that we are your child. Help us to respond with exclamation marks!'

Love is the witness

'Dear friends, since God so loved us, we also ought to love one another.'
1 John 4:11

Read 1 John 4:1–21

Repeatedly in John's letters to the believers, he urged them to love. God is love, he said. Whoever has been loved by God, will love. And others will notice! Some years ago, I visited Iris in India. She was born to a wealthy family in Chennai, and then she lived for 45 years in the jungle of Orissa, doing medical and gospel work. For the first 15 years, Iris and her husband Paul were very busy, treating patients and sharing their faith. But for 15 years, nobody from the tribal people came to faith, or asked for baptism. They were both discouraged and wondered if they should go home. But then Paul became very sick. The family travelled south, and Paul had an operation, and he died in the middle of it. Iris was 42 at the time, and they had four young children. Everybody said to her, 'Don't go back to the jungle. Stay in Chennai, set up a medical practice, make yourself comfortable.' But nine days later, Iris and the children returned to the village in the jungle, and she went back to treating patients and sharing her faith. The people noticed and said to each other, 'You see, she loves us. That's why she came back. The God she loves must be real.' Within six months, there were 36 people asking for baptism, and now there are 5,000 believers in the town. There is a time for relentless, persevering love, which can only come from God.

- - - - - -

Pray

'Lord, your love for us is everything, and so we thank you that we can respond in love. Please bear witness through our love today, even when it seems small.'

He hears us

'This is the confidence we have in approaching God; that if we ask anything according to his will, he hears us.'
1 John 5:14

Read 1 John 5:1–21

Some years ago, I spoke at a local high school in Australia. I talked about the great, consuming love of God, and the cost he bore to make us his, through Christ. I also talked about the incredible nature of prayer, and the way God listens to us, and responds to our prayers. Afterwards, a 12-year-old boy came up and said to me, 'I agree with you about God. It sounds good. But how do I know for sure that God is listening to *me*?' It was a good question, and perhaps something we all wonder. How do I know for sure that God is listening to *me*? What if he isn't? What if he just listens to the important people, or the louder ones, or the ones who have it all together? That's why this reminder from John is so important. *'This is the confidence we have in approaching God: that if we ask anything according to his will,* **he hears us***'* (5:14–15). God hears us. It's still true. And back in John's day, he had spent years with Jesus, watching the way Jesus listened – to the outcast woman at the well, and the bleeding woman without a name, and the blind man without hope, and the children who had been pushed away. He gathered them, and he listened to them. That's how we know that God listens to us . . . all of us.

- - - - - -

Pray

'Lord, we thank you that you hear us, and that our confidence in the way you hear us can lead us to pray, more and more.'

The vision of Jesus

'Do not be afraid. I am the First and the Last. I am the Living One; I was dead, and now look, I am alive for ever and ever!'
Revelation 1:17–18

Read Revelation 1:1–20

Of all the parts of the Bible that are difficult to understand, the book of Revelation has to be the hardest of them all. Most scholars agree that it was written by John in about AD95, at a time when some of the Christians had experienced persecution under the Roman emperors. But Revelation is, in fact, the most hopeful book ever written. Back then, the believers needed deep encouragement. They needed to know that God was sovereign and ruling . . . and that one day he would restore all of creation, completely. So, John's vision began with a striking image of Jesus himself, sovereign and glorious! It was not dissimilar to Daniel's vision, hundreds of years earlier. John wrote, *'In his right hand he held seven stars, and coming out of his mouth was a sharp, double-edged sword. His face was like the sun shining in all its brilliance'* (1:16). In fact, when John saw Jesus like that, he *'fell at his feet as though dead'* (1:17). We need to pause and re-read that. The vision of Jesus was so incredible that John fell at his feet as though dead. We may not fully understand apocalyptic literature, or God's timeline, but we understand awe. We know what it's like to be so overcome that we have no breath at all. That's how John felt, one thousand-fold, in front of Christ. Perhaps we need that reminder today.

- - - - - -

Pray

'Lord, we easily feel dwarfed by the society around us. Renew in us today a breathtaking vision of Jesus in all his glory and brilliance and endless rule.'

To the seven churches

'I know your deeds. See, I have placed before you an open door that no one can shut. I know that you have little strength, yet you have kept my word and have not denied my name.'

Revelation 3:8

Read Revelation 2:1 – 3:22

Part of John's vision included seven specific words from Jesus to seven specific churches in the ancient time. Each of the churches needed a different encouragement or challenge. For example, the believers in Ephesus had persevered and endured hardship, but they had forgotten their first love. The believers in Pergamum had remained true to Jesus, but there were false teachers among them. The believers in Laodicea were lukewarm and apathetic. But my favourite letter is to the church in Philadelphia. Back then, the church was small and weak. It was not outwardly impressive. But the word from Jesus was deeply encouraging. *'I know that you have little strength, yet you have kept my word and have not denied my name . . . Since you have kept my command to endure patiently, I will also keep you from the hour of trial that is going to come'* (3:8,10). The big theme in Revelation is faithful perseverance. Will the churches prove themselves faithful in the end? Will they trust that the outcome for Christians will be glorious, despite current persecution? Will they cling on to a vast, heavenly perspective, when powerful emperors rule in front of them? And now today, the question is the same for us. We may feel outwardly unimpressive, but we want to cling on to God's vast, heavenly rule and promise, even amidst significant, ongoing, societal pressure to do otherwise.

- - - - - -

Pray

'Lord, we want to remain faithful. We want to trust you, daily. We want to be found in you, in the end. Help us to trust you more.'

Worship and the Lamb

'Day and night they never stop saying: "Holy, holy, holy is the Lord God Almighty," who was, and is, and is to come.'

Revelation 4:8

Read Revelation 4:1 – 5:14

There is nothing like the images of worship in Revelation. After the words to the churches, John saw God's heavenly throne room itself. On the throne was the Lord God Almighty, with the appearance of jasper and ruby, and the sounds of lightning and thunder. Surrounding the throne were creatures and elders, all bowing down before him in worship. Day and night they never stopped singing! *'You are worthy, our Lord and God, to receive glory and honour and power, for you created all things, and by your will they were created and have their being'* (4:11). What a sight and a sound! What a glorious, appropriate way to respond to the living God! But there was a problem. No one could be found to break the seals and open the scroll. They needed someone! John wept over the problem. But then, one of the elders said, *'Do not weep! See, the Lion of the tribe of Judah, the Root of David, has triumphed. He is able to open the scroll and its seven seals'* (5:5). Jesus was the amazing answer – the descendant of Judah, in the line of David, the Messiah who would rule for ever and ever! But then strangely, John saw a bloody Lamb, not a lion. The Lamb had been slain. But the slain, bloody Lamb was able to take the scroll. And everyone fell down before the Lamb, in worship, and they sang a new song.

- - - - - -

Pray

> *'Lord, today, too, we want to sing loudly. We want to say, "Worthy is the Lamb, who was slain, to receive power and wealth and wisdom and strength and honour and glory and praise".'*

'Then each of them was given a white robe, and they were told to wait a little longer.'

Revelation 6:11

Read Revelation 6:1–17

Incredibly, the Lamb was able to open the seals. He was worthy. But the seals, when opened, were confronting. There were images of war and mayhem and famine and death and martyrdom and waiting and an earthquake. The sky was rolled up and every mountain was removed. Judgement would come and the people would be laid bare, all of them – kings and princes, rich and mighty, slave and free. They would hide in caves and call on the rocks to fall on them. *'Hide us from the face of him who sits on the throne and from the wrath of the Lamb! For the great day of their wrath has come, and who can withstand it?'* (6:16–17). Who can withstand it? It's the most confronting image in the Bible. Judgement will come. But, incredibly, there is an answer. The previous chapters told us who could withstand it – those who put their trust in the Lamb. The price has been paid by Jesus. The wait is over. The answer is already there in the throne room of God. The answer is for us. And wouldn't it be amazing if, as a result of our lives and witness, there would be a few more people at the end of time who didn't have to run and hide in the caves – a few more people who could stand in front of God because they had put their trust in the Lamb – a few more people singing. Imagine that?

- - - - - -

Pray

'Lord, you are the glorious ruler and saving, restoring King, who has every right to judge. Thank you for Jesus, and that because of his sacrifice we will be able to stand.'

A great multitude

'After this I looked, and there before me was a great multitude that no one could count, from every nation, tribe, people and language, standing before the throne and before the Lamb.'

Revelation 7:9

Read Revelation 7:1–17

This is an incredible image of the body of Christ. At the end, the worshippers of God will gather from everywhere – from every tribe, and nation, and people, and language. They will all stand before the throne, and before the Lamb, and they will sing together. And the reason they can be there is Jesus. They have put their trust in him. He has saved them! It's God's incredible, sovereign plan, from the beginning of time. It's the multitude, singing in one voice. It's the greatest image in God's entire story. It's the reason and the answer. It's profound and breathtaking. It's the nations! For me, having lived in other countries and learnt other languages, it makes me cry. We will be together, before our God! We will be singing one song! We will be worshipping together, in truth! And those who have suffered greatly for their faith – the martyrs – they will be there too. There is an especially tender word for them. *'And he who sits on the throne will shelter them with his presence. "Never again will they hunger; never again will they thirst. The sun will not beat down on them," nor any scorching heat. For the Lamb at the centre of the throne will be their shepherd; "he will lead them to springs of living water." "And God will wipe away every tear from their eyes"'* (7:15–17).

- - - - - -

Pray

'Lord, this is the most beautiful thing we have ever read. Please write it on our hearts, so that every day it leads to hope and trust and action.'

The prayers of all God's people

'The smoke of the incense, together with the prayers of God's people,
went up before God from the angel's hand.'

Revelation 8:4

Read Revelation 8:1–13

On the days when we question whether our prayers are being heard, or noticed, or answered, we should re-read this chapter in Revelation. As part of John's vision, each of the seven seals was opened. And then, after the seventh seal was opened, John saw that there was silence in heaven for about half an hour (8:1). Imagine that! It's the only point in Scripture where silence in heaven is mentioned. In every other moment, there were the overwhelming sounds of singing and praises and trumpets and lightning and peals of thunder and worship . . . and then, suddenly, there was silence in heaven for half an hour. During the silence, an angel stood before the altar, and he had a bowl of incense with the prayers of all God's people. He poured the incense and the prayers into the altar and it went up before God (8:4). What an incredible image. Our prayers today, and from twenty years ago, and those uttered in tiny island villages, or high-rise apartments, in Bangladesh and Bosnia and Bolivia, in distress and joy and pain and fear, all of our prayers are being offered to God, in a timeless, endless manner. He is hearing them. They haven't vanished into thin air. They are being offered as incense to our marvellous God and Saviour. Every prayer that we've ever prayed, even those we've long forgotten, are part of a golden bowl, an offering before the throne of God, and he is delighting in them.

- - - - - -

Pray

'Lord, please let this image of your delight bring us to our knees, with a hunger and urgency to speak with you, more and more.'

Victory

'The great dragon was hurled down – that ancient snake called the devil, or Satan, who leads the whole world astray. He was hurled to the earth.'

Revelation 12:9

Read Revelation 9:1 – 19:21

Much of the imagery in Revelation is terribly confronting. We either want to skip it or break it into sections that we pretend to understand. Perhaps we're not meant to. Perhaps we're meant to simply be overwhelmed by the sweep of truth, including the most marvellous of all. In the end, God wins. He has the ultimate, eternal victory over Satan and evil. I have a friend who always reads the last page of a novel before she begins the book. She wants to know if the story will turn out alright in the end. Amazingly, the book of God – the grand saga of life and love and pain and beauty – has an all-consuming victory at the end. There will be justice. At the end, the ancient snake that appeared in Genesis 3 will be done away with. The Messiah, the Lord Jesus, will win. We don't fully understand his timeline or imagery, and we don't need to. All we need to know is that Jesus will rule. He will hurl the serpent to the earth. There will be great, endless victory. And that one, all-consuming, penetrating question from the beginning of time will be answered. God has absorbed the curse into himself, and at the end, Jesus will crush the serpent's head for ever. We can not only read the story, but we can *live* the story, fixing our eyes on Jesus, and the wonderful, victorious hope to come.

- - - - - -

Pray

'Lord, we long for the ending, but we ask that you would grow faithfulness and mercy in us in the meantime, that we might be part of your restorative purposes for the world.'

'This calls for patient endurance and faithfulness on behalf of God's people.'

Revelation 13:10b

Read Revelation 13:1 – 14:20

Back in the time when John was writing to the churches, there were some believers who were under persecution from the Roman Empire. There were others who had become complacent or distracted. And John's vision spoke to them all about the seriousness, as well as the hope, of the gospel. They needed to remain faithful. They needed to persevere. Hard times would come, as well as distracting, morally tempting times. And it's the same message for us, in our time and place. We have friends who served for 21 years in Pakistan, Oman, Jordan and Yemen, with their two children. Twice they were forced to leave the country by the police and not told why. They had to pack up their whole lives in a week and move on. But they kept serving. They moved to another country and they began again. They persevered. When I asked them how they did it, they quoted this verse in Revelation. *'This calls for patient endurance and faithfulness on behalf of God's people'* (13:10). They said that their natural preference would be for an easy, results-orientated life . . . but sometimes God calls us to faithful perseverance, to stay in the battle, even when it's hard. It will be hard! Their testimony spoke to me. God also wants us to persevere in our life and faith and witness, in the places he has allowed us to be. He calls us to daily, patient endurance and faithfulness.

- - - - - -

Pray

'Lord, we thank you for the way you lift our eyes and help us to keep going in the battle. Please help us to persevere today.'

No more tears or funerals

> 'They will be his people, and God himself will be with them and be their
> God. "He will wipe every tear from their eyes. There will be no more
> death" or mourning or crying or pain.'
>
> Revelation 21:3–4

Read Revelation 21:1–27

In the end, after Jesus has the final victory, he will return in glory and restore absolutely everything. The world will be healed. There will be a new heaven and a new earth! It will be like the Garden of Eden, only better. It will be our true home, or the place that we have always longed for. It will be like a beautiful city – a place of harmony and work and worship and love, for all the nations! I remember sitting in Nepal one day, at the leprosy hospital. The patients, who had never heard of Jesus before, were quiet. An older Nepali man was explaining to them about Jesus and his life offered for us, and the hope of heaven. He read from Revelation 21. *'I saw "a new heaven and a new earth," for the first heaven and the first earth had passed away, and there was no longer any sea. I saw the Holy City, the new Jerusalem, coming down out of heaven from God'* (21:1–2). As he read, the patients slowly began to lift up their stumps of hands, and they stared at their missing fingers, and tears rolled down their cheeks. They cried, imagining being made new in Christ, being whole, being with God for ever, restored.

- - - - - -

Pray

> *'Lord, let your words bring tears and thankfulness – for your glorious promise
> of the city to come, where you will be our light. Thank you that the nations
> will be there together. Thank you that the gate will never be shut. Thank you!'*

Come!

'The Spirit and the bride say, "Come!" And let the one who hears say, "Come!"'
Revelation 22:17

Read Revelation 22:1–21

The last word in the Bible is not 'work', or 'try hard', or 'do better'. It's 'Come!' Jesus announced the new, restored world, and he issued a glorious invitation. He said, 'Come!' He, who is the Alpha and the Omega, the First and the Last, the Beginning and the End, said, 'Come!' He called out to those who were thirsty. And he calls out to us today, and to all those through the ages who have looked to him as their light in a dark world. He says, 'Come!' Sometimes, I ask my friends what they're looking forward to in a fully redeemed world. One of them, who lives with polio, said she's looking forward to running down the stairs. Another friend, who has a disabled daughter, said she's looking forward to seeing her daughter's face when she gets her resurrection body. Another friend, who struggles with singleness, said he's looking forward to flourishing relationships. In every part of life, there will be full and complete restoration. There will be no more fear. There will be no more fighting. There will be no more evil or funerals. There will be no more greed or injustice. *'The throne of God and of the Lamb will be in the city, and his servants will serve him. They will see his face, and his name will be on their foreheads. There will be no more night. They will not need the light of a lamp or the light of the sun, for the Lord God will give them light. And they will reign for ever and ever'* (22:3–5). For that reason, we can be utterly hopeful.

- - - - - -

Pray

'Amen. Come, Lord Jesus.'

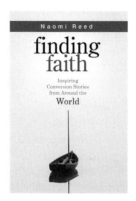

Finding Faith

*Inspiring conversion stories
from around the world*

Naomi Reed

A collection of inspirational stories from around the world,
sharing the exciting and life-changing transformation that Jesus
brings. From the flat, dry towns of Uganda to northern Iraq, from
the land of the native Australians to the former Soviet Union,
Naomi Reed shares moving accounts of ordinary people who
have put their faith in the Lord Jesus Christ. They all say the same
thing . . . God's love is amazing, and it changes everything.

978-1-78078-462-5

For more information about Naomi Reed:

www.naomireed.info

The Plum Tree in the Desert

Ten stories of faith and mission to inspire you

Naomi Reed

God is at work, even in the hardest places. From across Asia, the Middle East and North Africa, Naomi Reed has collected the stories of Interserve mission workers. These are stories of difficult situations in the mission field: some of victory and some that left the mission workers feeling they had failed. But despite the difficulties and perceived failures, each story speaks of the goodness of God and what it means to persevere and trust in him, even when it seems too hard. These stories give us a new perspective on those perceived failures and remind us that 'in all things God works for the good of those who love him'.

The Plum Tree in the Desert will build your faith and inspire you to action.

978-1-78078-141-9

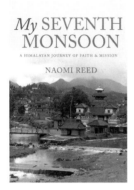

My Seventh Monsoon

A Himalayan journey of faith and mission

Naomi Reed

'My seventh monsoon was the hardest of them all. I sat on the back porch of our Himalayan home and stared as the rain streamed down all around me. I had never felt so hemmed in – by the constant rain, by the effects of the civil war and by the demands of home-school. As I sat there and listened to the pounding on our tin roof, I wondered whether I would make it through. I wondered whether I could cope with another 120 days of rain. And in doing so, I began to long for another season . . .'

From the view point of her seventh monsoon, Naomi Reed takes time to look back on the seasons of her life. As she does so, she shares with us her journey of faith and mission and reveals poignant truths about God and the way he works his purposes in our lives through seasons.

978-1-86024-828-3

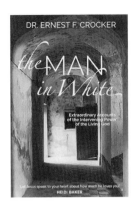

The Man in White

Extraordinary accounts of the intervening power of the living God

Dr Ernest F. Crocker

Many of us want to see Jesus, to hear his voice. We want a tangible experience of God.

As a Christian doctor and follower of Jesus, Ernest Crocker has been a witness to many interventions of God during his life. In The Man in White, he brings together an inspiring selection of testimonies from around the world of people who have seen God do extraordinary things in and through their lives. They include professionals, academics, a train robber, a surgeon facing decapitation for his faith, and those who have escaped the ravages of war.

These powerful stories inspire and challenge us to see that God is real and delights in being involved in our lives today.

978-1-78893-133-5

Blood, Sweat and Jesus

The story of a Christian hospital bringing hope and healing in a Muslim community

Kerry Stillman

What is a Christian hospital doing in a remote Muslim area of Cameroon?

Kerry Stillman shares her own experiences of working as a physiotherapist at the Meskine Hospital. A vivid impression of daily life is painted as the team deal with the threat of terrorism, the attitudes of local people towards Western medicine, their patients' health issues, and the challenge of sensitively sharing the gospel in a different culture.

Passionate, intriguing and uplifting, this is a colourful interweaving of cultures, beliefs and the power of prayer alongside modern medicine.

978-1-78893-148-9

Though I Run through the Valley

A persecuted family rescues over a thousand children in Myanmar

Pamela Johnson

At a time of ethnic cleansing and military dictatorship, being a Christian in a predominantly Buddhist Myanmar brought huge risks and danger.

Daring to trust God against all the odds, this is the powerful story of one family's sacrifice over many years to protect and show the love of Christ to many lost children in Myanmar.

978-1-78893-160-1

Finding Our Voice

*Unsung lives from the Bible
resonating with stories from today*

Jeannie Kendall

The Bible is full of stories of people facing issues that are
still surprisingly relevant today. Within its pages, people have
wrestled with problems such as living with depression, losing a
child, overcoming shame, and searching for meaning. Yet these
are not always the stories of the well-known heroes of faith, but
those of people whose names are not even recorded.

Jeannie Kendall brings these unnamed people to vibrant life.
Their experiences are then mirrored by a relevant testimony
from someone dealing with a similar situation today.

Finding Our Voice masterfully connects the past with the
present day, encouraging us to identify with the characters'
stories, and giving us hope that, whatever the circumstances,
we are all 'known to God'.

978-1-78893-037-6

A-Z of Prayer

*Building strong foundations for
daily conversations with God*

Matthew Porter

A–Z of Prayer is an accessible introduction that gives practical
guidance on how to develop a meaningful prayer life. It presents
twenty-six aspects of prayer to help you grow in your relationship
with God, explore new devotional styles and deepen your daily
conversations with God.

Each topic has a few pages of introduction and insight, an action
section for reflection and application and a prayer to help put
the action point into practice. There are also references to allow
further study.

978-1-78893-062-8

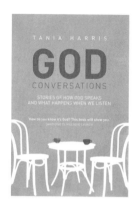

God Conversations

*Stories of how God speaks and
what happens when we listen*

Tania Harris

Stories of God talking to his people abound throughout the
Bible, but we usually only get the highlights. We read: 'God
said "Go to Egypt,"' and then, 'Mary and Joseph left for
Egypt.' We're not told how God spoke, how they knew it was
him, or how they decided to act on what they'd heard.

In *God Conversations*, international speaker and pastor Tania
Harris shares insights from her own story of learning to hear
God's voice. You'll get to eavesdrop on some contemporary
conversations with God in the light of his communication
with the ancients. Part memoir, part teaching, this unique and
creative collection will help you to recognize God's voice when
he speaks and what happens when you do.

978-1-78078-188-4

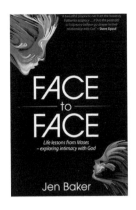

Face to Face

*Life lessons from Moses –
exploring intimacy with God*

Jen Baker

God longs for us to personally experience more of him, but
so often we refuse or feel unable to draw close to him. Even
the great hero of faith Moses hid his face from God, yet was
eventually transformed into someone who spoke face to face
with him.

Jen Baker explores Moses' life to see how he was able to
move from hiddenness to holiness and encourages us to follow
his example. Interwoven with personal testimony, Jen gently
challenges and shows us how to move out of the shadows into
the light of God's love.

Whether you feel distant from God or want to deepen your
relationship with him, *Face to Face* will help encourage you to
experience God in a new and powerful way.

978-1-78893-056-7

Authentic

We trust you enjoyed reading this book from Authentic. If you want to be informed of any new titles from this author and other releases you can sign up to the Authentic newsletter by scanning below:

Online:
authenticmedia.co.uk

Follow us: